Growing Up in the Midwest

Growing Up

IN THE MIDWEST

EDITED BY CLARENCE A. ANDREWS

The Iowa State University Press / Ames

ACKNOWLEDGMENTS

Meridel Le Sueur, "Budded with Child," in *Rites of Ancient Ripening*, Vanilla Press, Inc., Minneapolis, 1975. Reprinted by permission of publishers.

James Stevens, "A Prairie Town," from *American Mercury*, Sept. 1925. Reprinted by permission of *American Mercury*, P.O. Box 73523, Houston, Texas.

James Norman Hall, "The Woodshed Poet," from *My Island Home: An Autobiography*, Little, Brown and Co., Boston, 1952, pp. 3–10. Reprinted by permission.

MacKinlay Kantor, "I Think of These," from *But Look the Morn*, New York, 1947, pp. 137–42. Copyright © by MacKinlay Kantor. Reprinted by permission of Paul R. Reynolds, Inc., 12 East 41st Street, New York, N.Y.

Ellen Williamson, "Scotland in Iowa," from *When We Went First Class*. Copyright © by Ellen Williamson. Reprinted by permission of Doubleday & Company, Inc.

Langston Hughes, "One Christmas Eve," from *The Ways of the White Folks*, by Langston Hughes. Copyright © 1934 and renewed 1962 by Langston Hughes. Reprinted by permission of Alfred A. Knopf, Inc.

Hadley Read, "Saturday Night in Town," from *Morning Chores and Other Times Remembered*, University of Illinois Press, pp. 99, 101. Copyright © by the Board of Trustees of the University of Illinois. Reprinted by permission.

Robert Traver, "Fishermen at Night," from *Troubleshooter*, 1943. Reprinted by permission of author.

Patricia Hampl, "Views from the Hill," from *A Romantic Education*. Copyright © 1981 by Houghton Mifflin Co. Reprinted by permission of author.

Harry Mark Petrakis, "A Chicago Greek Boyhood," from *Stelmark: A Family Recollection*, David McKay. Copyright © 1970 by Harry Mark Petrakis. Reprinted by permission of Toni Strassman, agent.

Ruth Suckow, "A Little Girl's World," from *Midland Schools*, Dec. 1953. Reprinted by permission of Ferner Rall Nuhn.

Joseph Langland, "A Dream of Love." Copyright © 1977 by *The Massachusetts Review*. Reprinted from the book *Anybody's Song* by permission of the author and Doubleday & Company, Inc.

Dolores A. Quinn, "How Green Was My Alley," from *Chicago Tribune Magazine*, Mar. 23, 1980, pp. 30–32.

Garrison Keillor, "Drowning 1954." Copyright © 1976, *The New Yorker Magazine*, Inc. Reprinted by permission.

John R. Powers, "Some Great Moments in Sloppy Scouting," from *The Last Catholic in America*, by John R. Powers. Copyright © 1973 by John R. Powers. Reprinted by permission of E. P. Dutton. (A Saturday Review Press Book)

Gwendolyn Brooks, "The Life of Lincoln West," from *Family Pictures,*, by Gwendolyn Brooks. Copyright © 1970 by Gwendolyn Brooks. Reprinted by permission of Broadside Press.

James Hearst, "Emeritus." Copyright © 1977 by the National Retired Teachers Association. Reprinted by permission of *NRTA Journal*.

Library of Congress Cataloging in Publication Data
Main entry under title:

Growing up in the Midwest.

    1. American literature—Middle West. 2. Middle West—Literary collections. 3. Children—Middle West—Literary collections. 4. Authors, American—Middle West—Biography—Addresses, essays, lectures. I. Andrews, Clarence A.
PS563.G7   814′.54′0803277   81–8157

ISBN 0-8138-0250-4   AACR2

CONTENTS

The heart of the country—

There have been many attempts to define the Midwest. It has been seen as the land between the mountains: between the Alleghenies to the east and the Rockies to the west; between the Canadian border to the north and the Ohio River to the south, projecting westward along the northern Arkansas and Oklahoma borders.

Others would place the Midwest between the eastern Ohio border and the approximate line of demarcation between wet, humid conditions and the dry, high plains—the one hundredth meridian of longitude. Some would rule out Michigan's Upper Peninsula as more like the Old World than the New and the Boot Heel and Ozark regions of Missouri as more southern than midwestern.

Over the years I have listened to dozens of dry, abstract academic debates—is there truly such a place (will the real Midwest please stand up?); if so, where is it, what are its boundaries, what is it? Is it honestly different from something called the East, the West, or the South?

Of all the arguments, statements and assertions about the Midwest, I like William Carter's in *Middle West Country* (1975) the best because it expresses what I feel about this region in which I have spent nearly seven decades:

> The rural Middle West is more than a physical area. It is a region of the heart. A home place: sometimes narrowly disapproving, but nurturing and loving, and preserving the style of the era before America moved away to the city. A place of ice cream socials on warm summer evenings, of the autumnal smells of fresh cider and burning leaves, of snowy silences pierced by the zip of sleds, of the dewy softness of a newborn calf.

Robert McLaughlin in *The Heartland* described the Midwest as a place where "frame houses, with front porches as ample as a grandmother's lap, are set back on wide lawns and hold memories of a creaking swing, the tinkle of a ukulele, the gleam of white dresses moving in and out of screen doors."

the country of the heart

Social scientists and earth scientists, trying to define the Midwest in terms of spatial relationships, meteorological statistics, demographics, and other quantitative means usually end up skating on very thin semantic ice. While I sympathize with their concern for documentation, for measurement, for hard fact, yet I'm also sure that what Hawthorne once called "the truth of the human heart" can often strike closer to what we believe. Let's listen to the man I believe to be the Midwest's greatest writer, F. Scott Fitzgerald, in *The Great Gatsby:*

> One of my most vivid memories is of coming back West from prep school and later from college at Christmas time. Those who went farther than Chicago would gather in the old dim Union Station at six o'clock of a December evening, with a few Chicago friends, already caught up into their own holiday gaieties, to bid them a hasty good-by. I remember the fur coats of the girls returning from Miss This-or-That's and the chatter of frozen breath and the hands waving overhead, as we caught sight of old acquaintances, and the matching of invitations: "Are you going to the Ordways? the Hersheys? the Schultzes?" and the long green tickets clasped tight in our gloved hands. And last the murky yellow cars of the Chicago, Milwaukee & St. Paul railroad looking cheerful as Christmas itself on the tracks beside the gate.
>
> When we pulled out into the winter night and the real snow, our snow, began to stretch out beside us and twinkle against the windows, and the dim lights of small Wisconsin stations moved by, a sharp wild brace came suddenly into the air. We drew in deep breaths of it as we walked back from dinner through the cold vestibules, unutterably aware of our identity with this country for one strange hour, before we melted indistinguishably into it again.
>
> That's my Middle West—not the wheat or the prairies or the lost Swede towns, but the thrilling returning trains of my youth, and the street lamps and the sleigh bells in the frosty dark and the shadows of holly wreaths thrown by lighted windows on the snow.

And so I have turned to writers rather than scientists, to words rather than binary digits, to emotions rather than reason, to get at the truth of what the real Middle West is and what it meant to its native writers to grow up there. In so doing, I would admit that what follows is only partial definition rather than the whole truth—the whole truth about the Middle West would fill a library. As someone has pointed out, there are at least one hundred thousand books on Chicago alone.

I have chosen my twenty-two writers because of their track records and recollections and perceptions of growing up in the Midwest. With the exception of one beginning writer, all have published in magazines, newspapers, journals, and books—the most prolific of these authors has forty-five books to his credit. Their work has withstood critical evaluation with high marks. There are three Pulitzer Prize authors and a number of award winners, including a National Book Award winner. There are a number of honorary degree holders from prestigious colleges. Four of these writers have had their books converted to plays, musical comedies, and films, including two Academy Award–winning films.

I have ranged over the Middle West for these writings. Not every midwestern area is represented here—that was not possible. But big cities, towns, villages, and rural areas—all are here. Women and men are almost equally represented—that they are not is due to matters beyond my control. Occupational points of view are included—a jurist's, a farmer's, a professor's or two, a housewife's or three, an editor's, a radio "d.j." 's, an administrator's, a public relations worker's. Wealth is reflected here as well as poverty and income states in between. Ethnic groups are here—two blacks, a Greek, a Scotswoman, a woman who through her lifetime asserted her Jewish heritage, two persons of American Indian descent, a man whose father was a Jewish cantor.

And now for "my Middle West" I turn you over to the tender mercies of midwestern poets, playwrights, short-story writers, novelists, essayists, and journalists. I hope you like what they wrote. I do.

CLARENCE ANDREWS

Iowa City, Iowa
1981

Clarence A. Andrews has written and edited many articles and books about regional literature, including A Literary History of Iowa *and* Growing Up in Iowa. *He holds a Ph.D. from the University of Iowa and has been a visiting professor of journalism and adjunct professor of English there as well as professor of humanities at Michigan Technological University and adjunct professor of American thought and studies at Michigan State University.*

Growing Up in the Midwest

MERIDEL   LE   SUEUR

Meridel Le Sueur, a truly midwestern writer of distinguished verse, short stories, and novels, says of herself:

> I was born at the beginning of the swiftest and bloodiest century in a white square puritan house in the corn belt, of two physically beautiful people who had come west through the Indian Lincoln country.

Her father was an itinerant preacher; Meridel was "raised, not reared" in Oklahoma, Texas, Kansas, Illinois, the Dakotas, and finally, after 1915, in Minnesota. In her own words, hers was "a slow perpetual rotarian migration around the middle west, north and south." In time, her mother, Marian Wharton, a pioneer midwestern educator, divorced her father and married Arthur Le Sueur, a radical lawyer and the first and only Socialist mayor of Minot, North Dakota.
> *After one year of high school, shw was sent by her mother to the American Academy of Dramatic Art in New York City and lived in an anarchist commune with Emma Goldman. Then Meridel Le Sueur went West to Hollywood where she recalls in an article by Patricia Hampl in* Ms. Magazine *(4, no. 2 [1975]: 63):*

> I didn't know how to make a living except in the films. I did stunts. They killed people like nothing in the movies then. You weren't worth anything. But you could get five dollars—if you lived through it.

She reports that she did Pearl White's stunts in the famous serial, The Perils of Pauline.
> *She returned to Minneapolis to teach school, work on newspapers, write, and raise three daughters. She sold her first story to the* Dial *in 1927. Her next story, "The Harvest" (1929), was followed by two articles that make her lifelong lower class sympathies plain: "Women in the Breadlines" (1932), and "What Happens in a Strike" (1934). Her first book,* Salute to Spring, *a collection of stories (1940), was praised by the* New Yorker *as "distinguished stories about what we used to call the American proletariat . . . described with a passionate and convincing partisanship."*

Of her role as an artist of the working people, she wrote: "I am putting down exactly how I feel because I believe others of my class feel the same."

She was blacklisted as an author during the McCarthy era because she was identified as a radical. But she kept her sense of humor. Once she walked to the side of a car driven by an FBI agent who was following her. "You might as well give me a ride," she said. "We're going to the same place."

She was rediscovered several years ago by the feminist movement, and since then she has published a number of books of verse and short stories, all through "private presses." Among these are Harvest (1977) which includes the three early titles listed above, and Rites of Ancient Ripening (1975), from which "Budded with Child" was taken.

Budded with Child

Before your cry,
    I never heard a cry,
Headless ghost I rode the prairies,
The bodiless head screaming after me,
Skeleton, I searched for rose and flesh,
Lamenting in bereaved villages
Howling in stone cities.
I gave berries to strangers
I gave them fruits
    I gave them fruits
For stones and bones and broken words.
In the place where crying begins
The place of borders, the place of the enemy
I begot you, child,
Before you I did not know flowers out of snow
           out of snow,
Or milk of meadows out of drouth.

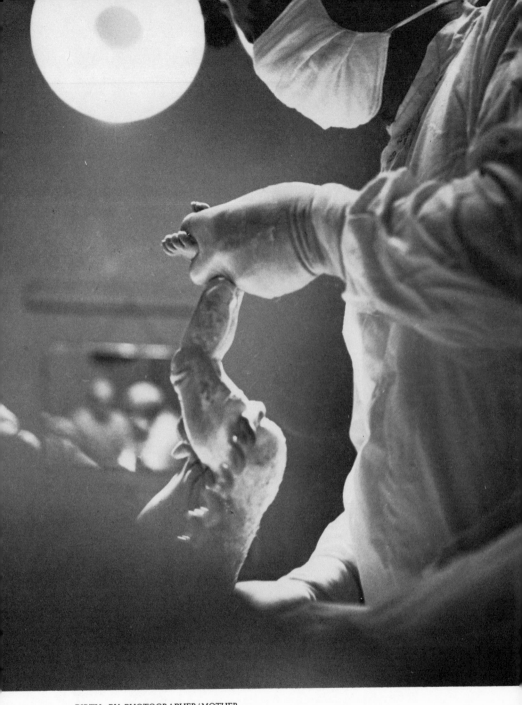

BIRTH, BY PHOTOGRAPHER/MOTHER.

Before your cry I never heard a cry,
Or globular breast, milk without summons.
Exiled I cried along the rivers
                caged in time and loss,
Empty pod I longed for winged seeds.
Till merged in earth's agony of birth
                leapt bridge
                        struck lyre
Impaled on earth and flesh's spring,
                budded with child.
Before you, child, I never knew the breast of milk
                the arm of love
                        the kerneled grain of groats
        and all for bread.
Before your face I never saw a face descending
                down my belly to time's horizon
Breast and skin multiplied into multitude
                                and benevolence.

EDNA FERBER

Edna Ferber (1887–1968), noted short-story author, novelist, and playwright and in her mature years a woman of the world, was very much a midwesterner. She was born in Kalamazoo, Michigan, and her formative years were spent in Chicago; Appleton, Wisconsin; Ottumwa, Iowa; and Milwaukee. Hers was a migrant life, like those of Meridel Le Sueur and R. V. Cassill.

In a 1922 Liberty article, we have Miss Ferber's own word for her midwestern quality: "Why do you always write about Chicago or some such Middle-Western wilderness?" Ferber reports "an occasional bored inquirer" as writing, "Why do you always choose commonplace middle-class people as your characters?"

To questions such as these, Ferber replied:

> A middle-class person living in Appleton, Wisconsin, or Chicago, Illinois, naturally wrote about middle-class persons living in Chicago or Appleton. Never having been rich or poor, the rich and poor were strange fields and pastures. . . .

She added that her "Bad Fairy" had given her "a smart clip over the head with her magic wand" and said:

> Yours shall be the commonplace middle-class name of Edna. All your life shall you be cursed with the inability to be dazzled by the romantic rich or thrilled by the picturesque poor. Never shall you be seen wandering, wet-eyed, around the slums of [New York's] lower East Side looking for what non-writers call copy; and though you peer hungrily into the perambulators and limousines of Park Avenue it shall avail you nothing. Not a Thing. Always for you, a tough young garage mechanic on his afternoon off shall appear more interesting than a Van Bibber on his polo pony.

She granted that she was becoming a cosmopolite—but she could rationalize that change:

> And though I now live in New York City, the City of Sophistication, I'll never be more than an onlooker in it. First Nights and Literary Teas, and Pomeranian Pups and Sable Coats, and Roof Bungalows will always be things I shall View With Alarm, mingled

with a feeling of unreality. And when it comes to writing I turn back to the town with a little human awkwardness left in it.

Ferber's first short stories and early books were set in the Midwest: Dawn O'Hara, The Girl Who Laughed *(1911),* Buttered Side Down *(1912),* The Girls *(1921),* So Big *(1924),* Show Boat *(1926),* Cimarron *(1930),* Come and Get It *(1935).* So Big *won a Pulitzer Prize and was filmed three times;* Show Boat, *as a novel and as a musical play by Jerome Kern and Oscar Hammerstein II, became a part of American folklore.*

Lennox Bouton Grey in a University of Chicago dissertation entitled "Chicago and the Great American Novel: A Critical Approach to the American Epic" (1935) commented that in the two decades during which Ferber used the midwestern scene, no American writer "surpassed her in the profitable talent for catching the current fluttering of the American pulse . . . a sign of timeliness that is her strength and weakness."

Ferber said of the following essay, taken from her 1917 novel, Fanny Herself, *that it mirrored her girlhood days, particularly the experience of being a Jewish girl in the non-Jewish Midwest, as accurately as anything she ever wrote. I agree; it is more detailed and interesting than accounts of her girlhood in her 1939 autobiography,* A Peculiar Treasure.

A Jewish Girl
on the Day of Atonement

SHE WAS A STRANGE MIXTURE of tomboy and bookworm, which was a mercifully kind arrangement for both body and mind. The spiritual side of her was groping and staggering and feeling its way about as does that of any little girl whose mind is exceptionally active, and whose mother is unusually busy. It was on the Day of Atonement, known in the Hebrew as Yom Kippur, in the year following her father's death that that side of her performed a rather interesting handspring.

Fanny Brandeis had never been allowed to fast on this, the greatest and most solemn of Jewish holy days. Molly Brandreis' modern side refused to countenance the practice of withholding food from any child for twenty-four hours. So it was in the face of disapproval that Fanny, making deep inroads into the steak and fried sweet potatoes at supper on the eve of the Day of Atonement, announced her intention of fasting from that meal to supper on the following evening. She had just passed her plate for a third helping of potatoes. Theodore, one lap behind her in the race, had entered his objection.

"Well, for the land's sakes!" he protested. "I guess you're not the only one who likes sweet potatoes."

Fanny applied a generous dab of butter to an already buttery morsel, and chewed it with an air of conscious virtue.

"I've got to eat a lot. This is the last bite I'll have until tomorrow night."

"What's that?" exclaimed Mrs. Brandeis, sharply.

"Yes, it is!" hooted Theodore.

Fanny went on conscientiously eating as she explained.

"Bella Weinberg and I are going to fast all day. We just want to see if we can."

"Betcha can't," Theodore said.

Mrs. Brandeis regarded her small daughter with a thoughtful gaze. "But that isn't the object in fasting, Fanny—just to see if you can. If you're going to think of food all through the Yom Kippur services—"

"I sha'n't!" protested Fanny passionately. "Theodore would, but I won't."

"Wouldn't any such thing," denied Theodore. "But if I'm going to play a violin solo during the memorial service I guess I've got to eat my regular meals."

Theodore sometimes played at temple, on special occasions. The little congregation, listening to the throbbing rise and fall of this fifteen-year-old boy's violin playing, realized, vaguely, that here was something disturbingly, harrowingly beautiful. They did not know that they were listening to genius.

Molly Brandeis, in her second best dress, walked to temple Yom Kippur eve, her son at her right side, her daughter at her left. She had made up her mind that she would not let this next day, with its poignantly beautiful service, move her too deeply. It was the first since her husband's death, and Rabbi Thalmann rather prided himself on his rendition of the memorial service that came at three in the afternoon.

A man of learning, of sweetness, and of gentle wit was Rabbi Thalmann, and unappreciated by his congregation. He stuck to the Scriptures for his texts, finding Moses a greater leader than Roosevelt, and the miracle of the Burning Bush more wonderful than the marvels of twentieth-century wizardry in electricity. A little man, Rabbi Thalmann, with hands and feet as small and delicate as those of a woman. Fanny found him fascinating to look on, in his rabbinical black broadcloth and his two pairs of glasses perched, in reading, upon his small hooked nose. He stood very straight in the pulpit, but on the street you saw that his back was bent just the least bit in the world—or perhaps it was only his student stoop, as he walked along with his eyes on the ground, smoking those slender, dapper, pale brown cigars that looked as if they had been expressly cut and rolled to fit him.

The evening service was at seven. The congregation, rustling in silks, was approaching the little temple from all directions. Inside, there was a low-toned buzz of conversation. The Brandeis' seat was well toward the rear, as befitted a less prosperous member of the rich little congregation. This enabled them to get a complete picture of the room in its holiday splendor. Fanny drank it in eagerly, her dark eyes soft and luminous. The bare, yellow-varnished wooden pews glowed with the reflection from the chandeliers. The seven-branched candlesticks on either side of the pulpit were entwined with smilax. The red plush curtain that hung in front of the Ark on ordinary days, and the red plush pulpit cover too, were replaced by gleaming white satin edged with gold fringe and finished at the corners with heavy gold tassels. How the rich white satin glistened in the light of the electric candles! Fanny Brandeis loved the lights, and the gleam, and the music, so majestic, and solemn, and the sight of the little rabbi, sitting so straight and serious in his high-backed chair, or standing to read from the great Bible. There came to this emotional little Jewess a thrill that was not born of religious fervor at all, I am afraid.

The sheer drama of the thing got her. In fact, the thing she had set herself to do to-day had in it very little of religion. Mrs. Brandeis had been right about that. It was a test of endurance, as planned. Fanny had never fasted in all her healthy life. She would come home from school to eat formidable stacks of bread and butter, enhanced by brown sugar or grape jelly, and topped off with three or four apples from the barrel in the cellar. Two hours later she would attack a supper of fried potatoes, and liver, and tea, and peach preserve, and more stacks of bread and butter. Then there were the cherry trees in the back yard, and the berry bushes, not to speak of sundry bags of small, hard candies of the jelly-bean variety, fitted for quick and

9

secret munching during school. She liked good things to eat, this sturdy little girl, as did her friend, that blonde and creamy person, Bella Weinberg.

The two girls exchanged meaningful glances during the evening service. The Weinbergs, as befitted their station, sat in the third row at the right, and Bella had to turn around to convey her silent messages to Fanny. The evening service was brief, even to the sermon. Rabbi Thalmann and his congregation would need their strength for to-morrow's trial.

The Brandeises walked home through the soft September night, and the children had to use all their Yom Kippur dignity to keep from scuffling through the piled-up drifts of crackling autumn leaves. Theodore went to the cellar and got an apple, which he ate with what Fanny considered an unnecessary amount of scrunching. It was a firm, juicy apple, and it gave forth a cracking sound when his teeth met in its white meat. Fanny, after regarding him with gloomy superiority, went to bed.

She had willed to sleep late, for gastronomic reasons, but the mental command disobeyed itself, and she woke early, with a heavy feeling. Early as it was, Molly Brandeis had tiptoed in still earlier to look at her strange little daughter. She sometimes did that on Saturday mornings when she left early for the store and Fanny slept late. This morning Fanny's black hair was spread over the pillow as she lay on her back, one arm outflung, the other at her breast. She made a rather startlingly black and white and scarlet picture as she lay there asleep. Fanny did things very much in that way, too, with broad, vivid, unmistakable splashes of color. Mrs. Brandeis, looking at the black-haired, red-lipped child sleeping there, wondered just how much determination lay back of the broad white brow. She had said little to Fanny about this feat of fasting, and she told herself that she disapproved of it. But in her heart she wanted the girl to see it through, once attempted.

Fanny awoke at half past seven, and her nostrils dilated to that most exquisite, tantalizing and fragrant of smells—the aroma of simmering coffee. It permeated the house. It tickled the senses. It carried with it visions of hot, brown breakfast rolls, and eggs, and butter. Fanny loved her breakfast. She turned over now, and decided to go to sleep again. But she could not. She got up and dressed slowly and carefully. There was no one to hurry her this morning with the call from the foot of the stairs of, "Fanny! Your egg'll get cold!"

She put on clean, crisp underwear, and did her hair expertly. She slipped an all-enveloping pinafore over her head, that the new silk dress might not be crushed before church time. She thought that Theodore would surely have finished his breakfast by this time. But when she came down-stairs he was at the table. Not only that, he had just begun his breakfast. An egg, all golden, and white, and crisply brown at the frilly edges, lay on his plate. Theodore always ate his egg in a mathematical sort of way. He swallowed the white hastily first, because he disliked it, and Mrs. Brandeis insisted that he eat it. Then he would brood a moment over the yolk that lay, unmarred and complete, like an amber jewel in the center of his plate. Then he would suddenly plunge his fork into the very heart of the jewel, and it would flow over his plate, mingling with the butter, and he would catch it deftly with little mops of warm, crisp, buttery roll.

Fanny passed the breakfast table just as Theodore plunged his fork into the egg yolk. She caught her breath sharply, and closed her eyes. Then she turned and fled to the front porch and breathed deeply and windily of the heady September Wisconsin morning air. As she stood there, with her stiff, short black curls still damp and glistening, in her best shoes and stockings, with the all-enveloping apron covering her sturdy little figure, the light of struggle and renunciation in her face, she typified something at once fine and earthy.

But the real struggle was to come later. They went to temple at ten, Theodore with his beloved violin tucked carefully under his arm. Bella Weinberg was waiting at the steps.

"Did you?" she asked eagerly.

"Of course not," replied Fanny disdainfully. "Do you think I'd eat old breakfast when I said I was going to fast all day?" Then, with sudden suspicion, "Did you?"

"No!" stoutly.

And they entered, and took their seats. It was fascinating to watch the other members of the congregation come in, the women rustling, the men subdued in the unaccustomed dignity of black on a week day. One glance at the yellow pews was like reading a complete social and financial register. The seating arrangement of the temple was the Almanach de Gotha of Congregation Emanu-el. Old Ben Reitman, patriarch among the Jewish settlers of Winnebago, who had come over an immigrant youth, and who now owned hundreds of rich farm acres, besides houses, mills and banks, kinged it from the front seat of the center section. He was a magnificent old man, with a ruddy face, and a fine head with a shock of heavy iron-gray hair, keen eyes, undimmed by years, and a startling and unexpected dimple in one cheek that gave him a mischievous and boyish look.

TEMPLE ISRAEL.

Behind this dignitary sat his sons, and their wives, and his daughters and their husbands, and their children, and so on, back to the Brandeis pew, third from the last, behind which sat only a few obscure families branded as Russians, as only the German-born Jew can brand those whose misfortune it is to be born in that region known as hinter-Berlin.

The morning flew by, with its music, its responses, its sermon in German, full of four- and five-syllable German words like *Barmherzigkeit* and *Eigentümlichkeit*. All during the sermon Fanny sat and dreamed and watched the shadow on the window of the pine tree

that stood close to the temple, and was vastly amused at the jaundiced look that the square of yellow window glass cast upon the face of the vain and overdressed Mrs. Nathan Pereles. From time to time Bella would turn to bestow upon her a look intended to convey intense suffering and a resolute though dying condition. Fanny stonily ignored these mute messages, They offended something in her, though she could not tell what.

At the noon intermission she did not go home to the tempting dinner smells, but wandered off through the little city park and down to the river, where she sat on the bank and felt very virtuous, and spiritual, and hollow. She was back in her seat when the afternoon service was begun. Some of the more devout members had remained to pray all through the midday. The congregation came straggling in by twos and threes. Many of the women had exchanged the severely corseted discomfort of the morning's splendor for the comparative ease of second-best silks. Mrs. Brandeis, absent from her business throughout this holy day, came hurrying in at two, to look with a rather anxious eye upon her pale and resolute little daughter.

The memorial service was to begin shortly after three, and lasted almost two hours. At quarter to three Bella slipped out through the side aisle, beckoning mysteriously and alluringly to Fanny as she went. Fanny looked at her mother.

"Run along," said Mrs. Brandeis. "The air will be good for you. Come back before the memorial service begins."

Fanny and Bella met, giggling, in the vestibule.

"Come on over to my house for a minute," Bella suggested. "I want to show you something." The Weinberg house, a great, comfortable, well-built home with encircling veranda, and a well-cared-for lawn, was just a scant block away. They skipped across the street, down the block and in at the back door. The big sunny kitchen was deserted. The house seemed very quiet and hushed. Over it hung the delicious fragrance of freshly-baked pastry. Bella, a rather baleful look in her eyes, led the way to the butler's pantry that was as large as the average kitchen. And there, ranged on platters, and baking boards, and on snowy-white napkins, was that which made Tantalus's feast seem a dry and barren snack. The Weinbergs had baked.

It is the custom in the household of Atonement Day fasters of the old school to begin the evening meal, after the twenty-four hours of abstainment, with coffee and freshly-baked coffee cake of every variety. It was a lead-pipe blow at one's digestion, but delicious beyond imagining. Bella's mother was a famous cook, and her two maids followed in the ways of their mistress. There were to be sisters and brothers and out-of-town relations as guests at the evening meal, and Mrs. Weinberg had outdone herself.

"Oh!" exclaimed Fanny in a sort of agony and delight.

"Take some," said Bella, the temptress.

The pantry was fragrant as a garden with spices, and fruit scents, and the melting, delectable perfume of brown, freshly-baked dough, sugar-coated. There was one giant platter devoted wholly to round, plump cakes, with puffy edges, in the center of each a sunken pool that was all plum, bearing on its bosom a snowy sifting of powdered sugar. There were others whose centers were apricot, pure molten gold in the sunlight. Ther were speckled expanses of cheese *kuchen*, the golden-brown surface showing rich cracks through which one caught glimpses of the lemon-yellow cheese beneath—cottage cheese that had been beaten up with eggs, and spices, and sugar, and lemon. Flaky crust rose, jaggedly, above this plateau. There were cakes with jelly, and cinnamon *kuchen*, and cunning cakes with almond slices nestling side by side. And there was freshly-baked bread—twisted loaf, with poppy seed freckling its braid, and its sides glistening with the butter that had been liberally swabbed on it before it had been thrust into the oven.

Fanny Brandeis gazed, hypnotized. As she gazed Bella selected a plum tart and bit into it—bit generously, so that her white little teeth met in the very middle of the oozing red-brown juice and one heard a little squirt as they closed on the luscious fruit. At the sound Fanny quivered all through her plump and starved little body.

"Have one, " said Bella generously. "Go on. Nobody'll ever know. Anyway, we've fasted long enough for our age. I could fast till supper time if I wanted to, but I don't want to." She swallowed the last morsel of the plum tart, and selected another—apricot, this time, and opened her moist red lips. But just before she bit into it (the Inquisition could have used Bella's talents) she selected its counterpart and held it out to Fanny. Fanny shook her head slightly. Her hand came up involuntarily. Her eyes were fastened on Bella's face.

"Go on," urged Bella. "Take it. They're grand! M-m-m-m!" The first bite of apricot vanished between her rows of sharp white teeth. Fanny shut her eyes as if in pain. She was fighting the great fight of her life. She was to meet other temptations, and perhaps more glittering ones, in her lifetime, but to her dying day she never forgot that first battle between the flesh and the spirit, there in the sugar-scented pantry—and the spirit won. As Bella's lips closed upon the second bite of apricot tart, the while her eye roved over the almond cakes and her hand still held the sweet out to Fanny, that young lady turned sharply, like a soldier, and marched blindly out of the house, down the back steps, across the street, and so into the temple.

The evening lights had just been turned on. The little congregation, relaxed, weary, weak from hunger, many of them, sat rapt and still except at those times when the prayer book demanded spoken responses. The voice of the little rabbi, rather weak now, had in it a timbre that made it startlingly sweet and clear and resonant. Fanny slid very quietly into the seat beside Mrs. Brandeis, and slipped her moist and cold little hand into her mother's warm, work-roughened palm. The mother's brown eyes, very bright with unshed tears, left their perusual of the prayer book to dwell upon the white little face that was smiling rather wanly up at her. The pages of the prayer book lay two-thirds or more to the left. Just as Fanny remarked this, there was a little moment of hush in the march of the day's long service. The memorial hour had begun.

Little Doctor Thalmann cleared his throat. The congregation stirred a bit, changed its cramped position. Bella, the guilty, came stealing in, a pink-and-gold picture of angelic virtue. Fanny, looking at her, felt very aloof, and clean, and remote.

Molly Brandeis seemed to sense what had happened.

"But you didn't, did you?" she whispered softly.

Fanny shook her head.

Rabbi Thalmann was seated in his great carved chair. His eyes were closed. The wheezy little organ in the choir loft at the rear of the temple began the opening bars of Schumann's Träumerei. And then, above the cracked voice of the organ, rose the clear, poignant wail of a violin. Theodore Brandeis had begun to play. You know the playing of the average boy of fifteen—that nerve-destroying, uninspired scraping. There was nothing of this in the sounds that this boy called forth from the little wooden box and the stick with its taut lines of catgut. Whatever it was—the length of the thin, sensitive fingers, the turn of the wrist, the articulation of the forearm, the something in the brain, or all these combined—Theodore Brandeis possessed that which makes for greatness. You realized that as he crouched over his violin to get his cello tones. As he played to-day the little congregation sat very still, and each was thinking of his ambitions and his failures; of the lover lost, of the duty left undone, of the hope deferred; of the wrong that was never righted; of the lost one whose memory spells remorse. It felt the salt taste on its lips. It put up a furtive, shamed hand to dab at its cheeks, and saw that the one who sat in the pew just ahead was doing likewise. This is what happened when this boy of fifteen wedded his bow to his violin. And he who makes us feel all this has that indefinable, magic, glorious thing known as Genius.

When it was over, there swept through the room that sigh following tension relieved. Rabbi Thalmann passed a hand over his tired eyes, like one returning from a far mental journey; then rose, and came forward to the pulpit. He began, in Hebrew, the opening words of the memorial service, and so on to the prayers in English, with their words of infinite humility and wisdom.

"Thou hast implanted in us the capacity for sin, but not sin itself!"

Fanny stirred. She had learned that a brief half hour ago. The service marched on, a moving and harrowing thing. The amens rolled out with a new fervor from the listeners. There seemed nothing comic now in the way old Ben Reitman, with his slower eyes, always came out five words behind the rest who tumbled upon the responses and scurried briskly through them, so that his fine old voice, somewhat hoarse and quavering now, rolled out its "Amen!" in solitary majesty. They came to that gem of humility, the mourners' prayer; the ancient and ever-solemn Kaddish prayer. There is nothing in the written language that, for sheer drama and magnificence, can equal it as it is chanted in the Hebrew.

As Rabbi Thalmann began to intone it in its monotonous repetition of praise, there arose certain black-robed figures from their places and stood with heads bowed over their prayer books. These were members of the congregation from whom death had taken a toll during the past year. Fanny rose with her mother and Theodore, who had left the choir loft to join them. The little wheezy organ played very softly. The black-robed figures swayed. Here and there a half-stifled sob rose, and was crushed. Fanny felt a hot haze that blurred her vision. She winked it away, and another burned in its place. Her shoulders shook with a sob. She felt her mother's hand close over her own that held one side of the book. The prayer, that was not of mourning but of praise, ended with a final crescendo from the organ. The silent black-robed figures were seated.

Over the little, spent congregation hung a glorious atmosphere of detachment. These Jews, listening to the words that had come from the lips of the prophets in Israel, had been, on this day, thrown back thousands of years, to the time when the destruction of the temple was as real as the shattered spires and dome of the cathedral at Rheims. Old Ben Reitman, faint with fasting, was far removed from his everyday thoughts of his horses, his lumber mills, his farms, his mortgages. Even Mrs. Nathan Pereles, in her black satin and bugles and jets, her cold, hard face usually unlighted by sympathy or love, seemed to feel something of this emotional wave. Fanny Brandeis was shaken by it. Her head ached (that was hunger) and her hands were icy. The little Russian girl in the seat just behind them had ceased to wriggle and squirm, and slept against her mother's side. Rabbi Thalmann, there on the platform, seemed somehow very far away and vague. The scent of clove apples and ammonia salts filled the air. The atmosphere seemed strangely wavering and luminous. The white satin of the Ark curtain gleamed and shifted.

The long service swept on to its close. Suddenly organ and choir burst into a pæon. Little Doctor Thalmann raised his arms. The congregation swept to its feet with a mighty surge. Fanny rose with them, her face very white in its frame of black curls, her eyes luminous. She raised her face for the words of the ancient benediction that rolled, in its simplicity and grandeur, from the lips of the rabbi:

"May the blessing of the Lord our God rest upon you all. God bless thee and keep thee. May God cause His countenance to shine upon thee and be gracious unto thee. May God lift up His countenance unto thee, and grant thee peace."

The Day of Atonement had come to an end. It was a very quiet, subdued and spent little flock that dispersed to their homes. Fanny walked out with scarcely a thought of Bella. She felt, vaguely, that she and this school friend were formed of different stuff. She knew that the bond between them had been the grubby, physical one of childhood, and that they never would come together in the finer relation of the spirit, though she could not have put this new knowledge into words.

Molly Brandeis put a hand on her daughter's shoulder.

"Tired, Fanchen?"

"A little."

"Bet you're hungry!" from Theodore.

"I was, but I'm not now."

"M-m-m—wait! Noodle soup. And chicken!"

She had intended to tell of the trial in the Weinberg's pantry. But now something within her—something fine, born of this day— kept her from it. But Molly Brandeis, to whom two and two often made five, guessed something of what had happened. She had felt a great surge of pride, had Molly Brandeis, when her son had swayed the congregation with the magic of his music. She had kissed him good night with infinite tenderness and love. But she came into her daughter's tiny room after Fanny had gone to bed, and leaned over, and put a cool hand on the hot forehead.

"Do you feel all right, my darling?"

"Umhmph," replied Fanny drowsily.

"Fanchen, doesn't it make you feel happy and clean to know that you were able to do the thing you started out to do?"

"Umhmph."

"Only," Molly Brandeis was thinking aloud now, quite forgetting that she was talking to a very little girl, "only, life seems to take such special delight in offering temptation to those who are able to withstand it. I don't know why that's true, but it is. I hope—oh, my little girl, my baby—I hope—"

But Fanny never knew whether her mother finished that sentence or not. She remembered waiting for the end of it, to learn what it was her mother hoped. And she had felt a sudden, scalding drop on her hand where her mother bent over her. And the next thing she knew it was morning, with mellow September sunshine.

"*The midwest,*" *said Winifred Mayne Van Etten in* I
Am the Fox *(1936), was both "the richest agricultural area in the
Union" and the "Bible Belt, where all the rural virtues resided,
godliness, the sanctity of the hearth, thrift and bucolic content."*

In three short articles published in Henry L. Mencken's American
Mercury, *James Stevens, born in Albia, Iowa, in 1892 and who is best
known for bringing the Paul Bunyan legend to the attention of American
readers, explores the pragmatic problems of sustaining these "rural virtues in the highly visible society of a raw frontier town beset by a mobile
pluralistic population." His protagonist in his stories like the protagonists
of Mark Twain's* Adventures of Tom Sawyer *and* Adventures of Huckle-
berry Finn, *is an impressionable boy, faced with the strictures and temptations of an adult world.*

*In the 1933 "Medicine Men: Reminiscences," the youthful protago-
nist-narrator, who is a born storyteller in the best traditions of the frontier tall tale, is caught up in a verbal feud between a medicine man and
a Methodist minister—or, we might say, between sin and salvation. In
the 1931 "Downfall of Elder Barton," the boy finds himself in the middle of a quarrel over the three "Rs"—not of "Readin', Ritin' and
'Rithmetick" but of another set sometimes taken more seriously at an
earlier time—"Rum, Romanism, and Rebellion."*

*In the 1925 "A Prairie Town" which follows, the narrator, who is
"not naturally a good boy," wavers between sin and salvation, between
backslidin' and revivalism. Eventually his backsliding triumphs, and his
grandmother—a faint echo of Tom Sawyer's Aunt Polly—packs him off
to the Oregon farming country to join his father. "Sivilization" was
becoming too much for him as it had for Huck.*

*Although there is some of the exaggeration in these tales which we
might expect of the writer who had been attracted to the gigantic adventures of Paul Bunyan and his Babe, still they have an atmosphere of
credibility that suggests Stevens is hewing very close to the truth of the
business of growing up in a turn-of-the-century Midwest village. Their
literary quality comes close to Twain's and is at least the equal of that
other narrative of* Boy Life on the Prairie *penned by Hamlin Garland a
quarter of a century earlier.*

A Prairie Town

IN THE SPRING THAT FOLLOWED my fifth birthday I went to live with my grandmother in Moravia, a town of five hundred population in southern Iowa. Moravia itself was a farm town, but only four miles away to the north were Foster and Hilton, coal-mining towns, and a gaudy industrial life. The best farms about Moravia were in the level lands along the eastern and western roads. South of the town was a hilly country, with streams foaming through its little valleys, and woods of hickory and elm on its hills. Many kinds of wildflowers grew there in the Spring among the young grass; and the fresh greenery of unfolding leaves on the boughs, and the tickling smells of the stirring earth, and the exhilarating air, washed by April rains, made the hills magical in that season. In the Summer the creeks offered swimming pools in cool shade. In the Autumn crowds of boys went out on Saturdays, with bags over their shoulders, and rescued hickory nuts, walnuts and hazelnuts from the squirrels, their pestiferous rivals. In the years when the nuts grew scantily on tree and bush these creatures were intolerable in their piggishness, and every true boy would play hooky to rout them. In the Winter the hill country was the best for sleighing and tobogganing; the best skating ponds, however, were out in the flat farm lands to the east and west.

The tranquility of the usual country town of that time and region was not in Moravia, though it was far from being openly sinful, like the coal-mining towns. The Methodists, the Christians, the United Brethren, and the Cumberland Presbyterians had churches there; and out in the hill country was a Primitive (Hardshell) Baptist meeting-house, and a Methodist chapel. But it was only a few miles from the chapel to the sinful Soap Creek country, where the soap-crickers rioted and danced and played poker. With the soap-crickers on one side, and the coal-miners on the other, the righteous neighborhood of Moravia (the town was founded by the Moravian sect) had a hard time of it; and even the most pious boys didn't have a fair chance. Three railroads ran through the town, so there were many section men and other railroad employes lolling about, and hobos were always dropping in. Quite often farm boys would go over to work in the mines, and they were usually spoiled when they came back. Sometimes a gang of them would drive over from Foster, bringing kegs of beer with them—our town had no saloons—and then they would gather up their friends and have a beer-bust in some out-of-the-way place. All this made a pretty risky environment for me, as I was not naturally a good boy.

During my very first Summer in Moravia I learned to chew tobacco; and no doubt I did many other things which greatly worried my grandmother. At any rate, she started me in school when it opened on the first Monday in September, though I was a year too young for it. I could already read a bit, however. The old folks used to shake their heads and say it was powerful strange that the boy was smart, and yet so pesky mean. My earliest memories of grown people are mainly concerned with their wonder and admonishments about "the 'tarnal contrariness of thet child."

School had a good influence on me at first; not because of the study and the schoolma'm's discipline, but because of the boys, all of them older than myself. It was Sam Trub, a fat boy of seven, who first taught me to respect the authority of power. Whenever it was his will for me to do so, I had to stop by his place, sit down on the sidewalk, and tell him stories. I had to run errands for him. I dared not wear my Bryan button when he was around, for his grandfather, a Civil War hero, was what my Virginia grandmother called "A black Republican." Sam Trub's people were all strict Methodists, and he ridiculed my Hardshell Baptist connections at every opportunity. Whenever I rebelled against his dominance, he would upset me on my back, straddle his bulk over my belly, and tickle me. I was fearfully ticklish, and I had a great terror of Sam. He was a pious, church-going boy, and he brought me to Sunday-school. He also ordered me to chew no more tobacco, and during the whole eight months of school I did not touch the leaf. For a year and a half I lived in dread of him. I was docile in school, I attended Sunday-school regularly, and in the Summer of 1899 I marched in a procession shouting for McKinley—all because my fat young master so willed it. But in the Autumn of that year, as I shall relate, I was freed of Sam Trub.

In August Wild Jim and his partner came to Moravia. They were dressed in buckskins, with fringes on their sleeves and breeches, and they wore gaudy silk bandannas around their necks, and amazingly wide and lofty sombreros on their heads. Handbills advertised that Wild Jim would do some fancy shooting in Lathrop's field, and that his partner would then break any colt to the saddle in ten minutes. All the boys were excited about these heroes of the West, and the grown-ups talked a lot about them, too.

There was a big crowd on hand to see Wild Jim do his shooting. Big marbles—the kind with curling colored stripes which boys called "glassies"—and empty cans were thrown into the air, and Wild Jim missed hardly a shot. When he had finished his exhibition he made a speech in which he told how much greater a scout he was than Buffalo Bill, and how his shooting surpassed Wild Bill Hickock's; "only," said Wild Jim, "I was never the kind of a feller to go around shootin' folks like Hickock did, an' I ain't the kind of a feller to go showin' myself off in a miser'ble, unchrischun circus, an' braggin' all over about the scoutin' an' Injun-fightin' I done, like Cody. Mind you, I ain't sayin' a word against Cody; I learned him a lot, an' I know there's quite a bit to him. But I quit him an' let him go his own way when he started showin' off. That wasn't the style to suit an honest an' straight-forward ol' plainsman like Wild Jim. What I'm doin', gents, is sellin' the story of my life here; writ in a plain, simple way, it is; all fac's an' no brags. I been mixed in a heap of deviltry, an' knew the time when I'd as soon kill a man as look at him. I confess it all here, as a warnin'. I live a Chrischun life now; an' to prove it I offer you this fifty-cent book for twenty-five cents; one quarter of a dollar; or, as we say in the wild an' woolly West, two bits. Step right up, if you want to read the honest-to-goodness hair-raisin' fac's about Wild Jim an' life on the plains."

He had waved his hands and pranced around like a politician when he talked, and there must have been a hundred men in the crowd who bought his book.

Book-selling done, Wild Jim and his partner returned to the hotel, where a farmer had an unbroken three-year-old tied to the hitching rack. The two Westerners went into the hotel, and the crowd waited. It grew impatient, as the partner failed to show up with his saddle. Finally, old Wilber Trub, Sam's grandfather, raised a yell for him, and the crowd took it up. Then Wild Jim came out and made another speech. He flattered the town, saying he had not been in so Christian a settlement in ages. He flattered the men, saying he had never seen a crowd anywhere, not even in the wild and woolly West, which could appreciate fine shooting as this one did. He certainly hated to leave them, said Wild Jim, and his partner felt the same way; but business was business, and they had to catch the 4:30 train, and if his partner took time to break a wild horse to ride, they might miss it. So he just wanted to thank the Moravia people again, and he hoped they would all keep good, Christian feelings for him and his partner.

Wilbur Trub was a steward in the Methodist church, but he had no good, Christian feelings about him just then. He ran around to the back of the hotel, yanked a rail off a fence, and carried it out on his shoulder, shouting, "Fakers! Let's ride the fakers out of town on a rail!" The other old soldiers always followed Wilber's lead, and there were many of them in the crowd. They started parading back and forth behind him, and then he led them up the hotel steps. Before they reached the door Wild Jim's partner came out, his saddle slung over his shoulder. Wild Jim did not show up to make another speech. The partner really looked mean and wild, having a lean, yellow face, and a heavy black mustache above a thin goatee; but he never said one word all the time he was in Moravia. He strode sullenly through the crowd, helped to blindfold the colt, and swiftly saddled him. I have come to suspect that the partner was the real Wild Jim, and that the orator of the pair was some circus or vaudeville marksman with a talent for showmanship.

Anyhow, the partner was a real rider, and he soon quirted the colt into a bucking gallop that carried him into the main residence street of the town. His evil-tempered rider then put him over a dozen fine lawns and flower gardens that had no fences around them. The colt returned at a weary trot; and the partner dismounted, snapped the cinch loose, and carried his saddle into the hotel, without a word or a look for anyone in the crowd. It made us boys shiver just to look at him, and we were sure that old Wilber Trub was the bravest man in the country, to stand on the hotel steps as he did and glare at the wild Westerner. And as Wild Jim and his partner got into the hotel hack to leave, old Wilber shouted at them: "Wild West, or no Wild West, you'll never git the best o' Moravy, let me tell you!" When the hack was gone the people all crowded around Wilber Trub and shook his hand.

None of the citizens whose lawns were ruined complained very much; everybody was glad that Wild Jim and his partner hadn't got the best of our town. Wilber Trub was quite a hero for a time. And Sam—well, no boy could have any peace around him at all. He actually went so far as to make me go along the street where the farmers were gossiping one Saturday afternoon, and yell over and over, "Hurrah for Mr. Wilber Trub, the man who scared Wild Jim!"

Old Wilber ran a furniture store, and, despite his Methodism, he sometimes indulged in very unsanctified merchandising. This practice of his cost him his glory soon after he had acquired it, and reduced his grandson to humility. The old soldier had been a gay fellow among the girls in his youth, and he still had an eye for a pretty lady. A young widow came to his store one afternoon to buy a little red wagon for her son. She demurred at the cost. Old Wilber, so the town gossip ran, suggested that there were more ways than one for a young widow to get a little red wagon from Wilber Trub. Unluckily for him, the widow's sense of humor was stronger than her sense of outrage when she heard his proposal. She did not reject it with scorn and keep the shameful secret; she merely laughed at old Wilber, and then told the joke to all the Methodist ladies she met.

On the following Saturday night there was a show in the opera-house. The actors heard of the joke on the Methodist steward, and, regarding Methodist stewards as their natural enemies, they made the most of it. At the end of the first act of their melodrama two comedians came out before the curtain to entertain during the wait. One of them began to blubber and bawl,

"Oh! Oh! I've lost my wife; lost her for keeps!"

"Well, well!" said the other. "That's too bad. When did she die?"

"She ain't dead. But she's gone to Wilber Trub's to get one of his little red wagons!"

This rascal had a handkerchief which he had soaked in water. He pretended to cry into it, and then wring out streams of tears. How the soap-crickers, farm hands and coal-miners roared! More than one good churchman, indeed, also snickered over the affair, though the opinion was pretty general among the church people that the sinful element had exaggerated the story, or had even lied outright about it, to cast odium on a Methodist steward. The widow had been under suspicion for some time; and it was considered a brazen thing for her to come right out and tell of old Wilber's proposal as a joke. It was very likely, said the Methodists, that she had tempted him, and he had not yielded, and she had told the story to get even.

This might have been so. At any rate, the old soldier went about his business as though the gossip did not exist, and no one ventured to taunt him openly. But the dignity and authority of his position in the town were greatly reduced. His poor grandson was now the most scorned and despised boy in my class at school. The bigger schoolboys, sons of section hands and other laborers, made life wretched for him; and he got so that anyone had only to say, "little red wagon," in the most unconcerned way, and he would look pale and sick and seem to shrink in his clothes. Sam never tormented me any more, and finally I got up courage to make myself completely free of him.

One day I went around to Buckmaster's barn. A gang of the boys had Sam Trub cornered there, teasing him about his grandfather's little red wagon. He just stood leaning against the barn, looking down at the ground, and kicking up dirt with his toe. I joined in the teasing, and he took everything I said without reply. After a while I got still braver, and I slapped his face and invited him to fight. He put his hands over his face and ran away as fast as he could go. After that I was just about as mean to Sam Trub as he had ever been to me. I abandoned his Sunday-school, and I cursed the Republican party in his presence. Once, aided by the drayman's son, I forced him to take a chew of tobacco. This experience ended disastrously for me. The leaf sickened Sam, and in his woe he tattled. I was denounced to my grandmother and got a lusty switching, losing, beside, a fresh plug of tobacco.

But most of my days were carefree and peaceful then, and my life ran along uneventfully until I was nine years old. Then I was converted at a big camp meeting. No doubt my conversion was mainly a manifestation of my natural contrariness; for my grandmother was a Hardshell Baptist and did not believe in children getting religion. She herself often went to hear the Methodist minister preach, as the Baptist meeting-house in the country had no regular elder, and she had encouraged me to go to Sunday-school, but she would not take my religious notions seriously. When I became fully aware of this I set about to become a very religious boy.

After my seventh birthday I had developed quite an appetite for reading, an appetite which had to be satisfied mostly by my grandmother's books—the Bible, "Pilgrim's Progress," and "Swiss Family Robinson." I must have read the two last books a dozen times each, and I became very familiar with Genesis, Exodus, and Revelation, my three favorite books of the Bible. I never tired of the story about Joseph and his brethren; and I remember that I was always greatly puzzled by the part about Potiphar's wife, thinking of her as a terrible liar who did her best to get Joseph to go around lying with her. The Presbyterian minister lived next door to us; and I used to talk to him about Joseph and Potiphar's wife, assuring him that I was going to be like Joseph and never lie around with anybody. I declared that I would always stick to the truth, just as Joseph did. One day I overheard him telling some churchmen about my interpretation of the story of Joseph and Potiphar's wife, and then I was more puzzled than ever, for they all laughed about it. With all this reading, the Holy Spirit began to work in me, and even before the camp-meeting began I had returned to Sunday-school, and had quit chewing tobacco once more without urging from anyone.

The Lawson brothers were two very successful revivalists of that time. They were young Methodist preachers and had some education, but in their preaching they ignored the teaching of the seminaries and stuck to the Peter Cartwright tradition. Peter Cartwright was the founder of Methodism in the prairie States; his fame there, in the Civil War era, equalled Lincoln's; and his name was still venerated in Iowa when I was a boy. Dozens of stories about this roaring, heavy-fisted prairie parson were familiar to everyone. In prairie towns like Moravia the camp-meeting remained a respected institution. The Lawson brothers, like Peter Cartwright, thought that meeting a failure where saints failed to swoon and shout, and sinners did not roil, roar and prance. Jesse Lawson was a barrel-chested, black-maned pulpit-thumper, and, strictly following old Peter in every respect, he would use his sledge-like fists on any irreverent soap-cricker or coal-miner who scoffed aloud at his meetings. Luke Lawson was a plump and kindly man; there was no light of battle about him. He had a soothing, caressing baritone voice which always seemed about to break into sobs when he sang such hymns as "Come to Jesus." When Jesse had got the congregation into a shouting, hysterical condition with his thundered threats of hell-fire, Luke's healing and comforting voice would go out over the throng, dropping on the tormented sinners the balm of a sweeter promise. Their yells and screams would subside; weeping, they would press yearningly towards the mourners' bench. Jesse and Luke made a rare team.

The Methodists, the Presbyterians and the United Brethren held this camp-meeting in union. The big tent was raised up in a maple grove. It was early Spring, and the farmers drove in to attend. Basket dinners were served in the tent. Everyone seemed excited and happy, eating, gossiping, swapping stories, and fist-fighting when preaching was not going on. There was more fighting around such a camp-meeting in those days than in the saloons. The sinful element was always made resentful and bellicose by the harsh and violent manner in which it was denounced, and the saints were never reluctant to do battle for the true faith. Jesse Lawson wore several scars.

I remember the camp-meeting as a festival, with everyone having a glorious and exciting time. Some of the night meetings lasted until midnight, and the sanctified would often remain in prayer and song until dawn. The Lawson brothers achieved a great triumph in Moravia. Even some of the most case-hardened soap-crickers "went forward." There were many hallelujahs among the saints when Parvin Repp, the most notorious and amusing liar of the Soap Creek country, was taken unawares one night and carried to the altar. Parve, as he was called, would pack the office room of the livery barn every time he came to town. His stories of his attempts at suicide had been retold until they were familiar to everyone in town. Time and again, he said, he had tried to kill himself for fear of his wife's wrath over one of his errors. Always he failed miserably. Once he had absent-mindedly taken her best calico apron and made rags of it to use in oiling his harness. Not until it was in bits did the thought occur to him that Cynthy, his wife, would be powerfully angry about losing her pretty apron.

"There was nothin' else fer it," said Parve, "but to go drown myself. So down I went to ol' Chariton River; an' it had been rainin' fer quite a spell then; an' so much water had come up over the bottom lands thet I couldn't git to the river nowhere at all. So back home I had to go an' take the whalin' thet was comin' to me.

Another favorite yarn of Parve's narrated his conflict with Cynthy over her Plymouth Rock hens. They were fine, fat hens, and she was mighty proud of them, insisting that they have the freedom of the barn. One Winter day Parve brought his team in after some hard hours of breaking down cornstalks and gave the horses a rich feed of oats. Cynthy's hens flew into the feed-trough and scattered the oats in every direction. Parve went for them with an ear of corn and knocked all life out of one of them.

"I knew thet Cynthy would everlastingly go after me fer this," said he, "so I thought the best way out was to make an end of everything. It was around twenty-five below; so I tramps out into the orchard, climbs into a Ben Davis apple tree, with a mind to freeze myself to death. But do you know, it was so tarnation cold thet I couldn't stay there five minutes! Shiverin' an' a hobblin', I had to make it on to the house an' take my lickin'."

After Parve had come to the mourners' bench and confessed his lies and vowed never to speak anything but the truth again, there was no question about the completeness of the Lawson brothers' triumph. At the end of the ten-day meeting a host of saints, including more than two hundred converts, marched to the Milwaukee depot and sent the revivalists away with shouting and song. They carried the glamor of festival away with them. I remember the saints going homeward after the train had gone with the aspect of a crowd dispersing after a burial. Backsliding began among them at once.

My own conversion had brought with it a desire to preach; and it lasted long enough for me to select a text and compose a sermon. The text was from Revelation. These are the words of it, as I remember them; "And he took the book and ate it; and in his mouth it was sweet as honey, but in his belly it was bitter." I made a warm sermon from this text, comparing man's sins to the book. On earth, I declared, sins were sweet to the taste, as was the book in the saint's mouth; but after death, in hell-fire, sins were terribly bitter, as was the book when it had been swallowed. I practiced on this sermon until the church people began to talk about it. One Sabbath afternoon I preached it to the Juniors' Union from the pulpit of the United Brethren church. The minister said that I was sure to be a first-rate preacher some day, and he advised me to keep right on.

But the Spring days marched on, with an ever-increasing music and glitter; they flew the bright pagan banners of the prairie May; and then school days ended and frolicsome June smiled and danced around me. The fields were lush and green with timothy, clover and corn, the woods were melodious with singing birds, the waters of the ponds were warm and caressing, the town lots were noisy with ballplayers. Such a time was the Winter of the saints' discontent. Later on, in the toil and moist heat of the prairie Summer, Methodism would flourish again; but now all its powers of resistance were needed for mere survival. I was drawn back to ball-playing with unsaved boys in the afternoons, and to hanging about the streets and lingering in the livery barn at night.

My complete backsliding occurred at a Saturday afternoon ball game. I had already been nicknamed Preacher at school, and most of the Moravia men knew about my oratorical powers. The visiting team was late, and while the crowd was waiting someone suggested that the boy preacher give his sermon. Well, I thought, here's a chance for me to do some real good; I've been backsliding quite a bit, and maybe if I preach my sermon right powerfully I'll have a return of grace. So I cut loose bravely and preached my best for about fifteen minutes. I had a grand and frightful ending for my sermon, in which I made a fearful picture of hell, showing the sinner tasting the final fiery bitterness of sin. When I got to this ending I yelled at the top of my voice and shook my fist in the finest revival style.

Suddenly I noticed that the crowd, which was made up mostly of the sinful element, was all doubled up with laughing. I broke off, feeling that I had made an awful fool of myself. But Buck Schrock, the pitcher of the Moravia team, thumped me on the back and roared

BASEBALL TOURNAMENT, BRITT, IOWA.

that he'd be eternally gol-derned if I didn't have old Jesse Lawson down to the life. "Yes sir, bub; you got him acshully to the life. Dod-derned if I won't be your steward an' take you up a collection." So he did; and I got a dollar and thirty-five cents, as almost everyone put in a dime or a nickel. I felt pretty badly at first, thinking I'd done something wicked in giving the sinful element a chance to laugh at the Rev. Mr. Lawson. But I kept the money and bought some pop for my boy friends after the ball game, and that evening I went up town and bought half a pound of Star chewing tobacco. I was lost, and I knew it; and something told me that such being the case I might as well have as good a time out of being lost as I could.

For a nine-year-old boy, I made a lot of money out of preaching at ball games and around the livery barn that Summer. The church people talked about me considerably; some of them thought I should be stopped, but others were sure I would do some good. I was popular with all the boys, for I bought the good ones pop, and the bad

Iowa State Historical Department, Division of the State Historical Society

ones could always come to me when they wanted chewing tobacco. I enjoyed that Summer as I have never enjoyed another one, though my sins increased and my heart hardened as the greenery of the prairie fields vanished in the sun and Autumn came with its harvest of grain and fruit.

When the school term began I was on hand, but I had reached the stage where I went to school rebelliously. I chewed the leaf in class, using the inkwell on my desk for a cuspidor. I became enamored of Frank and Dick Merriwell, Nick Carter and Diamond Dick; and in the shelter of my geography I read the weeklies in which the adventures of those heroes were published. I resisted punishment, leaving the room by a window one time to avoid being whipped by the schoolma'm, and returning to the school in the custody of the town marshal.

In the Spring, a railroad gang came to Moravia to replace a condemned wooden trestle with a dirt fill. The gang had a steam shovel and other machines, a delight to see. I made friends with the men who ran the work train, and they would let me ride back and forth with them. The watchman who kept up the fire in the locomotive at night also took a fancy to me; and nearly every night I would sit in the cab with him for hours, hearing him tell his plans and dreams. He would assure me that "one of these days you'll see a big Compound steamin' down the track, an' I'll be pokin' an' scatterin' coal in her ol' fire box." When his talk became monotonous I'd dream my own dreams, pretending that the work train locomotive was hitched to the Overland Limited, and that I was a veteran engineer, taking the train through the wild western mountains; roaring around curves, fighting off train-robbers, staying with the engine in the great wreck which was no fault of mine. Twice I spent the whole night in the cab, scandalizing my grandmother's neighbors. I played hooky for two straight weeks, hanging around the work train, and riding freights to Foster and back. I swaggered before my grandmother and boasted that I would get a job in the mines.

"I am going to send you West to your father," she told me quietly one day late in April. "I've written him, and he's expecting you. So we'll get ready for you to go right away."

I shouted and danced over the promise of this unexpected adventure. It began in three days—days which, in my impatience, I thought would never pass. Then one night I was in a Kansas City train, a ticket and a baggage check pinned in my inside coat pocket, a vast card, bearing directions to the conductor, sewed on a coat lapel. I sat stiffly in my seat thinking excitedly of the storied West. Idaho was only three days and three nights away. The land of cowboys, Indians, desperadoes, and magnificent heroes like Diamond Dick! As the train pulled out I began to feel a little doubt of the pleasure of living in such a dangerous land. I pressed my face to the window and caught a last sight of the scanty lights of the prairie town. Then I leaned back in my seat and thought about the life I was leaving. It seemed pretty good. Apples and melons and clover . . . fields of timothy and corn . . . ponds of water and oaks and elms in bluegrass pastures . . . preaching and basket dinners in the maple grove . . . story-telling in the livery barn. . . .

A ten-year-old boy is driving three horses hitched to a disk, guiding them back and forth over the alfalfa field of an Idaho valley farm. A month out of Iowa, he is already used to the realities of western life. He is in a pioneer country, where boys as well as men must work. He has learned to carry duties and responsibilities. He must guide his team straight; he must hold a tight, steady line, and watch carefully, for Cyclone, the broncho, is apt to to break and run. The disk must be oiled every hour. The team must be watered and fed at noon and night. This ten-year-old worker has an importance that delights him, and it is the more pleasurable because it is so new. His thoughts stray curiously to his last days in the prairie town. What a fool that Iowa kid was, anyway! Preachin'—holy smoke! Playin' hooky an' runnin' around with a gang of tenderfeet kids that wouldn't know a hackamore from a latigo! Readin' Diamond Dick, an' thinkin' *that* was the West! Gosh-a-Friday! . . .

The disk-driver pretends for a moment: he sees Brownie Mc-Cune, Hod Marion, Dobie Lathrop, Gene Horner—all the important boys of the prairie town—come tramping up the road that winds through the sagebrush. They are just out on an idle jaunt. What a different fellow is this driver of three horses to the Preacher they knew! How they stare in awe as he tolerantly explains his difficult job to them!

The disk-driver sighs as the familiar figures vanish, and he feels a little lonely. Gosh! hasn't he changed sudden? How in the name of all and everything did it come about, anyway? His memories of his long train journey tell him nothing; his main recollection is his argument with a Methodist conductor who tried to snatch his plug of Star away from him. Then he'd met his father and his other folks in Idaho. He had got acquainted with the valley boys at their first meeting. He had awed them by pulling out his plug and taking a chew in front of all the grown people, and then offering it to the other boys. He told them it was Kansas City chewing tobacco, and the best going; nearly all the people back East chewed Kansas City chewing tobacco, he said. He had got on famously with the valley boys, but the country itself was harder to get used to. The houses and barns seemed unnaturally small among the towering Idaho hills, and those hills themselves had oppressed him with the sense of their monumental size. Then he was put to work. . . .

Suddenly the country and its life seemed perfectly natural to him, and the prairie town and his old life there were obscured in a mist that dropped before them as the curtain falls on the act of a play. The driver of three horses on a disk was dimly conscious that something like a miracle had happened, and he troubled his mind with some wonderings about it. But he was not troubled long, for he felt life moving and saw it shining all about him, and he was still a boy.

JAMES NORMAN HALL

James Normal Hall was born in Colfax, Iowa, in 1887 and graduated from nearby Grinnell College. After fighting in World War I as an infantryman with the British "Kitchener's Mob," and as a fighter pilot with the French Lafayette Escadrille, Hall sailed to the far lands of the South Pacific. There, on Gauguin's island of Tahiti, he married Sarah Terairéia Winchester, the daughter of a Polynesian mother and an English sea captain father. There, with Charles Bernard Nordhoff, a comrade from his Escadrille days, he coauthored Mutiny on the Bounty, The Hurricane (both filmed on several occasions), and ten other books; there he wrote his autobiography, My Island Home, and a dozen other books, including that most delightful of literary hoaxes, Oh, Millersville! In the latter, Fern Gravel—an imaginary small town Iowa girl—recalls her childhood adventures in a deliberately primitive verse style.

Hall died on his adopted island of Tahiti in 1961. Today his grave, high on a breeze-tossed hilltop, overlooks Maeva Bay, where both Captain Cook and Captain Bligh anchored their ships, and where scenes from the films of Mutiny on the Bounty were photographed.

But for all his four decades in the "faery lands" of the South Pacific, for all his World War I adventures, for all his world traveling, James Norman Hall never forgot his native Midwest. In book after book there are allusions to his Iowa boyhood, as in Lost Island (1944):

> My thoughts went traveling farther and farther away from the present moment; all the way back to boyhood, I saw our sitting room at home, as it was in those days, lighted by the hard-coal burner and just such a china-globed lamp as the one before me; the family seated around the table, my mother darning stockings, my brothers and sisters reading or studying next day's lessons. I saw myself with my father's finely illustrated edition of Scott's Poems on my knees as I read "The Lady of the Lake" for the first time:
>
> > Harp of the North! that mouldering long hast hung
> > On the witch-elm that shades Saint Fillan's spring . . .
>
> Nothing read in all the intervening years has stirred me as those lines stirred me in boyhood. . . .

In "The Woodshed Poet" James Norman Hall tells us how his life-long spirit of wanderlust and his feeling for distant romantic places were shaped by his boyhood adventures.

The Woodshed Poet

Look to the northward, Stranger,
Just over the barn roof, there.
Have you in your travels seen
A land more passing fair?

THOSE LINES WERE WRITTEN fifty years ago by a woodshed poet who lived in the little town of Colfax, Iowa—population 1749—in the heart of the prairie country. He was twelve years old and little knew, then, that the Stranger appealed to would, in the course of time, prove to be himself, looking to the northward toward the days of his boyhood and youth from his home on the island of Tahiti, in the South Pacific. But so it is, and despite the distance of time and space, I am happy to find that some of the memories of those days stand out as clearly as though the events of them had happened last week.

The Hall-family woodshed stood a little way back of the house on the northern slope of a hill that gave a wide view of the country in that direction. Both woodshed and barn have long since vanished, but I still see them in the mind's eye, their walls covered with the early compositions of the woodshed poet. "Look to the Northward," of four stanzas, was penciled by the woodshed window, overlooking the barn which was farther down the hill. The Stranger's attention was called to particular points of beauty in the landscape stretching away to the hills that bound it north and west.

Colfax, in the days before the arrival of motorcars, was one of those small country towns healthy, commercially, because the farmers living around them within a radius of from six to ten miles did their trading in them; and "trading" it was, in a real sense, for the farmers' wives brought with them fowls and eggs and homemade butter to be exchanged for various articles which the combined dry-goods-and-grocery stores of those days had to sell. The town had a reason for being that was later to be partly lost. As motorcars increased and dirt roads vanished the farmers' custom went to larger towns. Colfax, like many another small town, is now only the ghost of what it was in the eighteen-nineties and early nineteen-hundreds. There were no wealthy residents in the town, nor were there any poor. Modern conveniences were few. During my boyhood I remem-

BAND CONCERT, MAIN STREET, COLFAX, IOWA.

ber only two houses furnished with bathrooms and indoor toilets. All dwellings were heated either by wood stoves, potbellied stoves that burned soft coal, or those glorious bringers of indoor cheer, "hard-coal burners." Furnaces were then unknown except for a few in store buildings. As for house furnishings, most of them came, I believe, from Grand Rapids, Michigan, and a few other emporiums in or near Chicago. It was all in atrocious taste, and rocking chairs in particular were monstrosities that would have to be seen to be believed.

Our house, on its exposed hilltop where it took the buffetings of the bitter midwinter winds sweeping down from Canada, was a story-and-a-half frame building with a porch eight feet wide, trimmed with gingerbread scrollwork, fronting the dining room. The only water faucet in the house was in the cellar, for this was believed to lessen the risk of the pipe freezing in winter, but it froze nevertheless. All water was carried up to the kitchen. On a small back porch we had an icebox; but Iowa summers were as hot as the winters were cold, and those precious blocks of ice would vanish before the day was done.

But that old frame house was a home in the best sense of the word. Comforts and conveniences there were none, but they were not missed because we had never known them. What amazes me now, as I think of boyhood days, is how our mother managed to raise five children, three boys and two younger girls, doing practically all of the work herself when we were little. Only the family washing was sent out. Everything else she did, with the help of an occasional "hired girl." We children helped, of course, when we were old enough, but I still wonder how Mother managed when we were too young to be of use.

Around my tenth year when I began my literary career, my model was James Whitcomb Riley, the Hoosier Poet, and my secret ambition was to be called, some day, the Hawkeye Poet. Despite my admiration for James Whitcomb Riley, I had no desire to follow him in writing dialect poems. I wished to write of real people and real events, and a typical example written at the close of the Spanish-American War, when I was eleven, was preserved on the flyleaf of my school geography, *Cuba Librey,* I supposed, was the way *Cuba Libre* was pronounced.

Cuba Librey! Cuba Librey!
Ring the bells, a glad refrain!
Noble Dewey, fearless Teddy
Have defeated haughty Spain.

Now the volunteers from Colfax
have returned home from the war.
Only one of them was wounded;
On his shoulder is a scar

Where a Mawser bullet hit him.
Barney Winpiggler his name.
Some got sick, but only Barney
will be known to future fame,

For he shed his blood in battle
So the Cubans could be free,
And they are, for Spain is conquered
On the land and on the sea.

A kind of melancholy seizes me as I travel back in thought from the grim uncertainties of today to the deep tranquility of 1899, the time when these verses were written. How little war, or the threat of it, intruded upon the lives of Americans in the nineties! To boys of my day it meant the American Revolution, the War of 1812, and the Civil War: battles of long ago, forever past and done with. Except for the half-dozen volunteers from Colfax who took part in the Spanish-American War, throughout the entire period of boyhood we never saw a man in uniform save the ageing veterans of the Civil War who assembled at one of the churches for the Memorial Day service and then marched to the cemetery to the music of the fife-and-drum corps. War was no threat of the future but a fading memory of the past. It was something one read about in illustrated school histories: Paul Revere's ride and the battles of Lexington and Concord and Bunker Hill. It was Ethan Allen shouting: "In the name of the great Jehovah and the Continental Congress!"; it was Lincoln at Gettysburg; General Grant at the surrender of Lee's armies. War, to us, was associated with Iowa in May, with the fragrance of lilacs and apple-blossoms in the air, when our beloved and revered school superintendent, Dennis M. Kelley, standing in the local cemetery by the grave of a Civil War veteran, reminded us of the sorrow that had been and would never be again. As for the Spanish-American War, it was not a real war; Teddy Roosevelt had won it almost single-handed, at San Juan Hill. We Colfax boys were proud of Barney Winpiggler who had shared a little of Teddy's fame by getting wounded in the shoulder.

Of all the haunts of boyhood, the Hill was the one I most deeply loved. It was the highest of the wooded hills east of town. The Chicago-to-Denver branch of the Chicago, Rock Island and Pacific Railroad wound around the bases of the hills and just beyond was the "Deep tangled wildwood" bordering the river: a paradise for boys but no more so than the hills themselves. The view from my Hill was even more beautiful than that from the one where our house stood, and from the middle of April the forest floor was carpeted, first with hepaticas whose fragrance is the very breath of spring; then came violets, Dutchman's-breeches, dogtooth violets, jack-in-the-pulpits, cowslips, bloodroots and May-apple blossoms. And, in the autumn when the hills were ablaze with color, there were hickory nut, black walnut and butternut trees and hazelnut bushes loaded with spoil.

Whenever, during later years, I have returned home, I have always planned to arrive in mid-April, if possible, so as to be in time for the hepaticas, and within half an hour of my arrival I head for the woods. At the crest of the highest hill there is, or was, a great linden tree where I loved to sit looking out to the north over the bottom lands of the Skunk River.

Many boys of my generation, like the boys of Tom Sawyer's and Huck Finn's generation, went to bed betimes on summer nights, but not always to sleep. And we were quite as skillful at making exits through upstairs windows; or we could creep downstairs, shoes in hand, as noiseless as cats. Alas! Having emerged from our parents' dwellings, we found no Mississippi River flowing past our dooryards, majestic, mysterious, under the light of the moon. In summer the Skunk River was little more than a prairie slough filled with sand-banks, mudbanks, and the trunks and branches of dead trees that had been swept into the channel during the spring rains. But we were not without adventure. Our Stream of Travel was of a different kind but none the less romantic: the C.R.I & P. Railroad.

Number Six was due at Colfax at 10:45 P.M., but a good five minutes before that time it appeared around the curve westward, at the top of the Mitchellville grade, six miles away. The headlight proclaimed the glory of its coming, and the first faraway whistle was like a call to adventure in the summer night, sending shivers of delight up and down the spines of three of us more than ready to respond to it—Buller Sharpe, "Preacher" Stahl, son of the Methodist minister, and myself. Number Six took water at Colfax, and we waited beneath the water tank about fifty yards past the east end of the station. We would hear the fireman climb onto the tender and pull down the iron spout with the canvas nozzle attached; then silence, save for the plash of water pouring in and the gentle yet powerful breathing of the engine. Presently up went the spout, spilling the water remaining in it onto the ground just beyond where we were concealed. Then came the "high-ball"—that most stirring of signals—two short sharp blasts of the whistle. Peering out from behind the posts supporting the water tank we would see the conductor swinging his lantern from the station platform. The fireman gave a pull at the bell rope; the great wheels began to move, and at the first mighty "hough!" of the engine we skipped out, leaped on the pilot—or "cowcatcher" as it was called by the uninitiated—and vanished into the pool of darkness just beneath the headlight.

What were the adventures of later years, compared with those summer-night rides on the pilot of Number Six? There was happiness almost too great for the hearts of boyhood to contain. The deep-toned whistle echoed among the wooded hills east of town. The great engine, rounding the sharp curves along the serpentine stretch of track skirting the hills, communicated the keen thrill of excitement from its own huge body to those of the twelve- and thirteen-year-olds who felt themselves a part of it. The headlight threw shafts of glory into the wooded land along the river; then, the curves passed, we felt sharp nudges from behind as the train gathered speed, and the long shaft of brilliant light now reached far ahead along the right-of-way.

A great part of our enjoyment came from being so close to the bosom of Mother Earth, which gave us the keen sense of traveling at enormous speed and with effortless power. All the odors of the summer night were ours: the cool dank fragrance of bottom lands along the river, mingled with that of skunk, one of the healthiest of all smells; the perfume of drying clover hay; the pungent odors of weeds and field flowers lying in swathes along the right-of-way as the scythes of the section hands had left them; the mingled odors of manure, horse sweat and harness coming from barns. And, best of all, the deep-toned whistle of Number Six, and we traveling with it! It was splendid compensation for the many times when we heard train whistles from afar, the sound growing fainter and fainter until heard no more.

Grinnell, thirty-two miles from Colfax, was our usual destination. In the horse-and-buggy days a town thirty or forty miles distant was unknown territory to most small boys, with the romantic appeal that distance lends it, and this was enhanced with the hour approaching midnight, the strange streets empty, and most of the houses dark. The three of us would hasten away from the station and the business part of town, for the night constable would be making his rounds in that neighborhood and we had no desire to be questioned by him. In those days when trains carried all the traffic of the nation we could be sure of catching a westbound freight that would take us home before daylight. And so, carefree and curious, we wandered at ease along broad residential streets where maple trees and overarching elms were "chandeliers of darkness" against the starry sky. On one of the earliest of these journeys I had my first view of Grinnell College, or Iowa College as it was then called.

I have often thought of the importance of the effect those midnight rambles over the Grinnell College campus were to have on the events of my later life. I had the feeling of being in another world, as remote from that I knew as though it had been a thousand miles away. The beautiful lawns and the trees that shaded them; the buildings that looked so august and venerable compared with the mean little churches of Colfax, which, together with the schoolhouse, were the only public buildings in town—all of this stirred in me a vague longing.

The nocturnal visits of Sharpe, Stahl and me had all been summer ones when the College was closed; but upon one never-to-be-forgotten occasion we saw the campus on a night in early October, shortly after the students had returned. This must have been in the autumn of 1902 or 1903. We witnessed a torchlight procession coming along the street bordering the west side of the campus. Thirty or forty men were singing what I afterward learned was called "The Glee Club Marching Song":

> A band of brothers from old Grinnell,
> We march along tonight,
> Two—by—two, our arms linked firm and tight.
> Our songs arouse the sleepy town
> As we go marching on,
> Singing the love that binds our hearts in one.

On they went, their bodies casting huge shadows in the torchlight, the singing dying away far in the distance. At the time I remembered only fragments of the song, but having been born an idealist, a romanticist, even in boyhood anything beautiful heard or seen was immediately enhanced in the imagination and formed dream pictures in my mind. So it was on this occasion: the street bordering the campus was no ordinary street, nor the houses ordinary houses.

The whistle of a westbound freight would hurry us back to the railway yards. On the homeward journey we usually rode on top of a boxcar to have a better view of the countryside. Often the train was a fast freight that went thundering through Colfax, gathering speed for the long Mitchellville grade; but there was no need for concern: the grade conquered the best of them. When halfway up, the freight would be traveling no faster than a boy could trot. Sharpe, "Preacher" and I would hop off there, walk the three miles back and be safely in bed and asleep well before daylight.

MacKinlay Kantor, born in Webster City, Iowa, in 1904, has ranged over the Midwest and beyond for subjects for his nearly fifty books: Chicago (El Goes South, *1930); Missouri (*The Voice of Bugle Ann, *1935); Kansas (*The Jaybird, *1932); the Iowa frontier (*Spirit Lake, *1961); and the Civil War (*Long Remember, *1934). His first short story, "Purple," about an Iowa farm, was published in the* Des Moines Register *in 1920 when Kantor was sixteen. His first novel,* Diversey *(1928), was the first novel about the Chicago gangsters who had come to power with Prohibition. It was also the first novel published by Coward-McCann with whom he had a long, happy relationship. His verse novel,* Glory For Me *(1945), was filmed as the Academy Award–winning* Best Years of Our Lives *(1946).* Andersonville, *another of his several books about some aspect of the Civil War, won a 1956 Pulitzer Prize.*

Here, in an excerpt from a book that has been too long out of print, the autobiographical But Look the Morn *(1947), he tells how his interest in the Civil War and his country's past had its origins.*

I Think of These

IF I HAD BEEN BORN thirty-eight years and ten months sooner, I would have been born during the week when the Army of Northern Virginia crept west from Petersburg to silence its last pathetic snarlings at Appomattox. But I was born in 1904, and the historians of the future may declare that the generation born in 1904 did not know the taste of the Rebellion.

Until I live to hear them make that assertion, I cannot argue with them. It is my belief, however, that we of 1904 (at least those of us who grew into the towns which still had something of their pioneer youth and rawness) were far closer to the War Between the States

—far closer than the generation of 1956, now [in 1947] lying unrealized within the bodies of people in their teens, will ever be to the first Great War with Germany.

For, day by day, we have lost the threads that tied us to an America long shadowed by the wings of passenger pigeons. Thirty-five years ago there were hot campfires in the parlors of midwestern homes, ready to melt the past decades into a common paste for the asking. And when the Fords and Chevrolets came, and Douglas Fairbanks and William S. Hart and Theda Bara came, and when the town jeweler set up an aerial for wireless telegraphy on the roof of his store, and snared the SOS call of a ship in trouble off Havana; and, after that, when the generations of 1898 and 1900 went yelling away to Camp Dodge, and the generation of 1904 hated itself because it couldn't follow—

When all of those things happened, and the crueler things afterward, it is no wonder that the campfires in the little parlors went out. I venture no prophecy about the date of their rekindling, and I feel sorry for the babies of 1956.

Because I was born into a bold illusion, authentic and sententious, like the basso profundo of drums in front of the G.A.R. hall. The keepers of this illusion lived in nearly every house, and while some few of them were frail and querulous and waxy, many were young enough to take part in the fat men's race at the county fair, or to engage in a Saturday night fist-fight behind the Park Hotel.

The Civil War lived in Grandma's button-bag, and it was my great-grandfather who had put it there. On rainy Sunday afternoons I used to take the Civil War out of the button-bag and play with it on the floor. There were the large, brass buttons which had fastened Grandpa Bone's blouse down the front, and the smaller ones which had adorned his sleeves. There was a shoulder-strap, too, with its single bars of stiff gold braid; and upstairs we had a picture of him which would have terrified me if I had not known that, in spite of his angry eyes, he was an old soldier. And all old soldiers were kind to little boys.

Of course, there was the Waldron place across the river where we dared not go for walnuts because old Fritz Waldron would come after us with a cattle whip; and there were old Gamewell, who swore under his whiskey breath whenever the boys tagged him at his lawn-mowing work, and Dr. Sill, who would stop his buggy and threaten to call the marshal if a boy caught on behind. But in spite of these glaring and dangerous exceptions to the rule, we were all nursed in the belief that every old soldier worthy of the name was a man of genial and courageous parts, schooled in adherence to the Apostles' Creed, the Emancipation Proclamation, and "A Visit from St. Nicholas." And so help me, if ever paragon lived to support a common misapprehension, at least a dozen such paragons lived in that Webster City of the early Nineteen Hundreds. Astride their graves I will challenge posterity to deny it.

Perhaps I was enlisted in the Civil War from birth, first by the persistent sentimentality of my grandmother, and, second by the influence of a younger woman who had transmuted that earnest sentimentality into a fervent, scholarly interest in Americana of the Mississippi Valley.

She was my mother, and during the years which have passed since she left me, I find my debt compounding each week at an interest-rate which will bankrupt me unless I work harder than I have worked before. She covered our walls with pictures of bison, and battles, and log courthouses, and mill-stones. She weighted down the table in the living room with well-rubbed books, and stuffed the corners of the old secretary with yellow newspaper clippings.

The Sundays of my memory glitter and hum . . . I drank my first and happiest coffee from a black tin pail in Hamilton County's pastures and wood lots. Here was the old Chase mill dam, here was a mysterious brick house built in the middle of Briggs' oak forest, here was a high, gaunt strip of prairie where Sidominadotah had ridden with his Sioux.

The survivors of the Spirit Lake Massacre relief expedition and the Northern Border Brigade came to our house: stooped, bony old men with deep eyes and opinionated jaws, and tongues ready to gossip for hours on end. Amid their nasal reminiscences, I heard again the swift scream of fifes which had sounded when I was three years old and played with the button-bag.

Not the least of Mister Mac's [my father's] gifts to me was his father-in-law, Grandpa Wicks, an elderly cabinet-maker who carried memories of the infantry along with him in his tool satchel. Once Grandpa Wicks had been wounded—that was a few days before the surgeons made a one-armed carpenter out of him—and he lay for hours in the full torment of a Confederate sun. As in a thousand Civil War tales, so alike as to be almost Biblical in their ubiquity, Grandpa Wicks was befriended by a dying rebel, who poured down his throat the traditional measure of cold water.

The water was poured from a canteen; I was five years old when I heard this, and the metallic suggestion of the word canteen rang in my ears. Canteen . . . I had heard the lusty or cracked voices at the courthouse park a few weeks before, when the old guard of Hamilton County met in reunion.

We have drank from the same canteen, boys,
We have drank from the same canteen.

The nearest that I could come to it, at long last, was a tin can; I found one on top of the refrigerator, an empty coffee can. Canteen, can tin, tin can. I filled it at the pump and carried it with me to the hill above the cornfield that fell away below our barn. Spread-eagled flat against the blue-grass, I lay there with eyes closed until the sun seemed ready to shrivel the lids apart; and I was Grandpa Wicks for a while, and in the end I was a rebel, dying; and I poured the water slowly down my parched throat out of my tin can canteen.

That was how I suffered my first wound in the Civil War, though many were to come later—nearly twenty-five years later, in fact, when I wore out my eyes building up the historical background for *Long Remember*. And in contemplating those wounds, I am as full of self-satisfaction—selfish, petulant, childish pride—as any hollow-cheeked relic who ever lingered, rocking on the porch of a Soldiers' Home and denying shrilly that Grover Cleveland ever cut the soldiers' pensions.

And then there were John Kearns, who let me hold in my hand the ounce ball which had splintered into his femur at Vicksburg, and Park Banks, so slim and trim and dapper that he looked more at home squiring pretty school-ma'rms to the Knights Templar banquets than he did marching with the other veterans on Decoration Day. Close in the squad behind them strode Bob White, whose rank exalted itself in his aging mind until, at his death, he was convinced that he had commanded a brigade; and old Mr. Jacks with a face like an Indian; and the Hon. Wesley Martin, superintendent of our Sunday School. I am grateful to them for whatever heroic marches they may have made, but more than that, for whatever truths or lies any one of them may have told.

. . . There came a young man in a seersucker suit, who sat fanning himself in our living room, and explaining rapidly to my grandmother that she should buy *The Photographic History of the Civil War,* complete in ten volumes, edited by Francis Trevelyan Miller and published by the Review of Reviews Company.

Even in the MacKinlay household, coal for the kitchen range was more necessary than the brave stand of Major-General George H. Thomas, and Mr. Scriven's grocery bill leaped automatically to a position surmounting that of the battle of Resaca. There wasn't much money in the old toothpick holder on the clock shelf, and not much more in the bank.

The young man in the seersucker suit had a vast sheaf of photographs, loose-leaf pages or proofs, carried with him for purposes of demonstration. I like to think that he took heart wholly because of the earnest pleading with which I importuned my grandmother. "Anyway," he said, "I will leave these pictures here for a day or two, and you folks can glance through them. Madam, I am quite confident that by the time I come back you will have been convinced that you cannot afford to let the members of your household be without this beautiful set of books, bound appropriately in blue cloth, and stamped in gold."

After he was gone, I spread the pictures on the floor, and I do not think I got up until supper-time. And some kind of god, perhaps the same god who is alleged to be kind to dogs and old soldiers and newsboys, did appear unto that young man in a dream and tell him to go him into all the world and preach the gospel of *The Photographic History of the Civil War* to every creature. At any rate, he didn't come back. If our house had ever caught fire, and I had been there, those loose-leaved proofs would have been the first thing carried out.

And then it was late May again, and all the buggies and Ramblers and Overlands and Marions lined up along Prospect Street— Prospect Street, that began at a coal yard along the Illinois Central tracks, and ended at the cemetery. Here marched the Webster City band in the fullest spirit of its brass, and here rode Press Hyatt, ordinarily the plump proprietor of the Orpheum moving picture theatre, but on this day swollen to even mightier proportions as the colonel of the Fifty-sixth Iowa Militia. And here came the I.N.G.'s, and George Yaus with his bugle, and the ladies of the W.R.C., and a plethora of flags. And here marched, also, the old soldiers, and there were a good company of them in that year. Ahead of them, skirling, squealing, booming like a battery of three-inch rifles, staggered the drum corps.

I was ready for this music, now, although I had not known it before. I trotted alongside the drum corps, and pattered through the dust of the cemetery lane and in through the wide gate. When the last volley of the firing squad had sounded, I lit out for home; I acquainted my lips frantically, over and over, with the song which the drum corps had played—a song born in the stubborn, cock-sure spirit of the American eighteenth century.

GRAND ARMY OF THE REPUBLIC ENCAMPMENT, ELKADER, IOWA.

It was played at Monmouth and Lundy's Lane and Chapultepec, and ten million times in the Civil War. It is still played wherever there is one rheumy, creaking relic to be transported in a parade. Everyone knows the tune. Everyone says, "What? Oh, yes. I know. It's the song the old soldiers always play." And yet one American in a thousand, or perhaps in ten thousand, can tell you the name. Originally, I believe it was known as "Paul Revere's Ride," and Down East there are old men who declare it to be "The Gobby O." And every member of the National Association of Civil War Musicians insists that the correct title is "Jefferson and Liberty."

I whistled it all the way down the hill and along Ohio Street, and past the cedars in front of the old Martin place. I whistled it across the yard and into our dining room. My grandmother came quickly from the kitchen, with a dishcloth in her hands. Her eyes were very bright. "Honey," she said, "that tune . . . I never heard you whistle that before. It sounds like—"

I cried, "It's a swell tune! The old soldiers just played it up at the cemetery—old man Lee, and Dr. Homan, and everybody. Here's how it goes," and I shrieked the thing once more, until the cat ran and hid under the sofa.

My grandmother began to cry. "Pa used to play that," she said. And that was the first I knew that my great-grandfather, too, had been a Civil War musician.

"It is a dangerous thing to bother about the rich," said John O'Hara in his introduction to the 1945 Viking Portable F. Scott Fitzgerald. *"A writer who does it in this country . . . will find himself regarded as a toy."*

But Fitzgerald had written about the rich, "gave them the business" in O'Hara's words—and no one, in his or her right mind, has ever treated Fitzgerald playfully. "Let me tell you about the very rich," he wrote in "The Rich Boy" in All the Sad Young Men *(1926).*

> "They are different from you and me. They possess and enjoy early, and it does something to them, makes them soft where we are hard, and cynical where we are trustful, in a way that, unless you were born rich, it is very difficult to understand. They think, deep in their hearts, that they are better than we are because we had to discover the compensations and refuges of life for ourselves. . . ."

When we think of the rich in the midwest, we are most likely to think of those midwesterners who made vast fortunes: Henry Ford, a mechanic building Model Ts in Highland Park, Michigan; Augustus Swift, walking through his Chicago meat-packing plant in a leather apron and boots; John Deere, hammering out his first plowshare in Grand Detour, Illinois; George Douglas, Sr., thrusting his railroad across the prairies to Omaha; and Robert Stuart erecting his cereal mill beside those tracks, midway between Chicago and Omaha. But Fitzgerald's rich are from the second and later generations who inherited the wealth made by the Fords, Swifts, Deeres, Douglases, and Stuarts and their wealthy peers, and who never worked for a living.

Ellen Williamson is of a third generation—all girls. The family members like to joke about their money. They say that Walter Douglas—Ellen's uncle, who built the Douglas Starchworks in Cedar Rapids—made the money; George Douglas, Jr., Ellen's father, saved it; and William Douglas, "Uncle Billy," who married Harriet Ives of a prominent Cedar Rapids family, went off to Paris and spent it, "living it up" there.

Walter not only made money—he also made history. He was on the Titanic. *As the doomed ship sank into the bitter-cold waters of the north Atlantic, he kissed his wife, Mahala Dutton Benedict Douglas, goodbye, and handed her and her newly acquired French maid into a lifeboat,* then stepped back onto the ship's deck. *"I'll see you in Cedar Rapids,"* he said.

His body was later recovered and returned home for burial. Mahala Douglas was reputed to be the model for the protagonist in Carl Van Vechten's The Tattooed Countess *(1924), a novel set in Cedar Rapids. Van Vechten, too, was able to pursue a leisurely life as a writer and photographer because he inherited a fortune made in insurance and banking in the Iowa city.*

Ellen Douglas and her sisters grew up in Brucemore, the largest and most luxurious home in Cedar Rapids, a castlelike structure whose front lawn alone covered as much of the city's area as the lots containing twenty or thirty workers' homes in the Irish and Czech neighborhoods close by the city's factories. The home had been built by T. M. Sinclair, whose fortune was accumulated from employing many of these Irish and Czechs in his meatpacking plant on the far southeast side of the city.

Although living a life of material comfort, commuting among her homes in Italy, New York City, Traverse City (Michigan), and Cedar Rapids, Ellen Douglas Williamson has taken the time to write three books. * *They are not literary works of the kind authored by other writers represented in this collection, although her first book,* Wall Street Made Easy: An Unconventional Book to Profitable Investing *(1965), was described by one critic as "an uproariously funny book." That book and* Spend Yourself Rich *(1970), however funny they may be, are full of practical advice from a wealthy woman on making money without working. Her third book,* When We Went First Class *(1977), is Ellen Williamson's narrative of life among the very rich.*

I grew up in Cedar Rapids, knowing that if I could smell the Douglas and Stuart Quaker Oats Plant, "the largest in the world," the wind was from the north, and if I could smell the Douglas Starchworks, with a faint odorous overlay from the Sinclair plant, the wind was from the south. If I could smell both or all three, as I could on many a summer day, then I knew there was no breeze at all, and the stagnant summer air was hanging heavy over our working-class neighborhood.

My Uncle Ralph, from young manhood on, labored in the Quaker Oats plant; my father was an occasional millhand in the Starchworks. On

---

*I am unable to verify a report that she wrote several mystery novels under an assumed name.

the night of May 22, 1919, when a grain-dust explosion blew the Douglas plant sky-high above the city, he escaped being blown to eternity with forty-three others by only fifteen minutes. (All that was found of the man who replaced him that memorable night were his dentures.)

Brucemore was distantly removed from the falling debris, as well as from the odors that permeated our homes. In the years following the explosion, I would occasionally ride my bicycle out First Avenue East until I came to the place where the long slope of Brucemore's evenly manicured lawn and its long row of tall, blue spruce reached the edge of the Avenue. The air, blowing lightly from the south on a bright early summer day, would be sweet with green clover and blue spruce, and I would sit there awhile, breathing deeply and staring at the magnificent home on the ridge. Like Fitzgerald, beginning to write about his "Rich Boy," I would be filled with wonder about the very rich and how they were different from me.

Fancy and Rich in the Middle West

CEDAR RAPIDS, IOWA, had a population in 1837 of one: a horse thief by the name of Osgood Shepherd. In 1838 the population rose to five when he built a log cabin by the Cedar River and brought his wife there and their two children and his aged father.

Osgood vanished several years later, but other settlers were arriving and it was thought that he was caught at his racket. In those days it was easy to walk off with someone's bay horse, dye it black during the night, and sell it the next morning to a traveler or settler on his way down the river. When a good rainstorm came along, the black horse turned brown again, and thus originated the phrase "a horse of a different color."

In the year I was born—1905—Cedar Rapids had a population of about twenty thousand people. The Douglas family must have seemed an odd group to the other residents, for they never discarded their Scotch ways and customs, but stuck firmly by them. Not only did we have collie and sheltie dogs with names like Jeanie and Roderick Dhu, but we children drove around in a wicker-basket-type cart behind a cross little black Shetland pony called Neddie. Out by the barn and stables was a little round dog-kennel house with run-

MR. AND MRS. GEORGE BRUCE DOUGLAS, JR., DAUGHTERS
ELLEN [WILLIAMSON] *(left)* AND MARGARET [HALL], AND "A
CROSS LITTLE BLACK SHETLAND PONY CALLED NEDDIE" ON
THE GROUNDS OF BRUCEMORE, ABOUT 1910.

ways where West Highland terriers were raised commercially.

Why had the Douglases come to Cedar Rapids in the first place?
Because my grandfather George Douglas, a stonecutter and construction engineer who lived in Thurso, Scotland, was asked to come to
the United States and help to build a railroad that would run from
Chicago to Omaha, Nebraska. I've forgotten what the railroad was
called originally, but it was known for years as the Chicago and
Northwestern, and if you are familiar with it at all, you may have
noticed that the engines all run along on the left-hand tracks and the
engineers all look out of their cabs for signals through the left-hand
windows just the way they do in the British Isles. They say that when
the trains arrive in Omaha and have to cross over to the Union Pacific
right-hand tracks, there is a fearful switching and a cursing of grandfather Douglas to this very day.

Cedar Rapids, being just about halfway between the two cities, seemed to be the best place for Grandfather to settle, especially as a cousin of his, Robert Stuart, was already living there and with his two sons had started a small cereal plant which was turning out a variety of rolled and steel-cut oats. Grandfather put some money into the company, and as a result his railroad was given the business of shipping oats East and West.

The company did well, and around the turn of the century merged with another oat mill, known as the American Cereal Company. What should they name the new company? They found that one brand of the Douglas-Stuart Mills outsold all the others (actually they were all exactly the same but were packaged differently), and it was known as the Quaker brand. The name evidently sounded solid and honest and safe for babykin's oatmeal, so they named the big new company the Quaker Oats Company, and that is what it has been called ever since.

Our little bit of Scotland included a dour Scot named Ross who kept the horses glossy and well groomed. He was also excellent with the bagpipes and he piped my father and mother in to dinner every night when there was company. And while we children ate our oatmeal porridge and applesauce upstairs in the nursery with our Scotch nurse Miss MacDannel (known to us as Danny) the men in the family appeared for dinner in full-dress kilt. My father and his two brothers all lived near each other at this time, and it was a grand sight to behold them (I've been told), all tall and handsome, wearing the pleated kilts of the ancient Douglas plaid, the colors of soft blues and greens, and each with a short-waisted dress jacket of black or gray velvet or heavy silk twill (a material then called bombazine).

After dinner there was often a game of whist (that would be the forerunner of bridge) and I learned that gentlewomen in those times referred to the spade suit as "lily." The word "spade" or *"pique"* was considered vulgar, especially as the design started out as the fleur-de-lys. Besides whist there was music. My mother played the harp and the piano, and there was also an Aeolian pipe organ that played (when pumped furiously) rolls of music. (Several years later I remember pumping away at the thing myself while singing "Oh, Where, Tell Me Where, Has My Highland Laddie Gone" accompanied by the proper notes, thanks to the self-unwinding paper roll, with all the stops pulled out. The noise was like the dawn coming up like thunder indeed.)

Mother and her two sisters-in-law never dressed in kilts, at least not in the evening. They all three wore custom-made Parisian dresses from Paul Poiret, Worth, Patou, Callot Soeurs, Vionnet, always gowns from *La Haute Couture.*

My Uncle Walter, a handsome widower, was the most sought-after man in town and there were all sorts of scandalous things whispered about him. And sure enough, a married lady friend named Mrs. Benedict left Mr. Benedict, obtained a divorce (hard to do in those days), and she and Uncle Walter were married in Washington, D.C.

They returned to Cedar Rapids, and while the tongues wagged furiously, proceeded to enjoy every minute of each other's company. Mother told me that they were just plain in love the same as she and my father were.

The Stuart family (our Scotch cousins) were far more conservative than the Douglas clan, and were perfectly horrified when Uncle Walter married Mahala. Mrs. Robert Stuart announced that she would never have a divorcée in her house, especially one who smoked.

The Robert Stuarts were in Pinehurst at the time of this second marriage in Washington, and Uncle Walter took his bride down to North Carolina and moved into the same hotel, in fact into a suite on the same floor.

Aunt Mahala told me years later that she was scared stiff and shook in her shoes at the thought of meeting this straitlaced pair, but Uncle Walter merely said to her, "My dear Mahala, just be your natural attractive self, and you will take them into camp. Come on." And he led her down the hall, knocked on their door, and apparently cousin Maggie found her as intoxicating as Prohibition, for they became lifelong friends.

My memory of Father and kilts began shortly after I started to attend the public school in Cedar Rapids. We girls—my sister and I and the daughters of our coachman and head gardener—had brought our lunch boxes to a place under a big elm tree and sat down on the ground in a circle. Along came some older boys who began yelling at Barbara and me:

"You think you're pretty fancy and rich, doncha?" We said nothing.

"Well, you're all wrong," they shouted. "Your father is a *sissy*."

"Yah-yah!" They all jumped up and down. Barbara started to cry.

"Your father's a sissy, just a gol-darn sissy!"

I was furious and stood up spilling cookies and hard-boiled eggs every which way.

"He's nothing of the kind!" I exclaimed firmly. "Go away and leave us alone."

"He's a sissy!" one of them shouted back, and stuck out his tongue. "He wears *skirts!*" he said, and they all started swishing around like ladies, bowing to each other and pretending to pull skirts aside.

"He does *not* wear skirts!" I stamped my foot in great anger. "He wears *kilts. All* Scots wear kilts."

"They're *skirts!*" was the answer, and they ran off.

When I got home that afternoon I was still furious and couldn't wait until my father got home from the office to tell him what those horrid little boys said about him.

He was very amused. "They are just trying to make you mad, trying to get your goat," he said. "They know that you live in a big house and most of them probably live in smaller ones. They are envious and would like to live in Brucemore." He pulled out his pipe and lit it.

"I'll tell you what you do." He chuckled and took a puff before he spoke.

"Be very polite to them from now on. Don't ever show that you are mad. Smile pleasantly. Be sure you look boys, and girls too, straight in the eye. You're their *friend*. You *like* them. You've got a job to do but I know that you can do it. And no boasting *ever* about living in a large house."

He took another puff on his pipe and added, "By the way, should they say anything further about my wearing skirts, you might ask them *politely* if they know what a Scot wears under his kilt."

"What do they wear?" I asked, round-eyed.

"I'm not saying," he replied, "but we kilt wearers are pretty masculine, and that's a fact."

I never quite understood any of this until one summer years later in Gleneagles, Scotland, when I learned that it was considered a mark of honor not to wear anything under the kilt. There was one exception: a high-stepping drummer wore a brief pair of shorts of matching plaid.

Another time, shortly after this sissy stuff, someone else at school made a remark in front of me about my father, saying that he was the president or head of a whole lot of things, and asked me if it wasn't true. I said that I didn't know and was told that I was either lying or else a dumbbell. I hurried home and asked Dad what he did at his office.

"I'm a merchant," he answered, "and furthermore there are a lot of us in town, so it is nothing to get excited or conceited about."

Shortly after this I also remember coming home from school and telling my father that I had made a new friend.

"Her name is Thelma Mahannah," I told him, "and she asked me what you did when you went to work every day and I said that you were a merchant."

He nodded. "That's right."

"Then I asked her what her father did and she said that he was a piano tuner. Then she said, 'My mother and I think that he is the Best Piano Tuner in town.' She's awfully nice."

She sounds great to me," he said. "Someone I'd like to meet. The next time she comes here be sure to introduce me to her."

Brucemore: What was it like?

At first the property was just a big front lawn sweeping uphill to the stark three-story red-brick house standing bleakly at the top, a driveway to the left, and a sidewalk ascending to the right. That was all; behind the house it was strictly farm. There were stables and cow barns and a pond for ducks. There were fields of corn and alfalfa, chicken houses and a pigsty, and beyond was a dense woods filled with hazelnut bushes and walnut and butternut trees.

Gradually the farm receded. First the big white barn departed and an orchard with a playhouse and swings for us took its place, then a formal garden and tennis court appeared adjacent to the house, next a greenhouse and a squash court, then the pond became landscaped and a pair of white swans floated on the surface.

Today there is still a vegetable garden, which is hidden away behind the garage, and I noticed the last time that I saw it, it contained a mere three rows of sweet corn. Brucemore has become completely citified.

The house too has lost its stark Victorian look, thanks to the addition of many porches and terraces and surrounding trees. It still is a curious house both inside and outside. Each of its thirty-odd rooms contains a fireplace, and each one is different. There are two stairways to each of the three main stories and the attic, as well as the cellar, and there is also an elevator shaft. There are two basements, one with recreation rooms and laundries and a furnace room, and a lower one for storing vegetables and wine. There is a tunnel leading from the lower cellar over to the Garden House (a two-bedroom guest house) two hundred feet away. One can still crawl through it quite comfortably. Its purpose? It carried steam heat in a big pipe from Brucemore's two big coal furnaces.

Up on the third floor there is a small secret room with its own cozy little bay window looking down on the garden. Whyfore? Back in the 1920s a new and larger pipe organ was installed. The smaller pipes were all put in a third-floor guest room, the larger pipes being down in the cellar, and the bay window was walled off with an extra ten square feet, making it the smallest and most private room in the house. . . .

Outside, the workmen that were brought over from Ireland to build the house also left their individual touches. The four big stone chimneys are each carved in a different design. Each side of the house bears different stone or slate inlaid areas to relieve the monotony of the brick, and the lintels over the windows and doors are each carved differently. . . .

Parties at Brucemore were different in all sorts of ways from what we have today. First of all, most big houses, instead of the present-day recreation room in the basement, had a ballroom in the attic. I even remember five or six in Cedar Rapids and they were perfectly lovely. One was in the attic of the Walter Cherry house and it had pale pink walls with crystal and gold side brackets lighting it up, there being no windows. It had a little platform for a three-piece orchestra, a smooth parquet floor, sixty-odd gold chairs around the walls, and a skylight overhead draped with artificial roses and pink ribbons. The skylight opened up to cool us off when the dance floor was crowded, and there was an adjacent sitting room where the chaperones sat, and where stood the ever-present big cut-glass punch bowl, filled with ginger ale and fruit juices.

Besides dancing, I remember playing exciting games of musical chairs, and marching grand right and left: when the music stopped you danced with the boy facing you. There was also a circle two-step that mixed up the boys and girls, and a dance where couples were eliminated if caught holding a feather duster when the music stopped.

Some of these private dancing parties were called cotillions, and that meant that there were favors. Usually they were laid out on a table and consisted of a dozen fancy paper hats and some lovely Japanese fans and perhaps a dozen tissue-paper colored boas, and so on.

The girls sat on one side of the ballroom and the boys on the opposite. The hostess would choose ten boys from the ranks and ask each of them to take a favor to a dancing partner. After they had danced a short time, they would sit down and she would pick another group. We thought a cotillion was "divine."

The private ballroom was good training for us shy young people who felt awkward and strange all dressed up and having to dance with people of the opposite sex. The girls of that period went to dancing school to learn how to waltz and fox-trot and even daringly do the tango, but we usually danced with other girls. If there *were* any boys, there were never enough to go around and they were generally shorter and rebelliously surly.

Another nonexistent party today is the tea dance, or *thé dansant* as they were called in the higher social circles. They usually took place from 5 to 7 P.M., and a private tea dance could take place in the private ballroom too. Tea or punch was served, and ice cream and cake, and the girls wore short dresses, and the boys cutaways or dark suits with white shirts and sometimes gates-ajar stiff collars.

Holidays too were special times at Brucemore, celebrated with little or no commercial help, and none of that "only 14 more shopping days" publicity, so to speak. We made out Christmas lists in the middle of December, assembled the presents soon after, and proceeded to wrap them up on the twenty-third or twenty-fourth.

Christmas gifts were always wrapped in white tissue paper, tied up with red or green cord or ribbon, and usually carried a small Christmas paper seal or two to help stick the tissue flat. Most seals were a small wreath of holly with a red bow, or a head of Santa Claus or a small Christmas tree.

The present was tagged with an equally traditional white rectangular card on a red string, and on them we wrote conventional things like "Merry Christmas to Grandmother with love from So-and-so." Girl friends exchanged all kinds of presents with each other, but boys could send only flowers or candy or a book to girls they liked or else something comical and inexpensive. Once I received an innocent-looking cardboard box, and when I opened it, out shot a yard-long rattlesnake, made of a cloth-covered coiled spring, and the boy who had sent it had pasted a photograph of his face on the front end of the snake. It was a sensation. However, if a heavy beau sent anything like a gold bracelet, back it went with a polite note of thanks for the kind thought; it could not be accepted.

Christmas at Brucemore was a glorious affair each year, as our high-ceilinged house had a three-story stairwell and standing in it tall and towering was a really huge Christmas tree, about fifty feet high. It took the entire household to trim it with silver tinsel and red and gold ornaments and frosted white tree lights. It was always chopped down on December 24 and came in from our own woods, drawn by Maude and Dobbin, the farm horses, and when it was set up in the main entrance a few steps down from the front hall, the whole house smelled like a pine forest all through the holidays. There was only one drawback; it took up so much room that no one could come in through the front door, but luckily there was a side door that was close by, which was better than having to crawl in on all fours.

On Christmas morning when we were young we opened our stocking presents upstairs in the breakfast room, then had breakfast and got dressed, and then all descended together downstairs to the big front hall, where we all lined up in front of the tree, while Mr. Bidwell, the organist of the Presbyterian church, played Christmas carols.

All the servants came in, and everyone who lived on the place, and we all wished them Merry Christmas, and Mother and Dad gave the grown-ups shiny new gold pieces, each in a little velvet box or purse, and we sisters gave all the children big red-and-white-striped candy canes tied with red satin ribbon, and oranges and almonds in gold net bags.

After they left we opened our presents, greeted friends who dropped in and later ate a traditional Christmas dinner of turkey and flaming plum pudding, and welcomed visitors all afternoon at a traditional open house, ending the day with a cold buffet supper, deviled eggs and cold turkey and potato salad, which waited for us in the pantry.

The next day we put all the presents away, and except for the tree and the Christmas wreaths in the windows and at the doors, returned to normal. . . .

What were other holidays like in the good old days? The Fourth of July was completely different: we had firecrackers. Girls and boys woke up at dawn's early light and sneaked outdoors, lit a long, thin brown cigar-like object called "punk," something that burned very slowly; in fact, as I remember, a stick of punk lasted perhaps an hour. After getting the punk going, then we took out a long string of little red firecrackers called "lady crackers." These were much the best because they made the most noise in the fastest amount of time.

In our case, carrying the punk in one hand and the lady crackers in the other, sister Barbara and I arrived at a spot just below the sleeping porch where my father slept during the summer. There was a brick terrace there and we lit the long fuse to the whole bunch and ran as far away as we could before they went off. It was a glorious moment.

We also had torpedoes that we hurled to the pavement and if they landed properly they made one deafening roar that was extremely satisfactory. Besides these, there was another noisemaker called a son-of-a-gun. It was a small round pellet which one tossed to the ground and then stamped on it furiously with the heel and it made loud crackling noises, smelled very brimstonish, and flashed sparks.

Thus the day passed pleasantly, and when evening came things got even better. First we lighted sparklers and sent paper balloons aloft filled with hot air, then as it grew darker we shot off Roman candles, being careful not to point them at any friends.

By this time we had moved to the tennis court where the grown-ups took over, shooting off pinwheels and flowerpots and finally the favorite of all: a series of glorious rockets.

My special favorite, since it was mine alone, was my Halloween birthday. Long before the days of "trick or treat" my family always gave me a Witch Hunt. It was the most exciting event imaginable, for it took place outdoors through a wooded area crisscrossed by paths. Actually this was an uncultivated part of land out in the back side of Brucemore. Thirty or forty of us would start off in groups of seven or eight, each bunch of us following our own trail. One set of boys and girls followed a trail of regular yellow corn, the next a trail of white corn, another group went after candy corn, and so on. Along the way there were various exciting things to help us find the witch. A lighted jack-o-lantern apiece, a bushel basket of horns, one for each of us, and a sign that said, "Blow horns to scare witch, for she is near." At another spot there were apples in case we needed energy, and peanuts, and noisemakers appeared before us at regular intervals. As it grew dark it became more exciting, and finally there *at last* hung the witch, right in our path, tall and huge, dressed in black tar paper and tall black pointed hat with a terrible white face and gray yarn hair.

But she was always carried back near to the main house and onto a brick terrace where there was a big shallow pool, now empty of water for the winter and filled with dead leaves. In the middle stood a stake and the witch was tied to it, the fire was started, and the witch burned up most gorgeously, while we watched and ate doughnuts and drank cider. It was always a successful party, and the team that reached the witch first received a special prize. One year the winners all got black furry kittens, one apiece. How the rest of us envied them.

Once when I was very young a respectable and well-to-do bachelor cousin wrote from somewhere in Perth, Scotland, inviting himself to come and stay a month with his Iowa relatives. He was Sir Sholto Archibald Douglas-Hamilton; he was thirty-four years old, had never visited "the States," and wondered if he should bring his golf clubs or . . . were there no golf links available?

My father wrote and suggested that he spend the month of October at Brucemore, the autumn being the best season in the Middle West, and he added that there were several golf links in the vicinity, but he noted apologetically that compared to St. Andrews and Dornoch and so on, our links were new and primitive.

Sir Sholto arrived on an afternoon train in the early fall with all sorts of bags and valises and satchels, minus the golf clubs, and begged pardon for traveling with so little baggage. He was a large tweedy type with a bushy beard, a splendid Scotch brogue, and a warm smile.

When my father conducted him to our new car, a large gray open Stoddard Dayton, he was amazed. "By Jove!" he exclaimed. "You have a motah." He turned to my father. "And you have roads?" he asked.

My father nodded. The chauffeur got the luggage in somehow, cranked the motor, and off they went.

Sir Sholto seemed dumbfounded. "My word"—he pointed his finger—"you seem to have sidewalks. I say—er—it seems far more civilized than I had believed the Middle West to be." He turned to Daddy. "Cousin George, sir, are the Indians hereabouts friendly or otherwise?" He patted his bulging overcoat pocket. "I thought it best to come fully armed."

Daddy answered solemnly that there were in fact several Indian tribes in the vicinity, that on a clear night one could see the smoke from their tepees across the cornfields, and that they were friendly unless they drank too much firewater, which only happened on Saturday nights.

Sir Sholto was delighted. "They carry tommy-hawks, of course," he suggested.

"Tomahawks," my father corrected him. "And of course bows and arrows. Steel arrowheads nowadays," he added. "Cost plenty wampum."

"What sort of Indians?" Sir Sholto asked eagerly.

"The local tribes are the Tama Indians," Daddy said after a moment of busy thinking. "I think they must be Sioux or Dakota or a mixture of both."

Afte they had reached Brucemore and the auto had snorted up the long elm-shaded driveway to the house, he was welcomed by Mother and the brothers, his luggage was dispatched to his room, and he was told that dinner would be at eight, with a before-dinner drink served in the library (the word "cocktail" was not yet in use), and that Daddy's valet would have his dinner jacket laid out for him.

Poor cousin Sholto turned beet-red with embarrassment. "I say." He faced them bravely. "I've nowt but apologies. I—I thought that you were all a bunch of wild and woollies. I didn't bring any proper clothes—just rough gear for stalking Indians—aye, that's about it." He turned to Daddy. "You and your savages!" And he laughed uproariously. "Aye, and I believed it all until I saw your bonnie Brucemore."

He was a delightful guest and proved to be an excellent marksman and hunter. He taught Margaret the Highland Fling and the Sword Dance, and when he returned home he sent Mother a Black Angus Aberdeen bull and cow.

LANGSTON HUGHES

"One Christmas Eve" by the distinguished black writer Langston Hughes (1902–1967) is a different kind of Christmas story. It is not the usual one given over to nostalgic remembrances of Christmases past, or of feasting and merriment, or of the miracle of the Christ Child's birth that has been replicated in some modern miracle. This story's theme will be important to readers who knew poverty in their youth, or who were black, or who grew up outside the American cultural mainstream.

Hughes was born in Joplin, Missouri, and spent several of his formative years in Topeka and Lawrence, Kansas, before beginning his eastward trek (like so many midwestern writers) that ended in New York City's Harlem. There Hughes began his association with some of America's major writers and emerged as a significant figure in the Harlem Renaissance. And it was there that he met and collaborated with another transplanted midwesterner, Carl Van Vechten, novelist, critic, photographer, and literary patron of better interracial relations between artists. Van Vechten asked Hughes to write a number of song lyrics for the seventh and subsequent printings of Van Vechten's novel, Nigger Heaven *(1926), a story about a black writer in Harlem.*

Langston Hughes was a prolific and talented writer; he was the author of almost three dozen books. Not Without Laughter *(1930) is his partly fictionalized autobiography of his first twenty-five years. His poetry has been collected in* Selected Poems *(1959), and his plays in* Five Plays *(1963). His four "Simple" books are epitomized in* The Best of Simple *(1961).* The First Book of Negroes *was one of several books he wrote for young readers.* The Ways of White Folk *is a notable collection of his short stories, from which the following selection is taken.*

One Christmas Eve

STANDING OVER THE HOT STOVE cooking supper, the colored maid, Arcie, was very tired. Between meals today, she had cleaned the whole house for the white family she worked for, getting ready for Christmas tomorrow. Now her back ached and her head felt faint from sheer fatigue. Well, she would be off in a little while, if only the Missus and her children would come on home to dinner. They were out shopping for more things for the tree which stood all ready, tinsel-hung and lovely in the living-room, waiting for its candles to be lighted.

Arcie wished she could afford a tree for Joe. He'd never had one yet, and it's nice to have such things when you're little. Joe was five, going on six. Arcie, looking at the roast in the white folks' oven, wondered how much she could afford to spend tonight on toys. She only got seven dollars a week, and four of that went for her room and the landlady's daily looking after Joe while Arcie was at work.

"Lord, it's more'n a notion raisin' a child," she thought.

She looked at the clock on the kitchen table. After seven. What made white folks so darned inconsiderate? Why didn't they come on home here to supper? They knew she wanted to get off before all the stores closed. She wouldn't have time to buy Joe nothin' if they didn't hurry. And her landlady probably wanting to go out and shop, too, and not be bothered with little Joe.

"Dog gone it!" Arcie said to herself. "If I just had my money, I might leave the supper on the stove for 'em. I just got to get to the stores fo' they close." But she hadn't been paid for the week yet. The Missus had promised to pay her Christmas Eve, a day or so ahead of time.

Arcie heard a door slam and talking and laughter in the front of the house. She went in and saw the Missus and her kids shaking snow off their coats.

"Umm-mm! It's swell for Christmas Eve," one of the kids said to Arcie. "It's snowin' like the deuce, and mother came near driving through a stop light. Can't hardly see for the snow. It's swell!"

"Supper's ready," Arcie said. She was thinking how her shoes weren't very good for walking in snow.

It seemed like the white folks took as long as they could to eat that evening. While Arcie was washing dishes, the Missus came out with her money.

"Arcie," the Missus said, "I'm so sorry, but would you mind if I just gave you five dollars tonight? The children have made me run short of change, buying presents and all."

"I'd like to have seven," Arcie said. "I needs it."

"Well, I just haven't got seven," the Missus said. "I didn't know you'd want all your money before the end of the week, anyhow. I just haven't got it to spare."

Arcie took five. Coming out of the hot kitchen, she wrapped up as well as she could and hurried by the house where she roomed to get little Joe. At least he could look at the Christmas trees in the windows downtown.

The landlady, a big light yellow woman, was in a bad humor. She said to Arcie, "I thought you was comin' home early and get this child. I guess you know I want to go out, too, once in a while."

Arcie didn't say anything for, if she had, she knew the landlady would probably throw it up to her that she wasn't getting paid to look after a child both night and day.

"Come on, Joe," Arcie said to her son, "Let's us go in the street."

"I hears they got a Santa Claus down town," Joe said, wriggling into his worn little coat. "I wants to see him."

"Don't know 'bout that," his mother said, "but hurry up and get your rubbers on. Stores'll all be closed directly."

It was six or eight blocks downtown. They trudged along through the falling snow, both of them a little cold. But the snow was pretty!

The main street was hung with bright red and blue lights. In front of the City Hall there was a Christmas tree—but it didn't have no presents on it, only lights. In the store windows there were lots of toys—for sale.

Joe kept on saying, "Mama, I want . . ."

But mama kept walking ahead. It was nearly ten, when the stores were due to close, and Arcie wanted to get Joe some cheap gloves and something to keep him warm, as well as a toy or two. She thought she might come across a rummage sale where they had children's clothes. And in the ten-cent store, she could get some toys.

"O-oo! Lookee . . . ," little Joe kept saying, and pointing at things in the windows. How warm and pretty the lights were, and the shops, and the electric signs through the snow.

BLACK CHILD IN A WHITE WORLD.

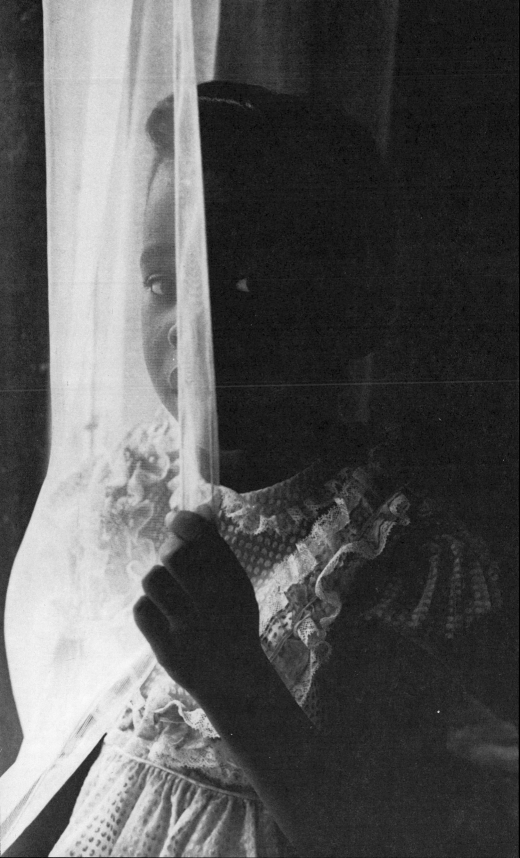

It took Arcie more than a dollar to get Joe's mittens and things he needed. In the A. & P. Arcie bought a big box of hard candies for 49c. And then she guided Joe through the crowd on the street until they came to the dime store. Near the ten-cent store they passed a moving picture theatre. Joe said he wanted to go in and see the movies.

Arcie said, "Ump-un! No child! This ain't Baltimore where they have shows for colored, too. In these here small towns, they don't let colored folks in. We can't go in there."

"Oh," said little Joe.

In the ten-cent store, there was an awful crowd. Arcie told Joe to stand outside and wait for her. Keeping hold of him in the crowded store would be a job. Besides she didn't want him to see what toys she was buying. They were to be a surprise from Santa Claus tomorrow.

Little Joe stood outside the ten-cent store in the light, and the snow, and people passing. Gee, Christmas was pretty. All tinsel and stars and cotton. And Santa Claus a-coming from somewhere, dropping things in stockings. And all the people in the streets were carrying things, and the kids looked happy.

But Joe soon got tired of just standing and thinking and waiting in front of the ten-cent store. There were so many things to look at in the other windows. He moved along up the block a little, and then a little more, walking and looking. In fact, he moved until he came to the white folks' picture show.

In the lobby of the moving picture show, behind the plate glass doors, it was all warm and glowing and awful pretty. Joe stood looking in, and as he looked his eyes began to make out, in there blazing beneath holly and colored streamers and the electric stars of the lobby, a marvellous Christmas tree. A group of children and grown-ups, white, of course, were standing around a big jovial man in red beside the tree. Or was it a man? Little Joe's eyes opened wide. No, it was not a man at all. It was Santa Claus!

Little Joe pushed open one of the glass doors and ran into the lobby of the white moving picture show. Little Joe went right through the crowd and up to where he could get a good look at Santa Claus. And Santa Claus was giving away gifts, little presents for children, little boxes of animal crackers and stick-candy canes. And behind him on the tree was a big sign (which little Joe didn't know how to read). It said, to those who understood, MERRY XMAS FROM SANTA CLAUS TO OUR YOUNG PATRONS.

Around the lobby, other signs said, WHEN YOU COME OUT

OF THE SHOW STOP WITH YOUR CHILDREN AND SEE OUR SANTA CLAUS. And another announced, GEM THEATRE MAKES ITS CUSTOMERS HAPPY—SEE OUR SANTA.

And there was Santa Claus in a red suit and a white beard all sprinkled with tinsel snow. Around him were rattles and drums and rocking horses which he was not giving away. But the signs on them said (could little Joe have read) that they would be presented from the stage on Christmas Day to the holders of the lucky numbers. Tonight, Santa Claus was only giving away candy, and stick-candy canes, and animal crackers to the kids.

Joe would have liked terribly to have a stick-candy cane. He came a little closer to Santa Claus, until he was right in the front of the crowd. And then Santa Claus saw Joe.

Why is it that lots of white people always grin when they see a Negro child? Santa Claus grinned. Everybody else grinned, too, looking at little black Joe—who had no business in the lobby of a white theatre. Then Santa Claus stooped down and slyly picked up one of his lucky number rattles, a great big loud tin-pan rattle such as they use in cabarets. And he shook it fiercely right at Joe. That was funny. The white people laughed, kids and all. But little Joe didn't laugh. He was scared. To the shaking of the big rattle, he turned and fled out of the warm lobby of the theatre, out into the street where the snow was and the people. Frightened by laughter, he had begun to cry. He went looking for his mamma. In his heart he never thought Santa Claus shook great rattles at children like that—and then laughed.

In the crowd on the street he went the wrong way. He couldn't find the ten-cent store or his mother. There were too many people, all white people, moving like white shadows in the snow, a world of white people.

It seemed to Joe an awfully long time till he suddenly saw Arcie, dark and worried-looking, cut across the side-walk through the passing crowd and grab him. Although her arms were full of packages, she still managed with one free hand to shake him until his teeth rattled.

"Why didn't you stand where I left you?" Arcie demanded loudly. "Tired as I am, I got to run all over the streets in the night lookin' for you. I'm a great mind to wear you out."

When little Joe got his breath back, on the way home, he told his mamma he had been in the moving picture show.

"But Santa Claus didn't give me nothin'," Joe said tearfully. "He made a big noise at me and I runned out."

"Serves you right," said Arcie, trudging through the snow. "You had no business in there. I told you to stay where I left you."

"But I seed Santa Claus in there," little Joe said, "so I went in."

"Huh! That wasn't no Santa Claus," Arcie explained, "If it was, he wouldn't a-treated you like that. That's a theatre for white folks—I told you once—and he's just a old white man."

"Oh . . . ," said little Joe.

MICHAEL BORICH

As a young poet, one among a myriad striving for the public eye and ear in an age when there seem to be more writers of poetry than readers, Michael Borich has commanded increasing attention. His first published poem, "Swimming in the Rock," appeared in The New Yorker *in 1974, when Borich was only twenty-five:*

> Emptying my body of its last breath
> I am free to walk the paths
> of rivers at such depths
>
> that mucky bottom sand sucking
> on my hollow, moving steps
> cannot keep up. . . .

His first book-length collection, The Black Hawk Songs, *was published by the University of Illinois Press in 1976.*

> In my sixty-seventh year I am prisoner
> of the whites. Between the spaces
> of barred metal, my people, my dead
> people, appear, sullen as judges.

Michael Borich is a native midwesterner with roots reaching back to before the white man's coming. His maternal grandmother was a fullblooded Sac and Fox Indian, and Borich has spent a good deal of time at the Tama Indian Settlement on the Iowa River—home of a remnant of the tribes that were massacred at Bad Axe Creek and then driven westward out of Illinois following the Black Hawk War. Borich was born in Waterloo, Iowa, in 1949, the older of twin brothers. He was educated in Waterloo's parochial schools and at the University of Northern Iowa where he studied with James Hearst, one of the Midwest's best poets. Borich has taught in Iowa public schools and presently teaches writing at the University of Wisconsin, Green Bay. His wife, Lynn, is also a teacher.

For a while, Borich was an emigré from the Midwest, earning an MFA degree and teaching at the University of California, Irvine, in that "brassy, laidback, free and easy and intense Southern California mindscape." Although he is persuaded that 90 percent of the Californians he met have the same basic motivations and desires as anyone in the Heartland, he revealed to a Des Moines Register *writer, upon his return to Iowa:*

> There is a sanity about life here in the midwest that is unique. The people and the seasons have something to do with that. I've come to realize that conservatism is more than a political label; a midwest conservative is a caretaker of time-proven beliefs. We are less trend-setters than trend evaluators. If we are rednecks, it is because we work hard. If we are traditionalists, so be it. To be narrow-minded is not to be intolerant, but to focus our energies.

Although Borich's teaching commitment requires that he spend his winters in the football and winter sports capital of northern Wisconsin, he spends his summers among his friends and relatives in Iowa.

Whatever Happened to Huck Finn?

MY STEP-GRANDFATHER was Huck Finn. Well, it's a bit more complicated than that, but anyone who knew Sam Clemens personally, knew that he had almost no imagination at all—he transposed, borrowed, or outright stole his most famous stories. When it came to creating characters, Sam couldn't help but draw entirely from real life; his early training was as a journalist, and a journalist he remained. Even his notorious jumping frog came from a true incident in a Sacramento newspaper—not from out of his head. And anyone who knew Hannibal in the days Sam was growing up, recognized "Huck" as Tom Blankenship, an unwashed, illiterate bumpkin. If Tom Blankenship didn't sleep with the hogs, he was purported to have at least visited them on occasion.

Suffice it for me to say, that when Huck headed out for the wilds away from civilization at the end of the book, years of lolling, fishing, dragging traplines, brought him north to Keokuk, and then up a smaller river to Des Moines, where he made and sold his home-made "likker" to the boys who worked in mines. Actually, he and my real grandfather lived in Highbridge—now a nonexistent criss-cross of highway lines on the map—my real grandfather was a miner.

On a wintry night in November, walking home across a high railroad trestle, my real grandfather fell to his death trying to haul up a friend who had slipped. Tom,. the Borich family's closest friend, moved in with my grandmother, providing as best he could for my father, who was two years old, and three other children.

Nobody seemed to care much about who Tom might have been; he was like any other breadwinner in the twenties and during the Depression who went on an occasional binge, beat his kids regularly, swore at his wife, brought home a side of ham once a year, and even showed up at Christmas mass to usher in the Holy Infant.

In 1921 the family roped all belongings into the redoubtable Ford and putted to Waterloo, where immigrant relatives came to fill up a battered two-story on North Barclay. My grandmother took over the homebrew business and even serviced the local police who nicknamed her Queen Mary. And Tom went to work for the Illinois Central as a switchman. My father grew through street brawls, sandlot football melees, school at St. Mary's and caddying at Sunnyside Golf Course, to three years of waiting for WW II to end in steamy India as a staff sergeant, to finally marry a fiery-haired dancer: an Irishwoman, name of Mulholland.

Shortly thereafter, two fat, twin boys arrived, bringing with them loads and loads of diapers, and an enormous milk bill. Fortunately, father worked for the Walnut Dairy. As my brother and I grew into the world, Tom, our grandpa, grew slowly out of it. When I was four, just before we moved into our first, new house on the west side of town, Tom began to smell more and more of ten-cent booze. Even Grandma Mary couldn't hide it from him. His nose, a bulbous scarlet, would twitch, and he'd either reach for a bottle under the damp couch, or tobacco spilling out of a tin. His eyes, sleepy like a hound dog's, flared slightly and rolled back when the coughing fits began. He would cough and cough, until you thought his lungs were coming up.

By then, the other children had moved to Chicago, all except my father who was up at 4 A.M. every morning to deliver the fresh cream and cottage cheese, and the bottles that would swell and pop their caps on cold porches. Only Mary and Tom remained in the weather-battered house which slumped down each year after the heavy snows. And Mela, the boarder from Croatia, who kept to himself in the backroom, remained. None of the neighbors, I'm sure, knew who really was dying of lung cancer in the darkened livingroom.

We made our dutiful, Sunday visits. In the summers we ate

fried chicken and cabbage rolls under the pear tree in the backyard. In winter, we played nickleback and seven-card stud and go-to-the-dump, whispering that grandma was a cheat, and the old man's hands were yellow with malaria. And he'd cough and gag, then excuse himself to go spit a hunk of something dark and odorless. He and my father talked silently, watching the street from their wicker rockers, until my brother and I fell asleep and were trundled home.

It was an unremarkable funeral. Blustery cold, overcast, I remember only the funeral tent billowing like a carnival, and the long cars winding ahead and behind, as we rode with our parents. And Tom lay down, with no cannons firing, no rivers nearby to carry him toward Cairo. He just lay down.

My father knew what to say, but he remained silent. And grandmother cried and brought out platefuls of food, and sighed and brought out more food. And after the funeral everyone went home. There were few possessions to pass along, no inheritance. But my father knew who Tom was; from living with the old man for thirty years, my father had breathed in that soft exhalation of freedom that Tom had never been able to recapture. And Tom was gone, and Huck was long, long gone. And Clemens was dead, and Nigger Jim still sat at the back of the bus, and grandma planted her garden, and my other grandpa coughed out his lungs, and my Nana Grace, as sweet as she was, shrank away. And brother Mark came along. My gemini and I burnt down a weedlot. And brother Matt came along. We fought mosquitoes for a week at Lake Okoboji. And brother Pat set up crib. I put a few dents in my forehead from rock fights. And finally, little sister Melissa arrived, nearly doing mother in by coming. And the six little peppers were red hots; we captured and lost and recaptured the neighborhood. We stole green apples and raspberries, hid in hedges, fired snowballs at passing cars from igloos, shoveled walks, delivered papers. Only when we sat around the dining table, chuckling as grandma dealt from the bottom of the deck, did I think about Tom. But I had my own rafts to build.

"One down, tag on a fly ball," Dad hollered from his third base coach's box. I nodded, trying to ignore the hecklers from the other bench.

"You're the winning run Mojie; watch a grounder to short," Pete Evans, my Dad's assistant coach yelled from first base. I pulled at my hat brim like Luis Aparicio, the Chicago White Sox shortstop, would do. I tromped second, as if kicking mud from my tennis shoes.

"Get off, get off," I glanced toward Dad as the pitcher took his stretch and looked back at me. "A couple more steps, come on, get off more." I could tell he was excited. Extra inning games always got to him, and now he was starting to get hoarse. The pitcher swiveled quickly and faked a throw. I went into the second baseman headfirst. But the ball didn't come.

"Balk, balk!" Dad and Pete charged the base umpire at the same time.

"You're crazy, sit down Borich!" The other coach was on his feet at the edge of the diamond.

Unsatisfied, Dad turned toward the home-plate ump.

"No, no, no, he took his foot off the rubber," the burly ump pulled off his face mask.

"He motioned toward second," Dad shouted weakly.

"His foot was off the rubber," the umpire said, turning away.

Dad paused, silent. He looked at me and shook his head. I shrugged, helpless. The pitcher thumped the ball in his glove.

"What's the count ump?" Dad was nonplussed.

"One and one. Play ball!"

I brushed my pants off and squinted toward home. My brother Milo was up. Not a power hitter, he could at least lace a single down the line or a blooper into short field.

"OK now, take a good crack at it," Dad called, his voice fading.

Milo spit in the dirt, took his stance and fanned at a slow, outside curve.

"One ball, two strikes."

"Choke up, choke up and just punch it!" Dad's voice cracked. He looked at me and back to Milo, who was mixing saliva and dirt in his hands. Mother sat at the end of the dugout bench with the scorebook, bouncing Melissa on her lap. I got off a couple of steps, watching the shortstop to my right, and the second baseman on my left who edged closer to the bag. The pitcher threw to home. There was solid wood on the ball, but it ricochetted just beyond the first base foul line and took a hop toward Pete Evans. Pete jumped back, startled.

"Foul ball!" both umps shouted simultaneously.

"Just straighten it out now." Every third word Dad said was inaudible. Milo spit again, looked to first and then third for any signs, and hunched down in the batter's box.

"A single will bring him in," my father warbled persistently. I flexed my legs, less confident of my performance than Dad. It was a brush off. Milo sprawled back in the dirt and sat up. Our bench exploded. "Ya goonhead! Whatsa matter, ya need telescopes?" Three of our players stood up. Dad motioned them to sit back down.

"What's the count ump?" Dad rasped.

"Two and two."

Milo called time and walked slowly down the third base line. He whispered something to Dad and looked at me. Dad took off his hat, scratched the back of his head and nodded. They turned slowly and walked back to their positions. The game at the adjoining field had just ended. Parents and players were trickling over to watch us settle the 1 to 1 tie. A sizeable crowd had gathered. The opposing bench started monkeying up again. Our bench heckled and razzed.

"Get ready to go Mojie," Pete was giving me a steal signal. I looked to Dad for confirmation. He watched Milo settle into batter's stance, but he too was signaling a steal. I measured my steps to second and then rehearsed what I would do as I broke for third. I crouched, sidestepping away from second. The pitcher didn't bother with a stretch, but wound up and threw. The ball popped back, low and fast just a step in front of me as I broke for third. I knew it had skipped past the shortstop. I saw pop waving me home as I hit the edge of third, and cut hard toward home.

"Hit it, hit it," someone yelled, and from the position the catcher was assuming, I realized the play was going to be at home. I flung out prone, headfirst, toward where I thought the plate should be. I heard the ball hit the pud as I barreled into the catcher and took him down, just below the knees. I heard his "Oof!" and then the umpire's "He's out!" I rolled over stunned. My whole front side was brown, except for my elbow which began to seep red against my shirt. At that point, I was vaguely aware of my father charging home and arriving in front of the umpire just an instant before Pete Evans. Pete, possibly more excitable in the short run, but definitely unable to sustain his volume or intensity as my father could, pushed Dad out of the way and jutted his nose inches away from the umpire's. He was screaming a gargle of words, and sputtering in the ump's face. My father shouldered Pete to the side, hissing and fuming at the ump also. And then, unprompted, Dad trotted three steps back along the third base line, spun quickly and came in low on his belly toward home, exactly as I had done. He lay out flat, slapping the plate. I couldn't quite catch what he was shouting, but it was obvious that his face reddened as he attempted to make his point.

"Damn right, ya damn right!" Pete enjoined.

"Got him on the shoulder!" Dad thundered.

Both benches gathered around home; even a few of the parents and ballplayers from the other diamond had come closer for, what appeared to me, a virtuoso performance of how the blind umpire had failed to recognize that the slow catcher had indeed failed to put me out. Regardless of who was right, just on the basis of Dad, still scooching forward in the dirt toward Pete, who was now pretending to be at once the catcher and the umpire—regardless of who even cared that the sky was darkening and dinner most likely was growing cold at home—regardless that the event was now more than just a game, I should have been safe. I wasn't. The umpire was adamant.

"You were right on top of them," Dad said, coming to his knees. "He was under him!"

"Out!" the umpire put his mask back on. Everyone turned away. I looked to Pete and then Dad.

"He was right under him." Dad's voice was going fast. "Got him on the shoulder," the voice came from years away, light-years.

"Play ball!"

Dad stood up right in front of the umpire.

"Play ball!"

In a daze, we brushed ourselves off. I stumbled over to the drinking fountain and sucked on warm water. I think we went on to lose, or the game was called because of darkness, I can't remember which. But just for an instant, as my father lay bellyflat in the dirt at Logan Field, I knew that the sky had opened and some barefoot, tousle haired kid looked up at me from home plate, slapped his hand on the ground and shouted, "He was safe, goddamit, he was safe!" You bet I was.

Wapsipinicon. Shell Rock. Crane Creek. Union Bridge. Sweets Marsh. Lake Okoboji. Mississippi. South Bear Creek. Black Duck. Hall's Eddy. Snake Bridge. Eleventh Street Bridge on the Cedar. To have not grown up with a fishing pole in my hand, and to have not felt the slimy chicken-bait, to have not felt catfish fin or handfuls of nightcrawlers we pulled from the flower gardens at Byrnes Park, and to have not sat by a drowsy, early morning river and listened for owls to carry away their field mice, would have been like Walt Whitman never going beyond the city boundaries of New York.

My father would read rivers as accurately as reading a newspaper. He could tell by the color of the water, the depth and speed of the current, if the fish would be slunk down in bottom mud. He knew where the deep holes were, where the snags would tangle his hooks, what the contour of the riffles suggested, if he had caught a crappie or a snapping turtle before his leader ever broke water, and if we happened to be on a railroad bridge miles from anywhere, he knew what time the next train would come by and where it would be headed.

As my brother and I hitched up our knee boots and struggled through the deep swale grass after my father who led us to the secret catfish spots, or chocolate brown back streams full of bullheads, we listened to the stories about the enormous channel cat on the Mississippi that was too big for the boat, the stringers of lake trout that no one could lift, the leaps off narrow railroad bridges onto the pylons and the baits, the lures, the sky that threatened to break into hail, the snakes in swampy grass, and the rivers falling unmistakably and relentlessly toward the Gulf days and days away.

"But the mayonnaise will spoil," my mother grumbles.

There's enough ice in the little cooler," father replies patiently as he brakes coming down the gravel slope toward Union Grove Lake.

"Why did the food have to go in the little cooler and your fish bait in the big one?" Mother slaps at a fly buzzing Melissa's head.

"Like I said," father is cool, even though a trickle of sweat is visible on his neck, "it's a special mix. We can have a picnic anywhere, but we don't have a lake in our backyard."

"Heh, Pat keeps breathing on me," Matt whines.

"I'm just trying to read my comic book!" Pat, ten years old, is slightly larger than Matt, who is twelve.

"Just sit still and look at the lake," father sighs.

"You want me to crack 'em on the head?" Mark leans forward from the far back of the nine-seater Chevy wagon which is beginning to fill with dust.

"Can't we roll up the windows? I can't breathe." Melissa is five years old.

"We're almost there," Dad says. "Look how pretty the lake is."

"I'm gettin' sick!" Melissa leans back against Mom.

"She's gonna throw up, I knew she would." Milo looks out the window and spits into the wind.

"Would you stop that!" Mom stares past Milo and out the back window as she speaks. "What kind of example is that for your younger brothers and sister?"

Matt looks up from his Superman comic book. "What'd he do?"

"Just a luggie," Mark says, rummaging in the picnic basket.

Melissa turns around and rests her chin on the dusty seat. She watches Mark, who slowly rips open the potato chips. "Hey, he's gettin' the chips. I want some."

"Put them back," Dad shouts as we coast in to the parking lot.

"I'm hungry!" Mark shouts back.

"Me too," says Pat. "I didn't have any breakfast."

"You ate three donuts on the way here," Milo snaps Pat on the back of his head.

"He hit me!"

"Dammit! Let's everybody get out of the car, carry the picnic basket over to that table, I'll bait our poles and we'll all catch a few fish before lunch." Dad wipes the sweat away from his eyes. "Besides, let's all just have a good time today, OK?"

Mom looks out the window and grumbles softly, "The mayonnaise is probably spoiled by now."

Milo climbs out the back window, and reaches for the small cooler. "Hey, who left the lid off the cooler?"

"What? The cooler . . ." Dad rushes around to the back of the car. "Oh, it's only the food."

"The food?" Mom walks slowly to the open tailgate as Matt and Pat rush off toward the lake.

"No, it's alright. The hamburger is just a little soggy." Dad unloads the poles and the larger cooler. "I'm glad I used the bigger cooler for the bait; this stuff spoils real easy."

"Would the fish care?" Mom drains the water out of the cooler. "We may have to eat those chicken livers and that, what is it, cheese bait, and use the hot dogs for the fish. What are these nightcrawlers doing under the potato salad?"

"They wouldn't fit in the other cooler," Milo says.

"Hey Mom, what's poison ivy look like?" Mark calls from a patch of bushes.

"I'm hungry." Melissa draws stick men on the dusty window of the wagon. "I don't wanna fish. I just wanna eat lunch and go swim. When are we gonna eat lunch?"

"Go have a sandwich now," says Dad as he carries the tackle box to the lake edge.

Mom follows after him. "What'll she have for lunch then? I just made one sandwich for her."

Dad looks through his lures and sinkers. "Let her have one of my hot dogs."

"You know she only eats peanut butter and jelly," Mom says.

Dad looks up at me. "You want to fish on the bottom or with a cork?" I say with a cork, and toss him my favorite bobber. "Get back from the lake Matt and Pat!" Matt and Pat skip stones out across the water.

"Yeah, you guys can't swim, and I'm not gonna jump in to save you," Mark says, with a mouthful of chips.

"Neither can you," says Milo.

"Bet I can. Bet I can swim better than them."

"So what, they can't swim at all." Milo baits his hook.

"Cast over by those trees," Dad tells Milo. "Early morning like this, they'll be deep in shade. Here," he hands me a pole. "Go get your line in the water. You won't catch any fish standing around."

I try to move far enough from Milo so our lines don't tangle, but not so far that I can't cast into the shade of the overhanging river maples.

"Hey, you're gonna cross me," Milo says as I make my first cast. But I don't take my finger off the release button soon enough, so my line plops three feet in front of me. I look down at the bird nest in my reel. As I untangle the line, I realize my bobber has vanished.

"Where's my bait?"

"You got a bite! Pull it in!" Dad jumps to his feet.

I yank my pole back over my head, but still my cork does not appear.

"Reel it in," says Milo.

"But look at my reel!" I hold up the tangle of filament. There's nothing to do, but pull at the loops of line and groan. Suddenly my red and white cork appears, but then it goes under again. I back away from the water's edge.

"Never mind," Milo says, as I'm about ten feet away from the lake. "Your bait's gone."

Mom and Melissa have wandered off to find a bathroom, Matt and Pat are fishing, Mark stares across the lake munching Melissa's peanut butter and jelly sandwich, Milo strings up his third bluegill, Dad is finally baiting his own pole and I've just untangled the last knot in my reel. I swat a mosquito which has finished with my neck.

"I wish we had a boat."

Dad makes his first cast, then lays his pole down against a crooked stick, and takes a Swisher Sweet out of his pocket. "Well, that's where the big ones are." He puts the small cigar into his mouth, but does not light it.

"I wish I had a canoe," Mark says.

"What for?" Milo turns to look at Mark. "You can't fish from it."

A LOST ISLAND LAKE CATCH.

"So?"

"And you're afraid of the water anyway."

"I'd go over the water."

"What if you tipped over?" Milo grins.

"You'd tip over, not me."

"You won't even put your face in the water." Milo laughs sarcastically.

"What do I do when I wash my face, huh, what do I do then?"

"You probably don't wash your face."

Mark pushes his glasses back up his nose. "Least I don't have pim-ples."

Milo rubs his chin. "These aren't pimples. It's just stubble, and a rash from shaving."

"You?" Mark scrunches his face. "You don't shave."

"What do you know?" Milo walks down the bank trying to un-hook a snag. "I got a tree," he says to no one in particular.

"Quiet, I got a bite," Dad picks up his pole and tilts his head slightly, listening, as if he could hear the fish circling his bait.

"Something's knocking my pole too," Pat says.

"Probably just you," says Matt.

"I caught the biggest one so far," Pat frowns.

"So what, it's still a pinhead."

"Bigger than yours."

"I caught the first one."

"Huh uh," grunts Milo. "I caught the first one, and the most so far."

Matt reels his line in.

"Leave your line in the water," Dad says. "That's where the fish are."

"Everybody else has the good spots," Matt pouts.

"You just got to have the skill," says Pat.

"Hey, he's biting good." Dad's arm tenses as he leans forward, intent on the tip of his pole. He talks to himself. "Now we just wait patient for him to grab it and run, oh boy, can I feel him nibble."

We all watch with silent interest. Mom and Melissa come back carrying firewood.

"You just let him play around," Dad continues his commentary, "until he get's good and grabby, and then, oh boy, look at him peck that bait, and then he get's real hungry and . . ." He jerks the pole back quickly. "Yep." He nods. "Got him."

"Is he a big one?" Pat asks.

Dad reels confidently, watching the line in the water come slow-ly toward him. Just as the fish is about to be exposed, there is a splash nearby to our left. We turn, startled to see Mark in the water. The fact of Mark being in the water doesn't register mentally. I realize there is another splash to my right. As my head swivels toward my father, whose head has just come up in the water, I can't quite seem to grasp what is happening. The probability of Mark's falling in hadn't occurred to me, but as father reaches my younger brother and holds him up, I see that Mark still has on his glasses, though his eyes are closed. Mother is soon at the water's edge, reaching for Mark's wet shirt. In a minute, Dad, still floundering in the slippery mud, lifts Mark up the bank, and Mom pulls him forward on his belly. He lies flat and starts whimpering.

"Jeez, what happened?" asks Matt.

Mark rolls over on his back, takes his glasses off and blinks up at us. Dad crawls up the slick bank.

"The bank gave way," Mark coughs.

"You must have gotten too close." Mom is unsympathetic.

"It just crumbled?" Matt asks.

"Yeah," Mark sputters and gags.

"What about your pole?" Pat kneels down next to Mark.

"It's in the water," he says listlessly.

"No, there it is," Milo points to the spot where Mark went in. The reel end of the pole is just visible in the mud. Dad, dripping, slogs over to the pole and lifts it up out of the dark brown water. Melissa begins laughing.

"Shut up!" Mark snaps.

Melissa giggles uncontrollably.

"Hey Mark," Milo says.

"What?"

"You look like a muskrat." He begins laughing too. "He does, doesn't he?"

Mark tries to spit the muddy taste of the lake out, as Dad takes off his clothes down to his underwear. He opens his billfold, and peels the soggy bills out, one by one, and spreads them on the grass in the sun. The ink on his driver's license is smeary.

"Well," he sighs. "We may as well make the best of it. Why don't we go over to the swimming beach?"

Mark sits up and squints blindly at him. "Not now. I haven't had lunch yet!"

My first job was newsboy for the *Waterloo Daily Courier*. I remember my feet icy as I awaken into an early morning of winter. There are sparrows, bruised and cold, that abandon their invisibility and sweep over the rooftops where light is just beginning to break. They look like smoke rising into the pale grey sky. The crust of crisp snow p-chucks when my stiff boots break through the top layer. The two bundles of wire-bound papers sit on top of the snow as patient, as immobile as grandmothers. There are no kitchen lights on in any of the houses along the street. The few cars left out are as quiet as sleeping sled dogs. When I snap the wire with my cutter, I can smell the fresh ink, the papers slightly damp with the scent of the pressroom.

It may be April, 7:00 A.M. on Easter Sunday and church bells are beginning to ring all over the city. Struggling under the paper bag, I plow through the thick dew with cut grass sticking to my bare feet. A dog barks two blocks away. Toys sprawl abandoned on front lawns. And the newspapers disappear one by one between the silent clasp of doors. If my twin brother is with me, he mirrors my movements on the other side of the street. If it is a morning when a Norther drops out of the high Dakota plains, swinging sharp blades of wind, then the stacks of papers are lugged into the back of our station wagon and my father drives over the slick streets.

More than a lyrical blanket of memory, the newspaper carried with it a great urgency. The first summer of my newspaper career, when I was eleven, money clinking in the collection bag seemed to be the most important reminder of getting the papers out on time. But one morning, folding papers in the half-light of the screen porch, I discovered the real import of what my role was. Secretly, privately, the still-warm print rubbing off on my hands, I saw behind the veil of youthful expediency. From the flat twenty-eight pages, I was shaping and folding the sacred grail, the cup of crystal, that I would deliver to the sleeping kingdom. And before any one of my sixty-one lieges found out how the world had been revolving in the past twenty-four hours, I knew. The revelation of having one foot in Palestine on the banks of the Suez and the other foot striding ashore from the bay at Cuba caught my breath in awe and thrust an immense responsibility into those full paper bags. Soon, I was rising a half-hour earlier each morning to read the entire paper, and always there was an item, a page, a story that imbued my route with such importance, that my friends, lost in their dreams of motorcycles and jacked-up cars, could not understand. I was carrying history.

One July evening when I was about twelve, my mother and I sat on the front porch watching lightning bugs flicker across the cool lawns. The sky was ablaze with stars. An occasional car would come down Vermont hill and drive slowly past us to the grocery store. Night birds fluttered in the high branches of our poplar trees. My father and brothers were in the living room playing cards, their conversation distant because of the soft whirring window fan. We sat for a long time in silence listening to the neighborhood wind down. I asked mother if she had ever wanted to live anywhere else.

"Well," she paused, thoughtful. "I always liked Florida."

The moon, swollen and milkgold, was just coming up over the rooftops. I stared hard, trying to see if the thin, dark cracks were roads across the vast seas of lunar dunes.

"The winters here are so long and bitter." She sighed. "And the hot, humid summers," she rubbed her hands together slowly. "But—"

She never finished her sentence. Something dark flew past us making a low, sad whine. My mother rose to go in.

"How about an ice cream cone? I've got strawberry ice cream with real strawberries in it." She was playing my tune.

HADLEY READ

Hadley Read was born on a farm on the Jewell-Stanhope road in 1918. A quarter of a mile east was the Garden Center rural school where Read got his early education; three-quarters of a mile west was the next farm. The Reads owned all the land along that mile stretch, running from the road a half-mile back to the fence line—320 acres of fertile Iowa soil.

It is of life on that farm, from 1928 just after Charles A. Lindbergh had flown the Atlantic in his Spirit of St. Louis *through those Depression years when fat steers sold for three cents a pound on the Chicago market, that Read writes in his nostalgic free verse form. It is the same period of time that R. V. Cassill writes about, but Read's verses reflect a far different attitude toward farm-town relationships than does Cassill's prose. In Read's world, farm and town are two sides of the same coin; the farm family, obviously prosperous for all the low farm prices, has relatives in the town. And the town offers "cosmopolitan" pleasures not found on the farm—seeing a movie, meeting friends, talking with girls, having a sack of popcorn.*

As a poet of farm life, Read contrasts strongly with James Hearst. Read's purpose, he says elsewhere, is simply "to tell how it really was." But Hearst in "Cows Bawl on Sunday" probes beneath the surface:

> The image of God
> in a warm mackinaw and rubber boots
> daily fights his way into the steaming barnyard
> into a multitude of hungry, angry, playful and determined animals
> through a cloud of raging sound
> to bring order out of chaos.
> Six times a week and rests not on the seventh—
> and there fails his divinity.

Until his recent retirement, Read was head of the Office of Agricultural Communications and assistant director of the Cooperative Extension Service at the University of Illinois at Champaign-Urbana. He is the author of three textbooks in addition to Morning Chores and Other Times Remembered *(1977), from which these verses are taken.*

Saturday Night in Town

Mom calls through the screen door.
A warning.
"Supper's ready in ten minutes."
I stand naked in the wash house.
My bath almost finished.
I pour soapy water from the tub over me.
The last rinse.
It's Saturday night.
We're going to town.
I reach for the towel hanging on the nail.
I wrap it around me and dash upstairs to dress.
I'll get almost dry on the way.
Clean shirt.
Denim pants with only one patch.
Downstairs.
Supper is on the table.
Canned pork, fried potatoes, gravy, biscuits.
Everyone eats quickly.
It's almost seven.
The picture show starts at seven-thirty.
We don't want to miss the comedy.
Or the serial before the main feature.
Perhaps a Tom Mix feature.
We won't know 'till it starts.
Mom says she'll do the dishes when we get home.

We pile into the car.
Arguing about who has to sit in the middle.
Dad drives slowly.
He has to compare all the cornfields with his.
I wish he would drive faster.
We park in front of Harry's Garage on Main Street.
Harry is Dad's brother who sells cars.

I have a dime for the show.
A nickel for popcorn.
So do the other kids.
Mom says to meet back at the car by ten.
The picture show starts in seven minutes.
We scatter.
I sit on the iron railing by the drug store.
Ronald comes along just in time.
We head for the show.
We decide to share one sack of popcorn.
That way we'll have a nickel for candy afterwards.
We sit behind some town girls by accident.

SATURDAY NIGHT MOVIE IN TOWN.

They pretend not to know we are there.
Anyway they have their own popcorn.
But it's just nice to be there.
The comedy is very funny and everyone laughs.
Mr. Barquist has to change reels before the feature.
He has only one projector.
So he has to change halfway through the feature too.
That gives us a chance to stretch.
We accidentally touch the girls in front of us.
They just giggle.
They probably think we did it on purpose.
The movie starts again.
Tom Mix does something I think I'll try sometime.
He swings down from his saddle and shoots from underneath his
     horse.
I forget now who he was shooting at.
But he hit whoever it was.

The show is over.
It's only nine-thirty.
Ronald and I sit on the railing again.
There is almost a full moon.
We talk.
We also wait to see if the girls will walk by.
They don't
so we decide to meet tomorrow and trap gophers.
I go back to the car.
Mom has bought groceries.
Dad is talking with Uncle Harry.
Pretty soon we drive home.
The car makes crunchy sounds on the gravel.
It's a wonderful feeling to go to town on Saturday night.

ROBERT TRAVER

The late Arnold Gingrich, founder and longtime guiding genius of Esquire *and author of books and articles on fishing, once called Robert Traver "the character's character," "the curmudgeon's curmudgeon." In the words of* Grey's Sporting Journal *(2, no. 2 [1977]:32-35), a magazine about fishing, Traver. . .*

is as much a part of Michigan's Upper Peninsula as the iron ore of his native Marquette County (and some would say as unbending). He likes people in moderation—say three or four. Tourists he cannot abide, and he vows darkly to "bomb the bridge," "the bridge," to any resident of the UP, being the one over the Straits of Mackinac that attaches the UP to the Lower Peninsula. He accepts, albeit grudgingly, the presence of browns and rainbows in his sacred brook-trout watersheds. Bass and pike he finds "unspeakable."

Robert Traver is the pseudonym behind which one of Michigan's best known jurists barely conceals himself; actually his identity has been no secret to anyone since the publication of Traver's best known book, Anatomy of a Murder *(1958). John Voelker was born in 1903 in the "remote and raffish UP," in the iron-mining town of Ishpeming, where he still has his home. With a 1928 law degree from the University of Michigan, he returned to his home area to practice law. He was married to Grace Taylor in 1930; they have three daughters. From 1935 to 1950 he served as prosecuting attorney of Marquette County, and from 1957 to 1960 he served as a justice of the Michigan Supreme Court, both elective offices.*

While he was still the county's prosecuting attorney, Voelker, a look-alike for former film actor John Wayne, began writing short stories with settings and characters drawn from the Upper Peninsula. A collection of these appeared in his first book, Troubleshooter *(1943). Following* Danny and the Boys *(1951) came one of his better books,* Small Town D.A. *(1954), a collection of lively, often ironic, anecdotes gleaned from his experience as prosecuting attorney.*

With the success of Anatomy of a Murder—*it was filmed in 1959 in Marquette County's resort town of Big Bay, and a Dell paperback went through at least ten editions—Voelker left the Michigan Supreme Court to spend more time fishing and writing, the latter usually in the winter when his favorite trout streams are frozen over! "I fish," he wrote under the guise of Robert Traver, "because I suspect that so many of the other concerns of men are equally unimportant—and not nearly so much fun."*

Of his later books, the best are Laughing Whitefish *(1965), a novel based on an actual court case (as was* Anatomy of a Murder*) involving the rights of an Indian woman in a world of white injustice; and three books—*Trout Madness *(1960),* Anatomy of a Fisherman *(1964), and* Trout Magic *(1974)—about fishing.*

Voelker says that when he began to practice law in the polyglot Upper Peninsula, an older judge advised him, "Young man, now you will have to learn to prosecute your cases in seven dialects," referring to the predominant immigrant populations in that rugged iron-mining, dairying, and logging country: Finns, Scandinavians, Italians, French-Canadians, Irish, and Cornishmen. Voelker eventually learned to swear a little in Chippewa Indian, but Scotch (the brogue, not the beverage, for which Voelker has an admitted fondness) totally eluded him. As a result, he says, the Scots whom he was called upon to prosecute went free.

So, in one of our author's funnier tales, did a Swede named Ole Paulson, charged with illegally netting twenty-seven brook trout—and out of season, to boot! Ole was haled before the court of Justice of the Peace Paulson by Deputy Sheriff Paulson. After the case had been lost because "who da hecks ever caught a gude Svede using vun of dem goldang homemade Finlander nets," Voelker (or Traver) took a second look at the names on the list of six good men and true, who had been recruited from a local saloon for jury duty. Five of them bore the name of Paulson; the sixth was Magnus Carl Magnuson. "How did this ringer Magnuson ever get on this jury list?" Voelker asked.

Deputy Paulson shrugged. "Ve yust samply run out of Paulsons," he said apologetically. "Anyway, Magnuson dare vere my son's brudder-in-law. My son vere da defandant, yew know!"

Fishermen at Night

WITH MY BROTHERS I stood in the crowded old parlor and looked down at my dead father. I stood there, curiously detached, apart from the scene, but not its meaning; an actor looking over the shoulder of myself, the bereaved son. I did not like this unbidden person there, prying into my heart, analyzing my feelings, cynically sharing in the death and burial of my parent. I was two people, one numb and choked, the other, the actor, appraising, cool, aloof, with a burning, almost fiendishly stereopticon vision. It was not the first or last time this person has dogged me in moments of stress.

I looked around the room. There were some wilted carnations giving off their ripe odor of death. There was a gaudy wreath from my father's lodge. TO OUR DEPARTED BROTHER. I considered the almost exquisite blunt crudity of the conventions people use to cover the horror of death. "Please omit flowers," I thought again, pondering this other vain, pathetic effort of wounded humanity to be alone in its grief. FATHER, said another wreath. "That would be from you boys," the actor whispered. "Isn't it barbaric? . . . And don't forget to pay your share, lad. It's just about five bucks."

I looked at my father, lying there, exhibited, on display, proof pitiful that he was indeed dead. How he would hate this final degradation, I thought. I would not have been surprised—would have cheered—had he suddenly sat up, cursing, and shouted them out of the house. But he did not. Instead he lay there, rigid and frozen—that great restless, lustful frame, that untamed, willful spirit . . .

"Don't he look natural?" someone whispered.

I wheeled with clenched fists. It was old lady Ryan, and she took my hand. I smiled and nodded my head, my eyes crowded with tears, with tears of gratitude and anger and humiliation.

People came and went. Some of the old Irish friends got up a chanting prayer. I stayed there, the actor and the son, on guard. It grew late. My brothers and some Irishmen went to the kitchen. The last vestiges of the wake. Charlie LeRoy, my father's old rheumatic bartender, came silently in the front door and shook my hand and stood beside me.

"Sorry for your trouble," he said. It is the local formula.

"Thank you, Charlie," I said.

Old Charlie stood looking at my father for a long time. He had known him in the tumult of their youth. We were finally alone. We three. Then Charlie turned to me, at last, with eyes of great wonderment.

"Robby," he said, "The old son-of-a-bitch really is dead, isn't he!"

Choking, I hurried to the kitchen for a bottle and returned. Charlie and I had a drink to his tribute, to the old man, to everything. Then Charlie said, "Good-by, Nick," and limped away. I stood there all alone—for even the damned sneering actor had finally gone away—looking down at the old man, at my old man.

It was quiet in the big frame house, except for the mumble and clink from the kitchen. I stood there pondering and thinking . . . of the time my father got drunk and gave me a dollar, and then took it back when he got sober; of the time an attractive and zealous female temperance worker had descended on our town to clean up its saloons, starting with my father's, and had instead wound up in an old iron bed over his saloon; thinking, too, of the marching generations endlessly lowering each other into the grave; of how chaotic may be the scenes of life, yet how inexorable the final drama; of the many times I had wished to grow up quickly so that I could thrash this man . . .

I stood there musing by my father.

We left the camp and cut down the hill into the waving grass of the ancient beaver meadows. My father pointed at a fresh deer track in the soggy trail and kept walking, his long legs swishing the wild grass. He was carrying his fly rod, set up, slowly smoking a briar pipe—an old, caked one with a hole worn through the bit. I drank in the fine smell and it was mixed with smells from the damp earth.

Over the little log bridge at the creek and at the far edge of the meadow, in the young poplars, we flushed two partridges, and we kept raising the rooster, who would fly ahead of us and land, and then turn, ruffling and bobbing like a young prize fighter, until we got too close. Finally it sped in heavy flight over a little hill and we could hear it drumming on the next ridge.

My father could step over most of the charred, weather-worn logs, skeletons of the giant white pines, while I had to climb up on each one and stand there for a little while as tall as my father, and then jump down and run after him, my leader box rattling against my creel.

We came out of the poplars and down below us there was a series of beaver ponds and a big beaver house stood in the reeds. There were no beaver. The sun going down made a reddish color on the water. The water was quiet except for the ripples of the trout rising to the hatching flies. A mist was beginning to spread over the ponds, and it was still; there was no noise, except for the frogs croaking and whistling and the splashing of the water spilling over the beaver dams into the ponds below.

My father stood there and packed and relit his pipe. He said, "Next year, Son, I'll put in a system here to furnish electric lights for the new camp."

I said, "Yes, sir." Finally I said, "Don't you think it's more fun to have kerosene lamps? Honest, Pa, I don't mind tending them. Don't you think machinery and things would sort of spoil it here— it's so pretty-like.''

My father laughed and walked ahead and I followed him along the edge of the ponds as we walked up to the big pond at the head of the dams. We worked through a thicket of tag alders and came out in the reeds at the edge of the big pond. The ground was soft and it shook when we moved. My father touched my arm and pointed across the water. A deer stood looking at us, standing in the tall reeds, its big ears up and forward, first one ear, then the other, sort of moving its head in the air, all the while looking at us. Suddenly my father clapped his hands and the deer blew and wheeled, and I saw its white tail straight up, bouncing and bouncing over the fallen old pine logs, and it was gone.

"A beautiful running shot, Son,'' my father said.

The trout were rising and my father knelt and looked at the water. He tied on a leader and a little black fly. I stood watching him. I watched his easy spiral casts as he worked out the line, straight up and forward to avoid catching the thick alders behind us, and then he placed the fly, and it floated down into the water like a thistle. There was a quick roll, and my father had him, the rod bending like a buggy whip, and I watched my father smile and he smiled so that I could see his teeth closed over his pipe and little lines by his eyes. My father slowly worked him in, smiling that way, until the trout lay still at his feet, and my father, not using the net, reached down and took him with his hand.

"Pretty tired trout, Son,'' my father said.

I could hear a whippoorwill make a noise across the pond.

I found a little black fly, and I fumbled in my hurry to tie it and pricked myself and my father said, "Be deliberate, Son.''

"Yes, sir," I said.

On my first cast I hooked the alders and snapped the leader, and my little black fly was twenty feet up in an alder. My father laughed and I could feel my cheeks burning as I searched in my kit for another black fly but there were no more.

I said, "Have you any more of those black flies, Pa?''

My father said, "Sh—don't talk so much. Work your own flies, Son.'' He cast his fly again, so easily, and just missed a beautiful strike.

I fouled my second cast in the alders and I had to bite my lip to keep the tears back when my father laughed again, showing his strong teeth clenching his pipe.

TROUT FISHING.

"You'd better go around and get out on the raft," my father said, pointing across the pond.

In the twilight I saw the logs of an old raft lying in the water amid the reeds. I scrambled through the alders and made my way across the matted arc of the beaver dam. I did not look at my father. It took me a long time to get around the pond and I could hear splashing and my father chuckling and I knew that the fishing was good.

I found a long jack-pine pole. I did not look across at my father, but quickly pushed the raft off into the deep water. Just as I was about to cast, the raft started to sink, over my ankles, my boots, up to my knees. I tried to push it back to shore and the pole caught in the mucky bottom and pulled me into deeper water. It was then that I heard my father laughing and I looked over at him and he was slapping his leg and laughing loudly with his mouth open. I worked hard with the pole, and then I couldn't touch the bottom. I tried to paddle with the pole, and it snapped off, and I held a little piece in my hand. The raft started to tip and the water was over my hips, and all the time I could hear my father laughing and laughing, roaring with laughter. Then I saw him holding his stomach, laughing, and I began to cry; I could not stop, and I stood looking at him, laughing so that the tears rolled down his cheeks. Suddenly I shouted, "You standing there laughing and watching your own son drown. . . . You—*you go to hell!*"

I started striking the water, the tears running down my face, and the raft started to rise and move slowly across the pond toward my father. He stood there holding his stomach, with both hands, bending up and down, laughing all the while.

"You go to hell!" I shouted again, crying harder than ever, and then he doubled up and leaned against the alders, shaking as though he were crying. As I wildly threshed the water, I prayed over and over for a gun so that I could shoot my father.

The raft was across the pond and I stepped off the raft on to the boggy bank and stood there dripping, looking up at my father, my fist clenched at my sides. My father had stopped laughing and he looked at me, and we stood there. I was not crying. Then he smiled a little and said, "That's a hell of a raft for a fisherman, Son. We'll have to get us a real man-size boat. Come on, we'll get back to camp and dry out and have a damn nice drink of whisky—what do you say, Rob?"

"We'll sure have to get us a boat. That raft's no bloody good. And we'll have a fine drink of whisky, Pa—a hell of a big drink, you bet."

It was dark on the way back to camp, and the meadow was thick with the mist. I did not mind shivering at all, and I took long steps, whistling to imitate the frogs. "Tomorrow," I thought as I walked along behind my father, "tomorrow I'll sure in hell get hold of the old man's pipe—and smoke the damn thing right in front of him, you bet."

PATRICIA HAMPL

"More than any other thing I can give a name," Patricia Hampl writes in the following piece, "the winter made me want to write." In the Upper Midwest's St. Paul, where Hampl was born and raised, winter consumes and rules. She has responded to that sovereign season by writing—to cover up the whiteness of the blank page, as she puts it. But winter, while it provoked a response, has certainly not been the sole influence on Hampl, who began writing as a young girl, sitting at the kitchen table and asking her mother "how to spell the hard words."

Born in 1946, she grew up in the part of St. Paul called St. Luke's parish. ("That's the way a Catholic would describe it.") Her middle-class neighborhood adjoined Summit Avenue, a majestic stretch of elegant homes built by industrialists in St. Paul's heyday before the turn of the century. Local history can be told by the moneyed inhabitants of those mansions. Most notable was James J. Hill, a Canadian farm boy turned Empire Builder, who parlayed an interest in agriculture and transportation into the Great Northern Railroad, connecting East and West with a network of rail lines. His massive four-story house, built at an estimated cost of $280,000 in 1887, overlooks the Mississippi River and downtown St. Paul and has thirty-five fireplaces, eighteen bathrooms, a two-story art gallery, and a ballroom.

This was the St. Paul F. Scott Fitzgerald described in his stories. Fitzgerald lived on Summit Avenue while revising the manuscript of This Side of Paradise. *To him the mansions were a reminder of the wealth and social standing he didn't have, and he called Summit Avenue "a museum of American architectural failures."*

It was along Summit Avenue that Hampl walked to and from parochial school, first St. Luke's and later Visitation Convent High School, and here, when she began reading Fitzgerald in high school, that the effect of his words—"The rich are different from you and me"—took hold. The broughams and trotters were gone, but the houses stood in testimony to the showy opulence that once reigned. In this excerpt she considers the wealth and legend of James J. Hill and what it meant to her, growing up a half century after Fitzgerald.

Hampl's father, a florist, and her mother, who worked for many years in the library at Macalester College, have long been supportive of her writing. She grew up surrounded by books; the world she discovered there—particularly in the works of Fitzgerald, Chekhov, Keats, George Eliot, Walt Whitman, D. H. Lawrence, and Katherine Mansfield—has influenced her own work.

In college at the University of Minnesota she turned from a major in music to English, and began writing seriously, contributing to a student magazine edited by Garrison Keillor. It was Keillor's encouragement and patience, she said, that enabled her to attempt "some really ambitious projects."

After college she enrolled in the University of Iowa Writers Workshop and graduated with an M.F.A. in 1970. She has worked as freelance journalist, editor, and writer. Hampl was founding editor of Preview, *now called* Minnesota Monthly, *the magazine from Minnesota Public Radio. She has had grants from the National Endowment for the Arts (1976) and Minnesota's Bush Foundation (1979).*

Her work has appeared in The New Yorker, Antaeus, American Poetry Review, Ms., Paris Review, The Iowa Review, *and* The Kenyon Review. *Her first volume of poetry,* Woman Before an Aquarium, *came out in 1978. Hampl, who is now working on a novel about two Catholic school girls growing up in St. Paul, does most of her writing during the summers in a rented cabin on the north shore of Lake Superior.*

Hampl lives in a Victorian row house in the shadow of the St. Paul Cathedral and the massive brownstone of James J. Hill. Hill's legacy lives on, but the term Midwesterner has changed. Once it was synonomous with pioneer, builder, founder; now, Hampl says, "You don't feel that greatness here." Midwesterners believe "that life goes on somewhere else. I was always happy but always reaching out. . . . We're reaching out to where we imagine the bright lights and magic are. Eventually," she adds, "it ends up as a general longing for life. It can make a person more acute, or lonely or dull. . . . What we need is a sense that we're living life here right now."

For Hampl, all the elements come into play in A Romantic Education: *her family, her Czech heritage, Catholicism, and the Hill legend. This excerpt is just a taste.*

—Terry Andrews

Views from the Hill

MY GRANDMOTHER, when she first came to St. Paul from Bohemia, got a job on the hill. To work on the hill was St. Paul lingo, meaning you were a maid or some kind of domestic help in one of the mansions along Summit Avenue or in the Crocus Hill area nearby. The hill was not just a geographical area; it was a designation of caste. It was also really a hill because St. Paul, like all romantic cities, draws its quality of personality, of identity, from its geography. Its topography mirrors its economy, its history, its image of itself.

There is a feeling of inevitability about the terraced hierarchal topography of the place, as if St. Paul was bound to be a Catholic city, an "old city" as Minneapolis is not, as if F. Scott Fitzgerald, born here, was predestined by this working replica of capitalism—the wealthy above, the poor below—to be obsessed by the rich.

I always took Fitzgerald's side in the exchange he and Hemingway are supposed to have had about wealth. He was the hometown boy. But beyond my loyalty, I felt his romantic cry that "the rich are different from you and me"—a pure St. Paul cry—was more to the point than the rejoinder Hemingway gave himself in the anecdote. *Of course* "the rich have money" as he said—but it doesn't end there. Romantics are rarely given credit for anything beyond the flourish, brilliant like spread plumage, of their style. But how often behind the indefensible rhapsody of a romantic statement—Fitzgerald's "The rich are different from you and me"—there is the hard fact of how people actually live.

The rich get to live differently. They are therefore different. Fitzgerald's line is less chumpy than Hemingway has made us think. It speaks the case for many people and explains in part why there is such a thing as a "celebrity" in our culture. His unguarded cry is true, even if he was "romantic about the rich," as people say. His statement speaks more truly than Hemingway who merely got the last word in a conversation. Fitzgerald wrote the book on the subject and made it stick; *The Great Gatsby* is "romantic" and it says the harsh truth: that the rich are different because we—the rest of us and they themselves—cannot help making them so.

In St. Paul, the metaphoric significance of "the hill" was further emphasized by the fact that the grandest of the mansions on Summit Avenue, the one with a view only rivalled by the Cathedral across the street, had been built by the city's chief resident, whose name was Hill: James J. Hill, the Empire Builder. Which is exactly how he was invoked in my family: the name, followed by the title. He had connected East and West with his railroad, the Great Northern; he had made St. Paul a railroad town, shifting its first allegiance, as a river town, away from the Mississippi so that even today the city turns its back on the river, as if it weren't the Father of Waters but a wet inconvenience.

This disregard for feature and advantage—the back turned on beauty—strikes me as American, but even more so as Midwestern. It is compounded of the usual pioneer arrogance and also, strangely, of diffidence: the swagger of saying we don't *need* beauty is coupled with the pouty lack of confidence of a wallflower who thinks of nothing else but beauty, but charm, what she lacks.

And so I became a snob in the midwestern way: the provincial anguish. My grandmother I feared, had migrated to Nowheresville. My family would have thought this nonsense. They loved Minnesota, preferred a "small city" like St. Paul, and without knowing it, caused me to love it eventually too. But I spent my moody girlhood aloof from my town, saving myself for the World. A Midwesterner to my toes.

My mother always sighed seriously, "God's country" when we crossed back from Wisconsin or the Dakotas after a trip. "Thank God," she said, "we have scenery." "This is paradise," my father told us every year as we went into the dark of the woods to fish at one of Minnesota's "10,000 lakes" and batted at mosquitoes. "Mosquitoes? What mosquitoes?" my father said, glaring at the child-traitor who spoke against paradise. "Look around you," he cried, gesturing with a casting rod. "This is heaven." He fished and my mother read her two-inch-thick historical novels.

We were not really the Midwest, my father explained; that would be Iowa or Nebraska, Kansas—hopeless places. We were the Upper Midwest, as the weatherman said, elevating us above the dreary mean. My father pointed with derision at the cars with Iowa license plates, hauling boats on trailers behind them, as we passed them on Highway 200 going north. "Will you look at that," he said. "Those Iowa people have to lug that boat all the way up here." My brother and I looked at the dummies in the Iowa car as we passed. "They're crazy to get in the water, they'll even fish in the middle of

100

GALLERY, JAMES J. HILL HOUSE.

the day," he said, as if the Iowa Bedouins were so water-mad that a school of walleye could toy with them in the noon heat, while my father coolly appeared at dawn and twilight to make the easy Minnesota savvy-kill. He pointed out to us, over and over, the folly of the Iowans and their pathetic pursuit of standing water.

Our supremacy came from our weather, and the history of our weather; the glacier had given us these beautiful clear lakes, my father explained. The glacier receded and—Paradise, with lakes. And as if the single great historical event, the glacier, had been enshrined as a symbol, in my family we were not to speak against the winter. Our cold was our pride. We watched the Today Show weather report and a shiver—not of cold but entirely of civic pride—ran though us as, week after week, some aching Minnesota town came in with the lowest temperature in the country. We did not delight in the admittance of Alaska, our icy rival, into the Union. We said nothing against it, but it was understood that it didn't really count, it had an unfair advantage which caused us to ignore it. "Didn't Alaska belong to Russia?" my mother asked. "I mean, isn't it strictly speaking part of Siberia?"

Much better to think of International Falls, the Minnesota border town known on the Today Show and elsewhere as "The Nation's Ice Box." We took pride in our wretched weather ("St. Paul-Minneapolis is the coldest metropolitan area *in the world*," my mother read to us from the paper) the way a small nation does in its national art, as if the ice cube, our symbol, were the supreme artifact of civilization. And like a small nation, we hardly cared among ourselves that the myths and legends, the peculiar rites of the land, were unknown and undervalued elsewhere, as long as we could edify ourselves again and again with the stunning statistics which constituted our sense of ourselves: the weather, the god-awful winters which were our civic, practically our cultural, identity. I didn't personally hate the winter; I hated that there didn't seem to be anything *but* the winter.

The cold was our pride, the snow was our beauty. It fell and fell, lacing day and night together in a milky haze, making everything quieter as it fell, so that winter seemed to partake of religion in a way no other season did, hushed, solemn. It was snowing and it was silent. Good-bye, good-bye, we are leaving you forever: this was the farewell we sent to the nation on the Today Show weather report. Or perhaps we were the ones being left behind, sealed up in our ice-cube for winter as the rest of the world's cities had their more tasteful dabs of cold, and then went on into spring. Even Moscow! even Leningrad! my mother read to us from the newspaper, couldn't begin to touch us.

"If you stepped outside right now without any clothes on," my brother said one day when we had not been allowed to go skating because the temperature was 25° below zero, "you'd be dead in three minutes." He sounded happy, the Minnesota pride in the abysmal statistic—which, for all I knew, he had made up on the spot. We looked out the dining room window to the forbidden world. The brilliant, mean glare from the mounds of snow had no mercy on the eye and was a mockery of the meaning of sun. "You'd be *stiff*. Like frozen hamburger," he said. "Or a frozen plucked chicken," regarding me and finding a better simile. "And when you thawed out, you'd turn green." The pleasure of being horrified, standing there by the hot radiator with my ghoulish brother.

We shared the pride of isolation, the curious glamour of hermits. More than any other thing I can give a name, the winter made me want to write. The inwardness of the season (winter is *quiet*) and its austerity were abiding climatic analogues of the solitude I automatically associated with creativity. "Minneapolis—a great book town," I once overheard a book salesman say with relish. And what else was there to do in the winter? Stay inside and read. Or write. Stay inside and dream. Stay inside and look, safely, outside. The Muse might as well be invited—who else would venture out?

The withdrawn aloofness of what had been, recently, leafy and harmless, now had a lunar beauty which was so strange and minimal it had to be foreign. But it was ours, our measure of danger and therefore our bit of glamour and importance. Or perhaps the relation between the winter and writing which I felt was a negative one: maybe I hated the season and wanted to cover up the whiteness; a blank page was the only winter I could transform. That's how little I understand winter, how it can bewitch its inhabitants (for it is more like a country than a season, a thing to which one belongs), so they cannot say and don't know whether they love the winter or hate it. And we always said "the winter," not simply "winter," as if for us the season had a presence that amounted to a permanent residence among us.

Spring didn't exist. I read about it in books which I read curled up on my grandmother's horsehair sofa, the English springs of the Bröntes, full of brave early flowers and all that English reawakening of life. Sometimes in St. Paul it snowed in May, once definitely in June. We skipped spring and plunged right into summer, maybe to get warmed up. "Don't plant until after the fifteenth of May," my father warned his customers at the greenhouse. They didn't always listen. "I told her," he would say at the dinner table, giving us the news of Mrs. Beauchamp's punishment by the season, as if her folly in planting her geraniums and petunias before May 15 and the result ("she lost a couple of hundred dollars there") were a working lesson in the effects of hubris in daily life. "I told her not before May 15. I said the twentieth would be better—in fact, why not just wait till June. What's the rush?" My father allied himself with winter and therefore could always feel righteous.

By April my brother and I were charmed no longer, but my mother and father were loyal. April 10, snowing a blizzard, and my mother looking out the window, said mildly, "Well, at least we get a change of the seasons." She and my father shook their heads over the appalling uniformity of the weather in places like Florida and California.

The winter and the conundrum of wealth ("the hill") became attached in my mind, became related in an unapproachable coldness. This may be because of the story I read by F. Scott Fitzgerald titled "Winter Dreams," which affected me strongly. The story is set in St. Paul. It is about wanting what the rich have—specifically, it is about Dexter Green wanting Judy Jones, the daughter of a rich man, with all her golden, buffaloing beauty. To begin with, I was overpowered by living—for the first time—in the setting of a story of fiction, a state of mind and life I sought and expected to find only on English moors and in other inaccessible places like New England. But here, as I walked home from school, was "the avenue" where "the dwellings of the rich loomed up . . . somnolent, gorgeous, drenched with the splendor of the damp moonlight." Summit Avenue, the hill, nearby.

The story hardly takes place in winter. Winter happens, for the most part, off-stage. The romance, the action, the betrayal—are all part of the summer and the long days at the lake. But the story's title is apt. For it is the dream of Dexter Green, with his self-mocking springish name whose mother, we're told, "was a Bohemian of the peasant class" who had "talked broken English to the end of her days," this dream of beauty and possession is the winter thing, the longing for the light which comes from long winter and its deep burial in a provincial city where, because there is wealth and winter, there are dreams—of beauty and beyond.

Like Fitzgerald, my grandmother found the rich different; unlike him, she didn't care. She worked as a maid or kitchen help in

various places, before and after she married, but her longest employ-
ment was in the house of Pierce Butler, a Justice of the United States
Supreme Court. She learned English in the classic way, by serving.
Asked to bring a broom, she appeared with an iron; she cleaned the
kitchen floor instead of the hallway stairs; she learned the language.
An odd, completely unsnobbish, result of this method of learning
was that she picked up several expressions and pronunciations that
went strangely with her Czech accent and grammar. She always said
tom*ah*to (though a potato was a potato), and when reprimanding
me, she said, like some first son of an English lord, a dandy at the
end of the last century, that I ''dasn't do that.'' She spoke Czech,
much of the time, to my grandfather, a man I remember mostly as an
icon of silence, stirring his tan coffee, adding endless spoonfuls of sugar that should have sent him bouncing hyperactively off the kitchen
walls but instead left him meditative and austere as if he'd been
sucking on a lemon. He played the concertina, but like many ama-
teur musicians, this did not make him sociable, but gave him an excuse not to talk. He was more presence than person to me, and I can't
remember his ever speaking directly to me, which is strange. He often went out on the back porch where he kept a parakeet and I clearly
remember his voice as he talked sensibly and softly to the bird, sometimes chuckling, as if he and the parakeet were recounting old times.
My grandmother banged around behind him in the kitchen and
sometimes called him The Crab. Maybe he was. Apparently my
grandmother had driven him mad during their long family years
when he gave her two dollars a day (or a week? I'm lost in the history
of inflation) from his wages as a packing clerk at a stationery supply
store downtown to run the household; she was one of those house-
wives who could not resist the wares of the Fuller Brush man, the coffee man, the matched-set-of-sharp-knives salesman, the merchants
with their stores in their suitcases. She bought and bought, and finally, in anguish, had to pay, had to ask for more than the two dollars.
There were scenes, my father said, which caused him to become the
kind of man who endorsed his paycheck and put it on the table for
my mother to take care of—perhaps to make it go away.

My mother said my grandfather was a gentleman. ''A wonderful
dry sense of humor,'' she said, approving. ''Very *Celtic*,'' trying to
claim him for the Irish though he too was a Czech immigrant. On
their fiftieth wedding anniversary he gave my grandmother a diamond ring (which she lost somehow in the washing machine) and a
card which he signed The Old Crab. They were deeply married: opposites. And although I don't remember him speaking to me, he

must have understood things about me. As a Christmas gift he once gave me a small desk, carpentered and varnished entirely by himself. When he was dying he said no, he didn't want the priest, priests were crooks. The Church had the last word, however; he was refused a burial Mass, which the family had requested. So we hung around the funeral parlor saying the rosary, and my mother, her loyalties badly at odds, kept whispering to me, "He went to heaven, of course he went to heaven."

My grandfather's stern face. Perhaps it wasn't stern, but what else is silence to a chatterbox child? Therefore: my grandfather's stern face. And then the city's great stern grandfather, James J. Hill with his monster house, his "Great Northern," the lordly power of a frontier magnate. Fitzgerald put him, name unchanged, in his story "Absolution"; he is compared to God, the simple obvious simile. Sinclair Lewis was also attracted to Hill as a character. He lived for a time in St. Paul in the Twenties, near the hill, writing a novel based on the personality of James J. Hill. He never finished it, and abandoned the project. Hill was probably a man better memorialized in architecture, not literature, in any case. What a piece of granite that face is in the formal photographs one sees now and again in St. Paul, and in the dark bust at the entrance of the James J. Hill Reference Library—his gift—downtown. The eyes are those of a just slightly toned-down Gurdjieff. The Empire Builder: naturally architecture was his art form.

His mansion is kitty-corner from the Cathedral, as if Fitzgerald was right: he and God were squaring off. The Hill house is a fortress, very dark, of rude dimension, with a black iron fence and a stone gate-keeper's lodge near the street. Inside he had an art gallery, a pipe organ, and to my surprise when I visited there in college, when the building was used by the Archdiocese for offices, a tiny cave of a study on the main floor, practically a secret room, it seemed to me.

There was nothing disappointing about the mansion of James J. Hill. It knew what it was: money, the bubble of being on top, not only on the hill but the hill itself, wrapped around by mortar and stone, endlessly hidden. That small, hidden room—where decisions were made, I thought solemnly as I stood there with someone pointing out the wood carving—was the moist kernel, the serious business, from which the rest of the outlandish tree had grown. It was devious and dark, and I loved it.

Next door was the son. Louis Hill, son of the Empire Builder, had constructed his own mansion. It was light, classical, with cool doric columns like pillars of fondant in front of the rosy brick structure. It was the rational mind, elegant, a little superficial, closer to the avenue than James J.'s pile, a denial of nightmare, anti-Gothic. Not a fortress but a manor. In the early Sixties it had become a retreat house and was named Maryhill. Our class was sent there for the "senior retreat" over a weekend not long after President Kennedy was shot. We weren't supposed to talk all weekend, and for the most part we didn't. We went to Mass in the ballroom on the second floor, the parquet floor smooth and intricate, fascinating to follow with the eye. Queen Marie of Roumania, the one who later advertised cosmetics for a while, had been a guest here in the Twenties. The Louis Hills were elegant and gave elegant parties. I felt effortlessly religious the whole weekend I was there for our retreat. It was winter (of course). I looked out the east window of the glowing yellow room toward the James J. Hill house, and not really seeing it and yet looking at it, contemplated the happy paradox of losing one's soul in order to gain it. I thought of St. Maria Goretti, as the retreat master had told us to: had she been just a prude? he had asked, throwing out the rhetorical question in a tough, thinking-man way as if he had himself just come away from considering this very explanation of her martyrdom at the hands of a *sex fiend* (who was also a *poor soul*). By degrees I arrived at the moving scene in which I astonished my parents (and she was always such a *talker,* my mother would say) by announcing my intention of entering the convent: I would enter this very one, I thought, staring out the lovely mullioned window to the other mansion. I would help run retreats, treading the parquet floors in sweet silence. I wanted badly to live in that house.

The St. Paul Cathedral—that is, God—had a better piece of real estate than the Empire Builder. It is poised on the crest of Summit Avenue, in a perfect angle to see and be seen. Archbishop John J. Ireland, a man with a country for a name, had seen to God's supremacy. The Cathedral, modeled on St. Peter's (and my mother told me early that St. Paul "like Rome" is built on seven hills), was erected as a monument of faith on the part of immigrants, mainly Irish, but all the nationalities were represented. Almost all. In the circlet of chapels running behind the main altar and dome, there are altars commemorating the patron saints of various groups, including "the Slavic peoples." The one intended for the Scandinavians was eventually dedicated to St. Therese of Lisieux because the Scandinavians turned out to be Lutherans. The first church in St. Paul had been dedicated by the missionary Lucien Galtier in 1841. "I blessed the new basilica," he wrote of the old church which no longer stands and which was not a "basilica," "and dedicated it to St. Paul, the apostle of nations." It was given to the immigrants in advance.

My parents were married in the Cathedral; it was my mother's parish. They used to say that the Cathedral was not finished, it would *never* be finished: that was in the nature of the thing. It was constantly being added to, changed, its details amplified, refined, deepened. In this way, I grew up with the Cathedral as an immense example of the creative act. The product itself was the atelier. The eternal was the progress of the fragment, of what was inevitably incomplete, unfinished. Its essence was longing and movement, not permanence and wholeness at all.

But it is untrue to say it in this way because my notion of all this was cloudy, unconcerned, a matter of unsorted sensation. Only now, as I remember what my mother and father said as we drove by (and it was said with pride)—*the Cathedral will never be finished*—do I see why I remember that casual statement at all. I remember because it contained what I was later to try to understand. The Cathedral will never be finished. Nor life, nor longing, the endless *reaching* we do. Therefore the metaphoric power of art.

Our Cathedral had its lore and legends, as the medieval cathedrals of Europe had their gargoyles: images in which the whole of life—not just the spiritual, not just the good, but the base as well—could be contained. My favorite story from the building of the Cathedral: one day the masons were bricking up part of a wall. It was summer, hot, parched. It was mid-afternoon, the worst time of thirst. They decided to sent for a pail of beer (to the Schmidt Brewery? I don't know, I don't expect things to be that neat). They sat, high above the city on their scaffolding, drinking cold beer from the pail. At which point Archibishop Ireland happened to come across the street—they could see him coming in the distance—to check, as he often did in an idle moment, on the progress of the Cathedral. The masons, drinking beer on the job, got instantly to work. They grabbed the pail of beer, wedged it into the unfinished wall and slapped brick and mortar as fast as they could. "And so," my father said, "there's a pail of beer bricked into that church to this day." Religion and the spirit of beer, Apollo and Dionysus, saints and gargoyles, empire builders and bishops, our endless story of opposites.

Even today now that the Cathedral *is* finished, my parents do not talk of it that way. It remains unfinished and they see its maintenance as part of its eternal emergence, not as a janitorial matter. They grew up with it high above them, visibly incomplete. They knew that the Depression or the War caused the abandonment of this chapel or that statue. And a window envisioned but not executed is still a window—a window, for them, unfinished and therefore eternal.

HARRY MARK PETRAKIS

People who like to dramatize the statistics of demographics say that Chicago is the third largest Greek city in the world, and they point to the 30,000 residents of "New Greek Town" centered within a radius of half a mile of the intersections of Chicago's Lincoln, Western, and Lawrence Avenues.

But there was an "Old Greek Town" once, a small urban area close to the west edge of Chicago's loop.* "If you want to know more about this Old Greek town," says Ron Grossman, an authority on Chicago neighborhoods, "you could do worse than to read the books of Harry Mark Petrakis."

Petrakis, as his name shows, is of Greek ancestry but was born in St. Louis (1923) and reared in a Chicago South Side neighborhood. His novels and short stories have their settings there: Lion at My Heart *(1959),* The Odyssey of Kostas Volakis *(1963),* Pericles on 31st Street *(1965),* A Dream of Kings *(1966),* The Waves of Night *(1969),* In the Land of Morning *(1973), and* Stelmark: A Family Recollection *(1970) from which the following essay is taken.*

Like R. V. Cassill, Petrakis has won an Atlantic First *award as well as an O. Henry Prize Story Award for his fiction. Petrakis's books have twice been nominated for the National Book Award. He has won the annual award of the Chicago-based Friends of American Writers, the Friends of Literature, and the Society of Midland Authors. He has an L.H.D. from the University of Illinois, his alma mater. He is well known in the Chicago area; he has taught writing in area schools and in the old bardic tradition he has read from his works on many occasions to Chicago-area groups.*

---

*The March 1980 issue of *Chicago* magazine places the setting of Petrakis's Chicago stories in the neighborhood of Chicago and Halsted. Internal evidence in Petrakis's work suggests Halsted and Harrison. In *Stelmark*, Petrakis says his Chicago youth (from one year of age on) was spent in a mixed ethnic neighborhood in the vicinity of his father's Greek Orthodox church at Michigan and Sixty-first.

A Chicago Greek Boyhood

THERE WAS ONE STOREKEEPER I remember above all others in my youth. It was shortly before I became ill, spending a good portion of my time with a motley group of varied ethnic ancestry. We contended with one another to deride the customs of the old country. On our Saturday forays into neighborhoods beyond our own, to prove we were really Americans, we ate hot dogs and drank Cokes. If a boy didn't have ten cents for this repast he went hungry, for he dared not bring a sandwich from home made of the spiced meats our families ate.

One of our untamed games was to seek out the owner of a pushcart or a store, unmistakably an immigrant, and bedevil him with a chorus of insults and jeers. To prove allegiance to the gang it was necessary to reserve our fiercest malevolence for a storekeeper or peddler belonging to our own ethnic background.

For that reason I led a raid on the small, shabby grocery of old Barba Nikos, a short, sinewy Greek who walked with a slight limp and sported a flaring, handlebar mustache.

We stood outside his store and dared him to come out. When he emerged to do battle, we plucked a few plums and peaches from the baskets on the sidewalk and retreated across the street to eat them while he watched. He waved a fist and hurled epithets at us in ornamental Greek.

Aware that my mettle was being tested, I raised my arm and threw my half-eaten plum at the old man. My aim was accurate and the plum struck him on the cheek. He shuddered and put his hand to the stain. He stared at me across the street, and although I could not see his eyes, I felt them sear my flesh. He turned and walked silently back into the store. The boys slapped my shoulders in admiration, but it was a hollow victory that rested like a stone in the pit of my stomach.

At twilight when we disbanded, I passed the grocery alone on my way home. There was a small light burning in the store and the shadow of the old man's body outlined against the glass. Goaded by remorse, I walked to the door and entered.

The old man moved from behind the narrow wooden counter and stared at me. I wanted to turn and flee, but by then it was too late. As he motioned for me to come closer, I braced myself for a curse or a blow.

"You were the one," he said, finally, in a harsh voice.

I nodded mutely.

"Why did you come back?"

I stood there unable to answer.

"What's your name?"

"Haralambos," I said, speaking to him in Greek.

He looked at me in shock. "You are Greek!" he cried. "A Greek boy attacking a Greek grocer!" He stood appalled at the immensity of my crime. "All right," he said coldly. "You are here because you wish to make amends." His great mustache bristled in concentration. "Four plums, two peaches," he said. "That makes a total of 78 cents. Call it 75. Do you have 75 cents, boy?"

I shook my head.

"Then you will work it off," he said. "Fifteen cents an hour into 75 cents makes"—he paused—"five hours of work. Can you come here Saturday morning?"

"Yes," I said.

"Yes, Barba Nikos," he said sternly. "Show respect."

"Yes, Barba Nikos," I said.

"Saturday morning at eight o'clock," he said. "Now go home and say thanks in your prayers that I did not loosen your impudent head with a solid smack on the ear." I needed no further urging and fled.

Saturday morning, still apprehensive, I returned to the store. I began by sweeping, raising clouds of dust in dark and hidden corners. I washed the windows, whipping the squeegee swiftly up and down the glass in a fever of fear that some member of the gang would see me. When I finished I hurried back inside.

For the balance of the morning I stacked cans, washed the counter, and dusted bottles of yellow wine. A few customers entered, and Barba Nikos served them. A little after twelve o'clock he locked the door so he could eat lunch. He cut himself a few slices of sausage, tore a large chunk from a loaf of crisp-crusted bread, and filled a small cup with a dozen black shiny olives floating in brine. He offered me the cup. I could not help myself and grimaced.

"You are a stupid boy," the old man said. "You are not really Greek, are you?"

"Yes, I am."

"You might be," he admitted grudgingly. "But you do not act Greek. Wrinkling your nose at these fine olives. Look around this store for a minute. What do you see?"

"Fruits and vegetables," I said. "Cheese and olives and things like that."

He stared at me with a massive scorn. "That's what I mean," he said. "You are a bonehead. You don't understand that a whole nation and a people are in this store."

I looked uneasily toward the storeroom in the rear, almost expecting someone to emerge.

"What about olives?" he cut the air with a sweep of his arm. "There are olives of many shapes and colors. Pointed black ones from Kalamata, oval ones from Amphissa, pickled green olives and sharp tangy yellow ones. Achilles carried black olives to Troy and after a day of savage battle leading his Myrmidons, he'd rest and eat cheese and ripe black olives such as these right here. You have heard of Achilles, boy, haven't you?"

"Yes, I said.

"Yes, Barba Nikos."

"Yes, Barba Nikos," I said.

He motioned at the row of jars filled with varied spices. "There is origanon there and basilikon and daphne and sesame and miantanos, all the marvelous flavorings that we have used in our food for thousands of years. The men of Marathon carried small packets of these spices into battle, and the scents reminded them of their homes, their families, and their children."

He rose and tugged his napkin free from around his throat. "Cheese, you said. Cheese! Come closer, boy, and I will educate your abysmal ignorance." He motioned toward a wooden container on the counter. "That glistening white delight is feta, made from goat's milk, packed in wooden buckets to retain the flavor. Alexander the Great demanded it on his table with his casks of wine when he planned his campaigns."

He walked limping from the counter to the window where the piles of tomatoes, celery, and green peppers clustered. "I suppose all you see here are some random vegetables?" He did not wait for me to answer. "You are dumb again. These are some of the ingredients that go to make up a Greek salad. Do you know what a Greek salad really is? A meal in itself, an experience, an emotional involvement. It is created deftly and with grace. First, you place large lettuce leaves in a big, deep bowl." He spread his fingers and moved them slowly, carefully, as if he were arranging the leaves. "The remainder of the

GROCERY STORE AT 4617 S.
ASHLAND AVENUE, CHICAGO.

lettuce is shredded and piled in a small mound," he said. "Then comes celery, cucumbers, tomatoes sliced lengthwise, green peppers, origanon, green olives, feta, avocado, and anchovies. At the end you dress it with lemon, vinegar, and pure olive oil, glinting golden in the light."

He finished with a heartfelt sigh and for a moment closed his eyes. Then he opened one eye to mark me with a baleful intensity. "The story goes that Zeus himself created the recipe and assembled and mixed the ingredients on Mount Olympus one night when he had invited some of the other gods to dinner."

He turned his back on me and walked slowly again across the store, dragging one foot slightly behind him. I looked uneasily at the clock, which showed that it was a few minutes past one. He turned quickly and startled me. "And everything else in here," he said loudly. "White beans, lentils, garlic, crisp bread, kokoretsi, meat balls, mussels and clams." He paused and drew a deep, long breath. "And the wine," he went on, "wine from Samos, Santorini, and Crete, retsina and mavrodaphne, a taste almost as old as water . . . and then the fragrant melons, the pastries, yellow diples and golden loukoumades, the honey custard galatobouriko.

Everything a part of our history, as much a part as the exquisite sculpture in marble, the bearded warriors, Pan and the oracles at Delphi, and the nymphs dancing in the shadowed groves under Homer's glittering moon." He paused, out of breath again, and coughed harshly. "Do you understand now, boy?"

He watched my face for some response and then grunted. We stood silent for a moment until he cocked his head and stared at the clock. "It is time for you to leave," he motioned brusquely toward the door. "We are square now. Keep it that way."

I decided the old man was crazy and reached behind the counter for my jacket and cap and started for the door. He called me back. From a box he drew out several soft, yellow figs that he placed in a piece of paper. "A bonus because you worked well," he said. "Take them. When you taste them, maybe you will understand what I have been talking about."

I took the figs and he unlocked the door and I hurried from the store. I looked back once and saw him standing in the doorwary, watching me, the swirling tendrils of food curling like mist about his head.

I ate the figs late that night. I forgot about them until I was in bed, and then I rose and took the package from my jacket. I nibbled at one, then ate them all. They broke apart between my teeth with a tangy nectar, a thick sweetness running like honey across my tongue and into the pockets of my cheeks. In the morning when I woke, I could still taste and inhale their fragrance.

I never again entered Barba Nikos's store. My spell of illness, which began some months later, lasted two years. When I returned to the streets I had forgotten the old man and the grocery. Shortly afterwards my family moved from the neighborhood.

Some twelve years later, after the war, I drove through the old neighborhood and passed the grocery. I stopped the car and for a moment stood before the store. The windows were stained with dust and grime, the interior bare and desolate, a store in a decrepit group of stores marked for razing so new structures could be built.

I have been in many Greek groceries since then and have often bought the feta and Kalamata olives. I have eaten countless Greek salads and have indeed found them a meal for the gods. On the holidays in our house, my wife and sons and I sit down to a dinner of steaming, buttered pilaf like my mother used to make and lemon-egg avgolemono and roast lamb richly seasoned with cloves of garlic.

I drink the red and yellow wines, and for dessert I have come to relish the delicate pastries coated with honey and powdered sugar. Old Barba Nikos would have been pleased.

But I have never been able to recapture the halcyon flavor of those figs he gave me on that day so long ago, although I have bought figs many times. I have found them pleasant to my tongue, but there is something missing. And to this day I am not sure whether it was the figs or the vision and passion of the old grocer that coated the fruit so sweetly I can still recall their savor and fragrance after almost thirty years.

R. V. C A S S I L L

When I first became a student in the internationally famous Iowa Writers' Workshop in 1951, R. V. Cassill was a new member of that faculty.

In profane moments over beer in an Iowa City pub where writers, would-be writers, and never-to-be writers assembled in extracurricular hours, the students dubbed the senior threesome of the workshop faculty the Father, the Son, and the Holy Ghost. On this scale, at that time, Cassill would have been somewhat lower than the angels, somewhat higher than the cherubim.

As time proved, he deserved better. He was no academic grind; yet he had graduated from the University of Iowa magna cum laude *and had been elected to Phi Beta Kappa in 1939. In 1947, after service in World War II, he had won an* Atlantic *First prize, and ten of his short stories had been accepted as his M.A. thesis at Iowa. His first novel,* The Eagle on the Coin *(1950), had won him grudging admiration from hard-hearted establishment critics.*

He has also taught at Monticello College, the University of Washington, the New School for Social Research, Columbia University, and Purdue University. Since 1966, along with Robert Scholes, he has presided over Brown University's well-known writing program.

His short stories are collected in Fifteen by Three *(1957),* The Father and Other Stories *(1965), and* The Happy Marriage and Other Stories *(1966). The best of his novels are* Pretty Leslie *(1963), based on a midwestern murder case;* Clem Anderson *(1961), the life and affairs of a gifted fictional writer;* The Goss Women *(1974), an account of a fictional artist; and* Doctor Cobb's Game *(1970), a novel based on the Profumo scandal in England.*

As this essay demonstrates, Cassill is a person given to deliberations and consequent insights into his own life and the lives of those he writes about. In the late 1960s these perceptions were recorded in In An Iron Time *(1969):*

> It seems to me I am speaking of reality when I say that I was born into the ethical life in and of the Midwest. In the candor of privacy, where proof is neither required nor relevant, I admit that all my notions of love and justice, the shape as well as the limitations of my sensibility were graven and determined for me by the Midwest

that preceded them. So that in my chosen alienation from the Midwest as I find it now, I am choosing that alienation in the name of the Midwest that made me. When I say, "To hell with the Midwest"—and that, in so many flat words, is what I have chosen to say—I am saying it in the name of the Midwest. It would take a braver man than I to say such a thing because he had been hurt and stung, impoverished, ignored, or denied what his vanity supposes to be his rightful place in the sun by his region or his country. Those things can be accepted, and when they're not accepted as the normal tax on patriotism, clearly the fault is with the man who won't accept them in the country or region that imposes them.

Cassill is married to the former Kay Adams, also a student in those halcyon days, who is now an established writer.

An Orbit of Small Towns

THE BOER TREK, the Mormon Migration, Gulliver's Travels, the Chinese on their Long March—I have an ingrained sympathy with all these tales of wanderers seeking themselves and home because of my family's orbiting among the small towns of Iowa. My mother and father had left the farms where they grew up in Davis County to be schoolteachers. Therefore I was born in Cedar Falls while my father was a student in the Teachers College there. The break from the farm had already been made, then, before I joined the migration, but it seems to me we were always headed back toward it as we moved away, governed by components of centrifugal and centripetal forces that permitted neither escape nor return.

As we moved from one small town to another in the years before I got back to Cedar Falls as a Teachers College freshman, we spiraled around some imaginary axis of desire that could be roughly represented by the geographical center of the state. We went round it through Sheldahl to Percival to Blakesburg in those years, never achieving the escape velocity that sent some of our relatives to the Dakotas or to California, never truly at home in the farm communities served by these little towns.

By title my father was superintendent of the school in each of these towns, but I take it as significant that in the first two at least, he kept some cows. Keeping cows was a practical measure, considering his salary. Beneath this practical rationale no doubt it expressed my parents' continuing obedience to the pieties and assurances they had grown up with on the farm. Cows were reliable, the whims and prejudices of small town school boards were not.

Because we had cows in Sheldahl, my older brother and I delivered milk to some of our neighbors. Some of my first memories of fear and challenge have to do with loading up a Boy Scout bag with quart and pint jars of milk and, in the chill of evening dark, pushing out across the gravel road alongside our yard to the first island of streetlight diagonally opposite, preparing to be bitten by dogs in every backyard I entered to leave the jars inside screen doors of our neighbors' kitchens.

It was not only the dogs of Sheldahl that intimidated me. The *people* of Sheldahl did. All of them. Because, however absurd it seems in the telling, I managed to transform my childish insecurities and ugly duckling definitions of self into the notion that I was a farm child trying to adjust myself to city ways. (In *Sheldahl?* Sheldahl, *Iowa?* asks my scornful wife, who grew up in Des Moines, or friends who grew up in Chicago, New York, or Boston. *Sheldahl* . . . with its constant population of three hundred people? I invite them to go back as an addled boy of four or five, who already knew the onus of starting school as "the superintendent's son" and try it for themselves. The alternative fantasy to supposing myself a farmer among city slickers was to nominate myself as a changeling prince, and I was then, as ever after, too modest for that dodge.)

The citizens of Sheldahl held me in scorn (I knew) because, if my parents could walk free in their adult disguises, the farmer's blood, the farmer's heart beneath their manners and their clothing were advertised in me by my shy clumsiness and every bargain basement or Monky Ward garment put on my back. No humiliation of later life compares at all with having to wear my *red* slicker down to the grocery store on a rainy night and go in among the loitering boys who knew what all the great world knew—that rainwear, on man and boy alike, was supposed to be yellow.

The bigger boys of Sheldahl were not only my superiors in sophistication and strength. They *lived there,* and we were only passing through. It would be a slow passage, in point of calendar time, for we dwelt among those tribes for seven years in actuality. Nevertheless, the alienation that I cultivated like a little dish of bacteria in laboratory broth gave a special poignancy to our summer vacations when, yearly, we drove down to the place of origin. South on the gravel roads below Des Moines and on the yellow clay roads beyond Ottumwa to the turnout of Ash Grove over the Bear Creek bridge, planks rattling under the wheels of the Model T, and the last climb up from Aaron Leonard's place to where my grandfather waited humpbacked and grizzled under the apricot tree by his front gate, with all the mystery and wonder of orchard and garden deep behind him. Home from the scornful city.

Once in the sixties when I was teaching my second stint at the University of Iowa, I brought my wife and children back to see that farm of wonders and itchy delights. It had been abolished.

The barn and house were still standing on opposite sides of the still ungraveled road, but the house was a windowless, doorless shell behind a long run of barbed wire without a gate, and sheep apparently roamed freely through it. The fruit cellar had caved in. The smokehouse, henhouse, and all the other outbuildings had collapsed or vanished entirely. There was no sign of the orchard or garden where the strawberry bed and the teepees of beanpoles had been. We poked around the outside of the barn and found the cistern my father, brother, and I had dug in the thirties. My initials were still scratched with theirs in the concrete cistern top. But the barn itself could not be entered. It was stuffed from dirt floor to roof beam with baled hay.

What this ruin meant was that farms like my grandfather's are no longer economically feasible—a proof of the progressive impoverishment of the state and nation, I understand. In America we will never be able to afford again the kind of life my grandparents lived there, to which their son and grandchildren could return in a Model T, driven down from Sheldahl.

But yet I had the sense, on that mellow October afternoon as my sons and daughter peered in through the cracks of the barn wall at the banal cubes of hay, that the old life had not gone very far—as if it were merely recessive in the earth, inaccessible to a corrupted memory, but biding so near at hand that the senses trembled like dogs dreaming beside a fire. I looked down the slope of the barnyard to the dried-up pond by the stand of hickories where Grandpa's hogs used to run, tempted with a fearful notion that if I walked down there I would see the pond full of caramel-colored water swarming with tadpoles, and I might smell a trace of gunpowder in the air of another year. For it was down there, across that water, that we used to fire my grandfather's .22 Winchester on at least one morning each summer when we came down from Sheldahl.

He kept the gun in a woman's black stocking under the bed in the room where we children slept. Odorous of oil and wood and the must of the farmhouse, it was a sacramental object. Firing it across the pond at red Prince Albert tobacco cans was the ceremony that brought all the sensations of our visit to a point of ecstatic fusion for me. The precise little crash of exploding cartridges, the smell of burnt powder on the hot drift of morning air, the abrupt reflex (sometimes) of cans struck by a bullet defined a sort of threshold between danger and responsibility, like the threshold between the humiliation of dreams and the dignity of wakening. With my father kneeling to embrace me—making sure the rifle was pointed in a safe direction, of course—I narrowed my world of anxieties into the concentration of sighting and pulling the sharply curved trigger. And by some miracle the world came back larger and more comprehensible from this reduction. The hickory grove, the hayfield rising as a backstop behind our targets, the red barn and gray outbuildings on the slope above us had a definition they had lacked before. And were more common thereafter, like everything else back in Sheldahl and other cities of the plain.

On that October afternoon with my disappointed children wondering what we had come looking for, I told them that we make a necessary bargain when we corrupt our senses with a sense of time. Eyes, ears, nose, and touch forget nothing, because they can't. It is only conscious memory that loses what is here, making the mortal decisions between then and now. It is a choice to believe what is here or what is gone with time.

What are you talking about, Daddy? they said.

What I can only tell you about, I said. What I smell and see and itch from here, but have mostly forgotten.

So while we shuffled around the dry ruin of the fruit cellar I told them how damp it smells when you go down for cream in the crocks. How the cistern water tastes of cedar shingles and moss. How it feels to be chigger-bitten in the evenings lying on quilts in the front yard, listening to the tree frogs and the grown-ups talking. The warning smell of the privy down beyond the gate, the smell of dusty feathers and ripening peaches in the henhouse, the fuzzy feel of apricot skin against lips and tongue while the juice squirts between your teeth.

The hand-hewn timbers of the barn and stalls feel slick where the mares Bird and Belle have rubbed their sides against them (and the other generations of horses whom you have never seen but who

R. V. CASSILL (AGE 5 OR 6) ON WHITE HORSE; BROTHER DON-
ALD (AGE 9 OR 10) ON DARK HORSE: COUSIN DE LAYNE
PROCTOR STANDING. WEST OF ASH GROVE, IOWA, 1924 OR
1925.

are just as present while the barn lasts). After rain, when the clay
roads are impassable for the Model T, Grandpa hitches Bird and
Belle to the spring wagon and we go into Ash Grove to get the mail
and deliver eggs and cream. The wet, obstinate clay builds on the
iron rims of the wagon wheels and on our tennis shoes as we walk behind the wagon and the farting horses. In Ash Grove my father's uncle Thurman (called Shum because that was the name he should have
had) runs the store, which is also the post office and gas station. The
temple-shadowed recesses of his store smell of rope and old cookies.
He has yellow metal cartons of cookies, fig newtons among them,
and the soda pop from his cooler sparkles like silvery fireworks in my
mouth as I sit on the concrete porch of the store dangling bare legs
against its sunwarmed side.

Shum has dark, purplish circles under his eyes, plump as
segments of ripe plums and his throat is a bladder of chuckles. On
Sunday he preaches in one of the Ash Grove churches, and when he
leads the hymn singing his marvelous, pumping throat sounds like a

jug band and three pedal organs. During his preaching my mother
fans me when I fall asleep, sweating against her side.

When I wake up again it is Time, and in Time you go
somewhere else.

Moving from Sheldahl to Percival was also a kind of return to
the farm, though not in any sense my parents would have wished it.
Out there in the extreme southwestern corner of the state, on the flat
floodplain of the Missouri River, Percival was hardly a detectable
town at all. Hardly more than a place of crossroads service for the
farms of the immediate vicinity. We lived in a farmhouse a quarter of
a mile out from this center. Again we pieced out our subsistence by
nursing, milking, and butchering animals because my father's salary
was cut even below what we had lived on in Sheldahl.

And if, in Sheldahl, I had abjectly seen myself as an infant
hayseed, in Percival this was turned right around, because here nearly
all my male classmates were farm boys. Their skills and assurance,
which I envied without much hope of matching, came from life on
the farm—riding horses, helping with chores and harvest, hunting,
fishing and trapping, and driving farm machinery or cars from an
early age. At around eleven I was the helplessly inept town boy
among them.

Outclassed again by sheer reality, I survived it by embroidering
it with fictions. I loved it too much to evade it. I simply retold it to
myself with satisfactory amendments. If the farm boys ran right over
me in our improvised games of football in the schoolyard, I limped
home to think about the budding career of the smallest, wiriest,
wiliest quarterback ever to make the All-American team. Me! When I
tried to sneak up on one of the great formations of geese and ducks
that sometimes landed in the flooded cornfields near our house, I
made no kills with my Steven's *Crackshot*. A big red-tailed hawk
used to land in the cottonwood in front of our house or on one of the
electric line poles across the road, and probably twenty-five times I
slipped out the back door with my gun ready and failed to get him.
But from knocking Spatsies out of the apple tree by the barn I
could—I did—go on to blasting Kodiak bears in the Alaskan
wilderness with .405. As for women—I knew by now that they had to
be trapped in the back seat of a car, and I certainly had no access to
the necessary vehicle. I had, instead, a harem of movie starlets from
fan magazines and corseted ladies from the Sears catalogue.

From reading the *American Boy* magazine I became "air-minded," as people used to say. As it applied to me, the term might well have meant there was little in my mind that would submit to the laws of gravity or other laws that might have limited my fictions. But in the sense generally intended it meant that I became a fanatic about airplanes, models and real ones.

One hazy summer morning when I was on the school ball diamond all by myself, chopping out perfect bunts and slashing the fiercest curves into nonexistent grandstands, I saw, coming down the river valley from the direction of Omaha, a 1910 Curtis biplane, riding low and slow on the impetus of a pusher propellor. This chugging, improbable contraption might have been believable in a museum—not out there in western Iowa making its way above farmers busy in their actual fields and a tale-stretching boy on a weedy ball field. At first I didn't believe I saw it. I thought I had really damaged my mind by tampering with the truth too often. For many years when I remembered it I supposed I might have made it up as I made up Kodiak bears and the submissive flesh of starlets. Now I believe they all had equal rights to existence in that visionary time, for all the past becomes fictive.

Yet the Curtis pusher can be documented, like the Howard racers and Waco biplanes we saw in those years at the air shows at Omaha and Red Oak. Speed Holman died in his black biplane at Omaha the day after we were there to watch him at his tricks. I believe that at the moment of his death I was on top of our fruit cellar, launching a rubber-powered model that tore itself apart in the wire fence around our yard. I believe this because I said so in a short story committed to print many years later. The shape of my fictions ever since has woven a fairly consistent pattern of passionate expectation, disappointment and, finally, amusement.

It has amused me ever since to think how I compromised inadequacy and talents to thrive in Percival where there was no niche either for the superintendent's cow-keeping family to fit in. To explain this trick of hovering, I must point out that landholding around Percival was then a little different from the egalitarian pattern that I suppose prevailed in most of Iowa's farm communities. Around Percival the big holders were three or four families who had enough to parcel it out among sharecroppers. They were not quite a baronial class, you might think, among the majority of farmers whose children came in to the consolidated school—not quite squires, but distinct in lifestyle and some of their connections. Not quite by accident nor quite by design, I was best friends with a boy from the chief of these families.

Carl lived exactly one mile straight west of our tacky place in an establishment of houses, barns, and granaries that even now I recall when I must picture the circumstances of gentlemen farmers. The main house was a three-story frame building, with porte cochere, set very deep in a lawn too big for mowing. He lived there with his grandmother and Uncle Mark, his mother being somehow engaged in Hollywood and/or New York, somehow involved with the theater or theater people, rarely stopping by to unload expensive presents on her son and leave behind whispers of wealthy decadence and metropolitan glamor.

The Sheldons lived in style on their farm. Mark raced his outboard motorboat in the regattas at Omaha and nearby Nebraska City. At one time he was being courted by salesmen trying to sell him a Stinson *Detroiter* monoplane. I was there twice when the husky plane landed in the field behind their big white barns and took him for spins out over the river to give him a taste of what it would be like to own it.

It was through Carl and my visits to the grand house he lived in that my omnivorous imagination was first fed by sniffs at style, and there I learned the American class distinction between leather goods and patent leather. Carl was a handsome boy (picture a juvenile Cary Grant) with the self-assurance to come to school in better clothes than the rest of us and get by with it. He wore a suede jacket when the rest wore sweaters. He rode in on a good looking saddle horse while some of the other farm boys came on plow horses or mules. His grandmother drove a Hudson. His .22 was a Remington automatic. He had a bow of English yew and a full set of authorized Boy Scout equipment. We shot his arrows over the tall grass of his lawn and used the Boy Scout cooking gear when we camped out in his uncle's log cabin among the willows by the Missouri shoreline. When he rode his bay horse for scampers on the flat roads, I pumped along behind on my two-dollar bicycle. He carried a condom in his wallet and told me secondhand stories of sexual or alcoholic depravities (so they seemed then) wafted to him from Hollywood, Omaha, and other sin capitals. I panted with envy.

I was, in a word, courtier to a young prince, and if this ambiguous station let me off some competitions with the working farm boys, it brought me to my most enduring humiliation. For Carl had a beautiful cousin I adored and for a long time hoped to kiss. I tried it once on the dark steps of the schoolhouse when I caught her arriving at a masquerade party. It was a glancing kiss at best, and from the sheer momentum of lunging at her I kept running—off the steps and over past the grain elevators and a half mile down the railroad tracks before my overtaxed heart brought me to a stop.

For me there seemed no turning back from the audacity and guilt that sent me racing into the night with the moon pursuing. But she and everyone else went on as if nothing had happened. Later that year some of us were dragooned into presenting an operetta. Carl and his cousin were chosen for the leading roles of Prince Charming and his darling. Poetic justice made me Cupid, grim enough in itself and worsened by the way I was dressed for the part in a costume my mother composed to make Cupid look decent enough for midwestern eyes. A red jumper and bloomers, around my forehead a band of crepe paper with a paper medallion bearing a red heart, and on my back, white paper wings. I still have a photograph that records this travesty for eternity—Carl and his cousin standing tall in the gravel schoolyard, holding hands and looking remarkably suave for eighth graders, while I kneel between them with my dinky bow and arrow, frowning sulkily to prove I knew even then how low my credulity and incautious passions could bring me.

Whatever anguish laces the comedy of stories I have written was woven in from Percival, too. For there I was learning not only the discrete precariousness of my own search for a way in or a way out, I was waking to the recognition of my parents, brothers, and sister as individuals similarly goaded, exposed and baffled by where, with the best of intentions, they had come. I began to see how my father felt at the mercy of school boards whose whim could spin us moving again. My parents had left the farm for what must have lured them as a better life. They moved from town to town in an unremitting grind of trying to hold their own. Moving was a doom visited on us by some obscure agency of wrath that measured us and found us wanting, a doom more harrowing than it need have been because, faced with it, my mother hardened her determination to yield nothing. No discarded toy, no outgrown piece of clothing or of broken furniture was to be left behind. She was obsessive about this, and while her reasoning was that you never knew what might come in handy in our next temporary home, I think she was truly moved by the impulse to scorch the earth behind her as her hopes had been scorched by the passing years. The outrage that harried her into painting, varnishing and wallpapering in one shabby rented house after another was aggravated when we had to leave it. So the intrafamily warfare about where we might live when we moved to the next town intensified with every displacement.

It should have cheered us all that when we moved from Percival to Blakesburg we were at last going into a house with an indoor bathroom. As bathroom the facility was welcome enough, though it functioned erratically. It was part of a plumbing system that depended on a pressure tank in the basement which had to be filled with a hand pump. The water came from a cistern, and in the drought years of the mid-30s there was precious little to pump out of it. So, whether to flush or not flush the toilet became a highly emotional decision of family politics. Not to flush was infidelity to our station in life, worse than a reversion to country manners. To flush was to waste water. It was Conservation of Resources versus the American Way. It was a new vocabulary for the resentments of being bound in the common shelter of a family.

It is funny how I think of that first house we inhabited in Blakesburg as a haunted house—funny because I am convinced that it was we who haunted it and that we in turn were haunted by having so hopefully marched outward from the poor hills of Davis County and now come back so close.

Over the county line a few miles south of Blakesburg were most of our surviving relatives. We were fewer than ten miles from my grandfather's farm. I could walk there easily in a long morning's walk, and I remember at least a couple of times when I hunted down through the fields arriving there by noon with a squirrel or a couple of rabbits I had bagged on the way, to be greeted by my grandmother ready to feed me on the good smoked ham and apple pie she had marked as my favorite food. They were fine times. But I could not come back there now with the privileges of childhood. Nothing had changed materially on that farm, but I saw it changed, saw how it had expelled us all and could not take us back. Smoked ham and apple pie were not my favorite foods. It was merely a formality of my grandmother's to say so and formality for me to agree, a ritual of commemoration without any real substance.

We came to Blakesburg in the drought years, the Dust Bowl years, when, sure enough, the red clouds of dirt from states farther west were blowing in the sky. In the summers I worked some for the farmers trying to save what they could of their crops. I chopped and shocked yellowing cornstalks in July for my uncle Delbert Roberts and understood something of the cruel and boring caprice of life on those submarginal farms. One afternoon when I should have been helping my grandfather get hay into his mow, I badgered and begged my way into Ottumwa to see "Lives of the Bengal Lancers." Coming out of the theater into the blast furnace heat of late afternoon I was stricken with a complex guilt that had as moral: *Watch as many movies as you can. Life is basically intolerable.*

On his farm some twenty miles from Blakesburg my Uncle Lou Glosser hanged himself that summer. The horror had not been unexpected. My mother's side of the family was knotted with some bloody snarl of unappeasable, oblique passions that brought several of them to premature death or insanity. When the quarreling with his grownup son became insupportable, Lou had spent some weeks visiting in the homes of his kin, including ours. I had sat in on a few sessions on hot porches, by night, while assembling relatives had tried to "cheer him up" or find some solution to the anguishes of his problems. I comprehended very little of the detail of what was said on such occasions; I am sure I understood that none of their remedies or affection reached through to the vast wrong he bore within him.

Lou had been more successful than most of his siblings who stayed on the farm. I remember once—this would have been way back in the 20s—when we were standing in the yard of his gaunt house on its gaunt hill, and he said to my father that, counting everything we could see, house, barns, land, he was "worth about eleven thousand dollars." He said it with a chuckle of pride, that chuckle which was so characteristic of his speech and that never came without a rasping note of fury that no one was allowed to register. I remember once when he showed my brother, my cousin, and me how to witch water with a forked peach branch. Linking arms with us in turn, he held one fork while we held the other and marched slowly toward his well in the barnyard. It worked with my brother and my cousin. It did not work when he tried it with me. Because I was afraid of some demonic current in him that might flow to me and resisted it? How will we guess what makes the dead branch quiver and tip down? I remember him standing in a dusty hayfield in the shade of bordering willows saying, "I can't sweat. I can't *sweat.*" Chuckling angrily as he said it. And once when he was staying with us that summer before his death he went up to the store with me when my mother sent me for cold cuts for supper. Gracelessly, relentlessly, he shoved a dollar bill on me to pay for them. "Hey, I'm not some old bum. Not an old bum," he said. I took the paper money from his hand just before it burned to ashes.

We were in the dining room of our haunted house when the phone rang. My father answered and then said, "Lizzy, it's for you." We all knew she would be unable to accept the news without spilling over on us, but that she would try to protect us from the boiling she could not contain. She did not cry out. She hung up the phone and turned with her mouth stretched terribly open, her hands reaching out for something to blame, to tear. She would never say he hanged himself, only that he was gone. She told me they would take me to my tennis tournament in Ottumwa on their way to Lou's farm that afternoon. In the hush of dreadful heat the house smelled of the unflushed toilet and the flowers she had planted to make it less hateful.

My parents always spared us what they could, but parents can never spare their children from themselves. There are wounds that run through generations like eroding rivers. In their canyons we take shelter from the pitiless day. We come from an old people and make gardens from their grief. I learned something like that from our return to Blakesburg, learning more than I understood then and more than I understand yet of how we endure in a current of faith, hope, and lusty forgetfulness. It has always seemed to me that in Blakesburg the irresolute parts of myself were bonded together into the permanence of the character I have had ever since. I got my range, learned what signified without displacing myself from the center of it all.

In Blakesburg I gave up the intent of being the smallest All-American quarterback (and saved it for a novel, written twenty years later). I found my real limits in playing guard on the basketball team. I outgrew the notion that masturbation was an end in itself. I learned to steal, to read well, to evade my enemies without shame, to scheme, to choose my religious denomination according to the girls who attended evening services in one church or another. I made friends with boys who were my equals in poverty, slothfulness, wit, lubricity, expectations, honor, melancholy, and poetic sensibility.

A letter from my friend in Percival spurred my erotic ambitions. He lamented that he had "wasted" his condom, at last, on a "little tramp" from a nearby town. After that the Blakesburg girls would have been doomed if they had not been—always!—a step ahead of me in wiles and the tactics of self-defense. As it was (and will always be in honored memory) there were randy hours of teasing, tugging, kissing, arm-wrestling, hand-inching, knee-nudging, thrilling and exhausting battle on the fire escape of the schoolhouse on summer nights, in haymows and empty boxcars on the railroad siding, on backyard quilts and in cemeteries. There was low-yield window peeping with my Bakelite field glasses. There were games of chalk-rabbit to celebrate the coming of spring, to find oneself with a mixed gang of boys and girls squirming under a porch while we waited for the hunters or for unexpected good luck. In the simmering, unsuccessful, endless pursuit there was always the stimulus of talking it over afterwards with friends, the golden lies about what you had been able to touch or pinch or snap before you were driven off.

My afternoon newspaper route nearly always terminated in Warner's cream station. There in the dairy smells, perched on ten-gallon milk cans, the bucks of Blakesburg habitually gathered to brag and chaff about the sporting life that followed high school. As the years went on I listened to these older fellows with growing skepticism and amusement at the bluff repartee about farmers' daughters, farmers' wives, old tales of castration by jealous husbands, the lore of venereal disease, this week's drama at the whorehouse in Ottumwa where the John Deere workers were the big spenders. Sitting back in the corner on my milk can, listening to these funny, heartbreaking stories of blueballs and the louts who hung around the hotel on East Main Street in Ottumwa hoping to cop a free feel from an off-duty whore, I dreamed these young men were already soldiers in some continuous war, members of a foreign legion. Those were the years of unemployment and CCC camps, times when most of these young men considered enlistment in the Navy to get a decent income, or moving west to Colorado or California to work where people still had money. They shared with me their faith that somewhere the women were different from the unyielding girls of Blakesburg and wherever that was was the great good place we had to move to. As sex education, it was low grade, but listening to them was vital in fusing legends of home and of wandering, a part of my literary education. How else would I ever have learned the voices of Odysseus's men, the grumbling and goatish expectancy as every wind beat them farther from home?

Delivering the Ottumwa *Courier* did a good deal for my social sense. It took me, literally, up and down every street in Blakesburg and gave me that intimacy with human types that only comes from the exchange of money. The dimes and quarters I gathered on my collection rounds on Saturdays seemed to come with a kind of blood warmth from deep in the mysteries of other families' lives. I learned how money really talks, the little yips of avarice, pride, potency, insult, and caring that people are careful to screen from their verbal language. That little bit of money coming from their hands to mine gave me a sense of communion I never got in their failing churches.

A couple of old, old men living together finally began to pay me from what must have been their collection of old coins, including a huge 1803 penny, half-dimes and two-cent pieces. Between those old men and me these coins were still currency and had not faded into the obsolescence of rarities, that money the only language I could conceivably have shared with them.

And if I got some vital communion with Blakesburg people from the little money I earned honestly from them, so did I from what I stole. I said that I learned to steal in Blakesburg, but I do not in any way at all want to suggest pride in the stealing or indifference to the wrong it was. Stealing is an injury to others—not to call it a sin. But maybe a distinction can be made between learning to steal (and learning from it) and the antisocial act in itself.

I would guess that in the time of our warfare on Blakesburg my friends and I did not steal more than twenty or twenty-five dollars worth of groceries, stamps from the Post Office, candy, cartridges, and gum from gum machines—though we also shot up Max Berry's cabin in the woods, shattering doorknobs, breaking windows, and knocking down his aerial by shooting off the insulating connections.

We raided dime stores and clothing stores in Ottumwa somewhat more heavily in a season of shoplifting until we learned that some of the younger Blakesburg boys were doing this so brazenly (and inexpertly) that the heat was on and the risk of being caught had probably skyrocketed. We cached a good deal of our loot in the furnace of the abandoned Baptist church at the west edge of town. Once when we had carried off a whole box of candy bars and hidden it there, we made it a duty to go every afternoon after school and eat away at the slowly dwindling and increasingly less appetizing stuff.

We talked—and it never got beyond the daydream stage—of stealing a car and driving it to Kansas City where we could sell it. And then, I suppose, continuing careers of crime and adventure around the globe to Hong Kong or Singapore.

Where this romanticizing fantasy actually led began to be revealed when my friend Paul Blake went off to Coe College in Cedar Rapids. There, as a natural consequence of crimes and dreams of crime in Blakesburg he inserted himself in a writing class and began to write poetry. I remember that I was working in Joe Shea's filling station the first summer Paul came home from college, and in the idleness of hot afternoons when no one came by to have his tank filled Paul and I lounged in the shade of the station alternately doctoring pennies to milk gum machines and discussing the prospects of becoming writers. To think of following in the footsteps of Hart Crane, Paul Engle, Ernest Hemingway seemed equally as desperate as taking up the trail of Pretty Boy Floyd or John Dillinger, and we sensed it would take desperate remedies to get us out of Iowa. I suppose we felt our shoplifting and pillaging had proved us adequate to what would be required of us to "live by the pen"—as Paul put it after his first year in college.

Marvelously unsophisticated as we were, no doubt we had laid hold of an essential metaphor in perceiving that the writer and the criminal are two stems from the same root, simultaneously outcast and monstrously intimate with family or town. So what I have to say abut my Blakesburg years is that, more than anything else, they gave me my temper as a writer, whatever I was to make of that preparation.

It was later in Iowa City, Paris, and New York that I learned to make this conditioning productive. When I thought I might die in a frigid, stark room on the Cité Falguiere, I knew what kind of writer I would have to be if I didn't. I would have to write as carefully and respectfully as I could about going to Uncle Lou's funeral and watching my mother force my terrified younger brother to go to the coffin and kiss the dead man. About the young men in Warner's cream station. About my Uncle Delbert howling for his son kicked to death by a horse in their pasture. About going to the World's Fair in Chicago with the Southern Iowa Farm Bureau Band. About the time some girls found us swimming in Mitten Creek. About Paul's encounter with a homosexual preacher interested in Scouting. About my fist fight after a dance in the Opera House above the hardware store. About a girl who clung with me to a buoy in Lake Wapello while I tried to peel her suit off.

It was not merely that these things were subject matter I could use. They were obligations. I was under a kind of life sentence to them. They were the counterweights to my attempts to disengage, as I suppose I had known they would be from the first time I really set foot out of the Midwest, hitchhiking to Colorado to join my friends Lawrence and Richard Dorothy.

Before I graduated they had quit high school to work in the resort town of Manitou at the foot of Pike's Peak. A few days after I had my diploma my father drove me five miles north on the gravel to the highway between Ottumwa and Albia. He parked discreetly around the corner to watch until I had thumbed a ride west. A salesmen in a black Essex stopped. I ran for his car without a wave to my father.

Three days later Lawrence, Richard, and I were climbing the eastern slope of Pike's Peak. Somewhere near the timberline we wore out and sat down looking back. In that late afternoon there was an immense blue shadow from the mountain out over the foothills and the prairies, but beyond this shadow, like another planet floating away, was the vast, many-colored curve of the earth in sunlight. I watched it roll toward the East with a clutch of panic and acceptance in my heart. It was already too far gone to see any trace we had made on it, even with highways and towns, not to mention griefs and fervid wishes. One wanted to put out one's hand to grab, however vainly, at the past before it was gone beyond Mars and Venus. I wanted to wave back to my father watching me leave in the salesman's car.

But even in that moment when the old planet rolled away, something trembled as if inside my eye while I watched it diminish— the tug of a fragile and familiar fiber binding me to the world vanishing in the indifference of time and space. I supposed then I was continuing the dubious trek my parents started when they dared leave the farm for Cedar Falls. I suppose that, like them, I will never break free of the old laws, the absurd gravity that keeps us spinning round what we do not return to.

RUTH SUCKOW

Ferner Nuhn, literary critic and Ruth Suckow's husband until her death in 1960, concludes that "A Little Girl's World" is apparently "the start of an unfinished early novel." It is written in the tiny neat script Ruth Suckow employed and Nuhn believes it comes from the years in which she was writing short stories and finding her way as a novelist. He adds that the story "reflects the love of places, the savoring of detail, the wonderful powers of recall which Ruth Suckow possessed."

But one might also compare the image of the small Midwest town and its family life at the turn of the century with the visual images in the film of Sally Benson's Meet Me in St. Louis (1944) and the film and stage versions of Meredith Willson's The Music Man (1960, 1962). For all the nostalgic charm inherent in those two portraits of midwestern life, Ruth Suckow's "A Little Girl's World" calls forth remembrances of times past with a great deal more sense of the reality, at least for some, of growing up in the Midwest. Certainly "A Little Girl's World" is an adequate rejoinder to those sour and acerbic critics of midwestern life who revolted from the village.

Until her death, Ruth Suckow was a distinguished regional writer, and many of her themes and characters have their roots in her native Midwest. Her first novel was Country People (1924), a story of rural life among emigrants from Germany; over the next thirty-five years there followed The Odyssey of a Nice Girl (1925), The Bonney Family (1928), The Folks (1934), and several collections of short stories. Strangely enough her strongest supporters were H. L. Mencken, that acidulous critic of American life, and Alfred A. Knopf, the New York publisher of much more exotic writers.

She wrote always, her critics noted, about "the sparrows of the Midwest." But in her work these ordinary people became extraordinary.

A Little Girl's World

LINDA LIVED IN EMMAVILLE. She thought that it was not the largest city in the world, but of course it was the most important. She judged every town by Emmaville.

Linda's father, who was Chas. E. Dalrymple, Attorney-at-Law, said that Emmaville was booming. He put the population at between three and four thousand, and the census man put it at two thousand five hundred. It had a new city waterworks, all-night electric light service, three business blocks, a main line railroad and a "stub road" (seven miles long, that connected Emmaville with nearby Paris), two school buildings, and six churches.

Lola Healey and the Big Kids were always saying that Emmaville was dead. Lute Healey said that the Soldiers' Monument in the cemetery ought to have been put up for the town, but Linda thought there was something going on in Emmaville all the time. There was school, which she was still young enough to enjoy, and Sunday School where she got a colored card each Sunday. There was the Lecture Course, and once *Uncle Tom's Cabin* in the Opera House. There were band concert nights, school programs, Sunday School exercises, and the Fair. There was mamma's club day, and church suppers. There was the Sunday School picnic and the Eastern Star picnic. There were birthday parties and surprise parties. All these, besides play every day!

All this seething life that Linda knew went on in a very small space. There were whole parts of Emmaville which she never considered as being in the scheme of things. There were stores like the harness shop, the feed store, and Nisson's Lunch, for which she saw no use. There was the whole unexplored region called vaguely "across the tracks," in which she thought that no one whom she could call a real person lived. "No one who is anyone," was what the ladies said. Her Emmaville was confined to a few definite places, which seemed to make up the sum total of the real universe. All other places were foreign, strange, and only half-existent.

First there was her own house.

It was the favorite type of house in Emmaville, then—white frame, with an ell and a porch. The only decorations (but which Linda considered very fine) were a border of cut wood-work along the ridge of the main roof and the ell, very much like tatting on a handkerchief; a triangle of wooden lace set in the front peak of the roof; and a pane of colored glass above the big front window.

In the summer, a foamy cascade of clematis blossoms covered the side of the porch, but in winter only a few dried stalks were left clinging to the rusty wire.

Linda's tricycle with a red plush seat was kept in a corner of the porch. There was a mat of brown cocoanut fiber before the front door. The pane of the front door was frosted, and the clear glass left made a picture of a Newfoundland dog set in a border of oak leaves.

A hard maple tree, red-gold and gorgeous in October, grew in front of the house. In the corner of the ell, on the wet, black ground, grew a thick bed of lilies-of-the-valley. In the early morning, Linda could run out and find the dark-green pointed leaves hung with wet silvery cobwebs—fairy washings she liked to think. When she put her hand into the leaves to find the stems hung with lily bells, they were so cool, so strange, she hardly dared to pick them. The pansies, too, close to the cold stone foundation of the house, with their pretty faces, were a kind of strange little people, not so much regular fairies as elves, perhaps, or beautiful, dressed-up Brownies. There was a snowball bush in the "side yard." Linda carried a bunch of the snowballs with the wet stems wrapped in tinfoil when she marched out to the cemetery on Decoration Day.

Every spring, Linda and her mother planted nasturtiums, sweet peas, and cosmos in the back yard, from seeds the congressman sent. Linda's father had a garden out by the stable, but every summer he said it was "too much" and got the Nisson boy to take care of it.

Linda loved the barn. It was Ned's house. Ned was a chestnut horse, blind in one eye, who loved his home so well that he always began to waltz on his hind legs when he got within two blocks of it. Here lived, too, Ned's one-seated buggy and the black shiny cutter with Santa Claus bells. She liked to sit in the buggy, in the gloom of the carriage room, with the cutter, the lawn-mower, the watering pot and the gasoline can shining faintly, with their ghostly memories of summers and winters past, and pretend that she was driving to Paris, or even, as her imagination kindled, to Des Moines, Dubuque, and Chicago!

"Gid up! Whoa!!" she would shout, see-sawing fiercely at imaginary reins. "Don't you know we won't get to Chicago before night if we don't go faster'n that?"

Sometimes she played that the buggy was a "horseless carriage," which was a mythical kind of vehicle much talked of (chiefly in derision) when Linda was a little girl.

The best part of the barn was the haymow. It had one high window draped with cobwebs and deceased insects, through which a long beam of light, like golden dust in which were dancing things, slanted across the hay. The hay was in a great loose pile. Sometimes it covered, perilously, the square hole through which it was shoved down into Ned's manger. It had a sweet, dusty, pungent smell.

Here, Linda and Gertie Healey would sit, drinking sugar-and-water through straws, and deciding about their wedding dresses and number of children. They talked about babies—Linda had always thought that angels put them into peoples' windows at night, but Gertie was strong on facts. Minutes and hours drifted past as lazily as the sunlight through the window. Mothers' voices were too far away to be heard the first time they called.

The haymow was a place divinely set apart for secrets, confidences, and the formation of clubs.

Linda's parlor was associated in her mind (and perhaps in her mother's mind) with callers, the Travel Club, and the Missionary Society. It had several articles which Linda trustingly believed to set a true standard of elegance—a piano with a dumb pedal, a mahogany center table with a Battenburg doily and a mottled-leather copy of *Hiawatha,* a rocking chair on a standard that pitched forward like a vessel in a storm, two mahogany chairs and a settee in "a set."

The carpet was a Brussels, dark brown, with pink blush roses spilling out of cornucopias. It was very precious. Linda had to spend half an hour in her bedroom if she carried bread-and-butter-and-honey into this room to eat. For this reason, it always tasted better to her in the parlor than anywere else.

There was an archway between the parlor and the sitting-room hung with long string of leather, knotted, and with beads at the ends that rattled and threatened to break when anyone went through. So only visitors were permitted to enter by the arch; the family had to go through the hall and in by the lesser door.

There was a combination desk and bookcase in the sitting room with several little balconies that made good places where paper dolls might take the air. The paper dolls had their home in twelve pasteboard shoe boxes in the bay window. There Linda played every night while her father read *David Harum* and Dickens, and her mother sewed. Linda had to be careful not to touch the ends of the big sword fern in the bay window, because if she did, they would never grow again. She wondered how this could be, and often longed to touch one and see if it came true.

In some ways the kitchen was the pleasantest room of all. This was partly because all morning long the sun fell in golden squares on the floor, from two high windows on whose ledges geraniums stood. Every year a new real estate calendar hung over the table, showing some very refined cows taking a foot bath in a purling brook. Dr. Price's Almanac, beside the sink, told fine things like the meanings of flowers, birth stones, and what people were like who were born in every month. Linda often wondered if all the people born in the

TURN-OF-THE-CENTURY SMALL TOWN ELEGANCE.

same month had to be exactly alike. She had found out that Miss Palmer, whom she and the other little girls disrespectfully called "Old Et Palmer," had been born in August, her own birth month. Must she then be just like Old Et? The Almanac said so, and that she had a hot temper and would be successful in money affairs. Old Et Palmer was not successful in money affairs. She had had the same hat, with a bunch of wilted flowers, always.

In winter when Linda would come running home from school over the creaking snow, all red and cold, she would take off her overshoes and put her feet up on the oven door, and sit there eating apples and reading *Tom Sawyer.*

Linda had a little room of her own upstairs which gave her a certain status. Gertie Healey had to share hers with her sister Mignon. The furniture was odds and ends now—a white-painted commode, an iron bed, an enameled rocker—but she was to have a real "bedroom suite" when she was twelve. Sometimes she thought it would be white with pink rosebuds, and sometimes of birds-eye maple. Anyway there would be a Princess dresser, which was probably the most elegant thing there was.

The most precious things were the shelf of children's books (the Alcott books, the Dottie Dimples, the Little Colonel books, *Alice* and *Tom Sawyer* and *Water Babies,* and the *Blue Fairy Book*), a white celluloid hair receiver in the form of a cornucopia laced with yellow velvet, the Japanese doll pin cushion whose body pulled out and left his legs dangling, and the paper parasol from the Japanese Festival at the church.

Linda revered her mother's room, with the golden oak bedroom suite and the china manicure set, but she always went into the spare room on tiptoe. It was so still and the bed spread was so white. It seemed as if the ghosts of all the people who had slept there were about. Linda used to creep up to the big white wardrobe, listen, and then jerk the door open suddenly. There was nothing in it but her mother's best black-and-white silk dress hanging, thin and ghostly, from a nail, but Linda could not help feeling that the Old Witch, Bluebeard, or Mary Queen of Scots beheaded might be shut up there. . . .

"Uptown" was another magic land to Linda.

She liked to go into A. C. Brown's Dry Goods & Notions, and look at the ribbon case and the fashion magazines full of paper dolls. She and Gertie Healey would each say what she would choose if Mr. Brown told them they could have anything in the store. Linda thought she would have a bolt of pale pink satin, but Gertie wanted the blue brocaded corset on the "bust form" above the counter. She said that Lola wore one now and she was going to just as soon as her ma would let her.

"It isn't nice to talk about corsets," Linda told her gravely.

"Why not?" demanded Gertie. "All women wear them. Your ma and my ma, and I bet the minister's wife does, too."

Whenever Gertie or Linda had a nickle they went to Peters's. They bought a penny's worth of each kind of candy because Sherman told them they got more that way—a yellow marshmallow banana, a candy egg in a little frying pan, a licorice pipe, and paraffin hearts with pictures pasted on them. Linda's father said that this was not nice candy. Sometimes he gave her little hard green squares dusted with powdered sugar that he bought at the drug store. Drug store candy was supposed to be the finest, but you didn't get enough.

Linda liked Peters's—liked the pyramids of cans on the high shelves, the great bunch of bananas hanging by the door, the wire vegetable stand with the water always dripping as if in a fountain. How she longed to have that for her paper dolls! It was her idea of a "watering place"—there was always a "watering place" in books. The paper dolls could have watered there.

It was fun to go to Sherwood's on Saturday when the people came in from the country—big-whiskered farmers in leather coats and boots, the women with "fascinators" over their heads, the little stolid-faced children who yanked their mothers' skirts and begged for candy.

There was no more wonderful place in town (unless it was the lumber yard) than Goldie's father's store. It was for the store that Linda played with Goldie. They used to go up and down between the long lines of furniture, saying which ones of every kind were theirs. Each had a favorite piece. Gertie's was a white enameled bed with rosettes and curlicues, Goldie's a mammoth leather rocker with tufts, and Linda's a real mahogany desk. One day the desk was sold, and Linda felt that she had been defrauded. She had always hoped that she would find money to pay for it in a purse some unknown had dropped, or that a wealthy stranger would see her looking at it and say, "Give it to the child."

Sometimes Mr. King gave them pieces of picture frame—gold or silver or shiny wood—for their little doll furniture. Or the traveling men gave them nickels.

There was one traveling man that Linda liked. He was tall and elegantly slim, and was the first person Linda had ever seen who she was sure had an olive complexion. He drew Linda to him and said:

"This one's my girl."

Most of the traveling men were nicest to Goldie because her father kept the store.

Goldie used to try to tempt the rest of them into the "back part" where the caskets stood on end against the wall. She said she wasn't a bit afraid, and proved it. Homer said he wasn't afraid to lie down in a coffin—he'd show 'em! But just then his father came and he said: "Well, I can't do it now. But I will."

"But he won't, old Big-Ears!" Gertie whispered to Linda.

Linda liked Boggs's meat market least of all. She hated to see the great backs and legs of meat hanging up in the back of the store under the deer's antlers. It made her cringe when Mr. Boggs in his terrible apron took a saw and went scrunch-scrunch though a slab of meat. Sometimes there were rabbits hanging up, dear furry rabbits with their pitiful ears pointing down, and geese with the pretty feathers on. She always traced her name in the sawdust on the floor, or pretended to weigh herself on the scales, while her mother bought the meat.

Papa's office was over Grant's Jewelry Store. Linda liked the feeling of her father's having an office, and of her being his little daughter come to see him. Gertie's father had no office. No one seemed to know just what Mr. Healey "did." He had a farm just out of town where he often drove. When Linda came as her father's daughter, it made her feel quite superior to Art Bishop, the clerk.

Art Bishop parted his hair in the middle, with two long curving locks that enclosed his forehead like a pair of parentheses. He wore a little brown felt hat, a red string tie, and coats and trousers that were not a match. He always wanted to stroke Linda's hair and to kiss her, and he laughed when she wiggled away from him. He called her his girl. Once Linda said to him:

"What about Mabel Somers?"

Then he got red clear into his collar.

Linda had seen him out buggy-riding with Mable Somers and Lola Healey said that they went together.

"He's a Smart Alec," Gertie said, when Linda told her about it.

The Hotel was very grand. It was called the Perry House. It was of red brick, on the corner of Main Street. It had velvet furniture inside. There was something splendid and awe-inspiring about a Hotel. Selma Hollis and her father and mother had dinner there every Sunday. It made Selma so important. She was always telling what she had at the Hotel.

Linda's father wouldn't pay over twenty-five cents, he said fiercely. When they went anywhere it was to Mrs. Bowman's up over the Eagle office. But Gertie could not even go there. Mr. Bowman waited on the table, and he always stuck his thumbs into the gravy bowls.

The creamery was another fine place.

It was down a little hill from Main Street, and a whole block away you could smell the queer steamy air.

Every Saturday morning, when there was a long line of people waiting at the little window with pails, Linda always had to go. At first she hated it, but after she got bigger she liked it, because she had to pass the Eagle office where John Cooper worked. John Cooper was the devil—printer's devil, that is.

Then there was the Opera House over the bank; the Central School of red brick; and the Church. The Church was of red brick, too, and had stained glass windows. The Baptist Church did not. Goldie King went to the Baptist. The Sunday School room opened off from the "big room" with folding doors. It had pale green walls, an organ, a colored lesson chart, and red chairs. Linda wanted to sit in the "big room" with the Bible class.

Linda and Gertie and Mary Brown were in Mrs. Sexton's class.

They had junior leaflets, and some day would have intermediates. They always were in the "Exercises" on Christmas and Children's Day. Linda was the best speaker and so she always had the leading part. Gertie didn't care, but it made Mary Brown very bitter.

Linda always hoped the Superintendent would have them sing *At the Cross, at the Cross* in opening exercises.

They all felt very important when he said, "The only perfect attendance was in Mrs. Sexton's Class."

After Mr. Dalrymple bought old Ned, Linda grew to know the country around Emmaville, besides the Fair Grounds, the cemetery, and the West Woods.

She went driving nearly every day after school, squeezed into a little triangle of seat between her mother and father. She liked best to go on the Cornville road. It was across the Dry Run, over the old iron bridge that rattled and shook and thundered under Ned's hoof beats (Linda always thought, what if the bridge should break down! but her father said it never could); then past Flaherty's place, with the little wooden horse set on the barn for a weather vane, and on to Cornville. Cornville wasn't a town at all. It was nothing but a square pink school house and a little white church.

Just as they were out of Emmaville, Linda felt that it was strange country, and that anything might happen. It was wonderful.

In the spring, the water roared and foamed in the Dry Run under the bridge. There were puddles in the road, and the buggy was all splashed. The air and all the ground smelled sweet and good. The farm orchards were in blossom.

In the summer, wild roses, sweet clover, yellow mustard flowers, brown-eyed Susans, and then goldenrod, grew along the road. The fields of oats and barley were like great green-gold seas, with winds that started, and ran a little way, and then made them break into great billows. The corn was high and green, with a milky smell, and the ears that Linda called "corn babies" all had long silky hair.

But in the autumn, the cornstalks were dry and dead-yellow, and the long pointed leaves rattled as if they were trying to keep the wind out. There was a smell of dust and apples and bonfires. Then the end of the road was lost in purple haze, and Linda could never be sure where it led.

And in the winter, when the bells on the cutter made the only sound in the whole still world, the snow lay like wreaths on the Christmas trees in Mason's Grove.

Hugh Sidey, a fourth generation journalist and author, is a native of Greenfield, Iowa. He began his career on the family newspaper in south central Iowa before he moved on to the Council Bluffs Nonpareil (1950–1951), the Omaha World Herald (1951–1955), Life (1955–1958), and Time (1958–). In 1966 he began writing Time's column "The Presidency," and in 1969 he became Time's Washington Bureau Chief. He is the author of John F. Kennedy, President (1963); A Very Personal Presidency: Lyndon Johnson in the White House (1966); These United States (1975); and Portrait of a President (1975). Sidey is one of only three winners of the James W. Schwartz Award for distinguished journalism awarded to graduates of Iowa State University. The others are Donald Jackson, historian and editor, and Robert Bartley, Pulitzer Prize-winning editor of the Wall Street Journal.

No history of the Midwest can ignore the impact of the printing press and the local newspaper on this region. Among those who came West with Jacobus Teunis Vandemark, hero of Herbert Quick's Vandemark's Folly (1922), were editors hunting opportunities for founding newspapers, dragging their dismantled Washington presses with them. Before the Territory of Iowa was legally established in 1838, there were newspapers at Dubuque, Davenport, and Burlington.

Sidey's essay doesn't focus on those early Iowa newspapers. He first became aware of the newspaper's influence on his family life, and its potential for his own, at the beginning of the Depression. What follows is an important essay that shows us not only those two influences (the Adair County Free Press is still published by Hugh's brother) but the significance of the newspaper for life in a rural Midwest town. The essay provides instances of technological advances adopted by town newspapers that made them an even more important part of the town's life—as the week-by-week historical record and as an integrator of the town's social, personal, and business life.

Finally, if we wonder why and how it is that a boy born in a small midwestern town can become an important figure in one of our globe's most important centers of power, or how and why a person acquires the background enabling him to affect the ideas of millions of others, that story is here. "Fourth Estate in Greenfield" is a significant case study of the pervasiveness of a father's example and the power of the work ethic in developing what once upon a time we hailed as character.

Fourth Estate in Greenfield

THEY BECAME GREAT FRIENDS. But when I was first led to "the office" as the family reverently called the narrow brick building in which each week the *Adair County Free Press* was conceived, written, assembled and printed, those clanking, hissing machines in the rear were awesome monsters. That one of my parents or a member of the staff would hover attentively near me as I surveyed this intriguing landscape did nothing but reinforce the notion that a misstep and I would be eaten by those huge gears that rolled and meshed in their creative ritual that I soon understood was the center of our small universe.

Undoubtedly I went to the office in a baby carriage and as a toddler but first memories registered about the age of three or four. From that close to the floor, there was nothing in Greenfield, Iowa, quite so worthy of study as the newspaper press, a Miehle flatbed, that even in those years was primitive in the trade. But it was the rock on which all else rested. The two metal steps up to the feeding platform were worn smooth from the countless trips of the pressmen weighted with newsprint hefted over their shoulders and flopped dramatically down on the feeding board, smoothed out and riffled, so that each sheet then could be lifted with a deft—almost dainty—grasp of thumb and forefinger. A quick twist of the wrist would then trap a cushion of air that would travel beneath the sheet and separate it from the pile just long enough that the sheet would slide into position for the grippers which would snatch it, pull it around the drum, and then roll it over the freshly inked type. It was so fast, yet so precise for such ungainly shaped pieces of metal and wood that I remember looking for minutes at a time (a rather long attention span for one so young) into the press's maw. I would see the clean white surface of the paper wind around the drum and then on the next revolution it would be something to read, cleanly stamped with furrows of black ink with figures and letters and faces and stories. Before any of that could register with meaning on my eye, however, the sheet was delicately peeled from the drum and slid down the graceful fingers of the rake, then was lifted in a great arch—the air pressure holding the sheet in place—to be deposited with a firm thump as a printed page on the pile of others already printed.

There was poetry in that old press, or at least as I look back after almost half a century I think that I felt it speak to me even before I comprehended it fully. Certainly I surveyed all the other mechanical ceremonies of a small town—the light plant with its churning diesels, the waterworks with its cascading sheets of muddy fluid, the garages with their hydraulic lifts, even the depot with its steam locomotives switching and thrashing with more force than anything in my experience. But nothing was quite so proud and kingly as the old Miehle. How many words had it printed—millions, of course. It had come to the *Free Press* second hand from one of those hideous dark shops where job printing was done. No soul, or heart there. But when it was rescued in late middle age it began even longer service as a member of the Sidey family and of course we felt its words and pictures now formed a part of the central current of human history—at least that tributary in the great Middle West, U.S.A. The Miehle told stories of the people with whom we lived and worked. It was not simply metal and bolts and wood. It breathed life. Why else did the townspeople line up each Wednesday afternoon and wait for the sign of life in the press, then lay down their nickels and scoop up a finished *Free Press* and go off as if they had just found rare treasure. In fact, they had. Vaguely, in those years when I first laid eyes on that machine and its explosive labors, I believe I understood that.

The family newspaper was the center of our lives. It was, at least in the early years, far more pervasive a force than God and far more believable. Though God was considered to be a member of the household, He was a hard Fellow to catch and He was always falling down on the job, or at least not reading the messages correctly that were sent up nightly from bedside. God was much too vague for a small boy just entering the first years of memory. But the newspaper was the force in our universe, very tangible and very comforting. The family metabolism was shaped by it. The waking, eating, studying, going and coming, sitting and visiting all were affected by the necessities of publishing. The first of the week was the time of creation when Dad was not to be bothered. He was gathering ads, writing stories, making up the pages, and seeing that the early press runs were out of the way. The pace built to the Wednesday night climax. We called that night press night. Actually there already had been one other press time for the Miehle but the final run was press night. In those early years of mine, when we were gripped hardest by depression and drought, the paper was rarely larger than eight pages. That meant the Miehle was pressed into service twice during the week. It could print four pages each run. For a regular eight-pager, the sheets of newspaper were flopped and the final four pages printed on the back side. The folding and trimming ritual yielded the finished product, which was rushed to the front office and the impatient customers. Press night was sacred. Nothing could intrude, Dad was required at the office for as long as it took to get that final paper printed; in those days when machinery was less reliable, the entire night might be consumed in the struggle.

The paper cast its spell in other ways. I began to feel almost from the first contact with the office that we were involved in the public's business. All kinds of people wandered in and out of the building. They wanted to tell about family dinners and the graduations of their children, and so they stopped by and left that trust with Dad. They worried a lot with him, too, about crops and prices and politics, about illnesses and mortgages. Everybody's business seemed to be our business. If a farm was to be sold, the owner came by and carefully went over the list of his things that would go into the sale ad. When a barn burned, Dad was called within minutes after the fire department got the message. Camera in hand, he rushed off. Auto accidents were his province too, no matter how late at night. When bad weather threatened, Dad stalked the tyrant. He was angry with himself the day that a tornado swept out of the sky northwest of town, raced across the fields flattening crops and smashing barns and homes. From the north end of town it had been visible for a few minutes, a hideous black-green cauldron of clouds that sent down its funnel with hail and rain. All the time Dad had been in the Greenfield library catching up with the new magazines and books.

Dad catalogued sports and debates, attended the big trials, and photographed the best fishes caught during the week. He always carried his small pad and he would take it out right after church, or around the town square when he ran into somebody who wanted to leave with him some of those ''items'' of small town life. Brought together in the newspaper they really were small town life. Because we were a newspaper family we were tucked in a corner of that singular stage. Our moods went up and down with those of the town. We shared the tragedies and we knew about social turmoil and did not dare tell, although at times I fear that I broke the rules. But above all there was an obligation to serve, to take part in the public drama and somehow give something back for the special trust we had been given.

What had we been given? When I look back these days I marvel at how little it was in a material sense. Yet there was exuberance despite depression and drought and grasshoppers and all the human miseries that seemed to accumulate in the world in the 1930s; hope and the freedom and the feeling that things would be better seemed to carry people along. There was humor and prayer, there was sacrifice, and there was, of course, misery, but always there was the promise that the next day might be better. There was the richness of space, air, and sunshine. For boys, especially, those years were still flavored with the frontier. The idea of adventure lay just beyond the horizon. On some evenings the local farmers would drive their cattle or sheep to the depot which lay at the far end of our street. And for a moment the animals would fill the street with their baa-ings and bleatings and something inside a youngster would stir at the sight and the sounds. It was like the books about the Old West with their line drawings and tales of the Chisholm Trail. Once or twice an animal would break from the herd and plunge up the embankment in front of our house and run across our lawn, intensifying the excitement.

The desperation of those times was an adult affliction. We children were spared those dark and brooding thoughts about the future. Life was good in the backyards and out along the railroad tracks with the wild strawberries and the black-eyed Susans. The outdoors was a resource to be used as far as a boy's imagination would carry him. From the first years, the feeling for the land, the rhythms of the seasons, the smells and sights of the changes in sky and trees were implanted in my consciousness. Dad and playmates were part of this ritual. Almost as soon as we could travel any distance on our small legs, we began Sunday hikes. After church and Sunday dinner we would change into our old clothes, supply ourselves with apples, cookies, and an occasional Hershey bar, and then congregate around Dad. He always seemed to wear an old suede jacket with holes in the sleeves and a felt hat with frayed edges. He was the tour guide for as many as a dozen of the neighbor boys who had by now learned the Sunday schedule. When the weather was good, the word would filter down the streets like magic. By 1 P.M. our backyard would have the day's collection and Dad would emerge with a smile to announce the plan, usually about a two-mile trek out along the old Burlington right-of-way to the ice hill turnoff, then through the creek that in earlier

KENNETH SIDEY, IN FRONT OF THE FOLDER, AND HIS BROTHER JOHN, SHOP FOREMAN, FEEDING THE FLATBED PRESS, 1946.

times had filled up the ice pond which had furnished the town's refrigeration, up the steep incline that we used for coasting in the winter, and over into the fairways of the Greenfield Public Golf Course. Beyond those manicured stretches of grass lay a patch of timber that to a five- or six-year-old seemed like real forest. In the fall it yielded hazelnuts, in the summer wild plums. Always, there was a low-hanging branch from an oak on which we could rock up and down as if we were riding a horse.

The creek beds had snapping turtles and we could expect the patches of strawberries to attract bull snakes. In the fall the large weeds were so hardy that their stalks made marvelous spears. We could spend hours scrambling up and down the gulleys and ravines, pulling up the weeds and heaving them in friendly contests. Sometimes a beebee gun showed up on these excursions and occasionally one of the mature participants came along with a .22 rifle. But there was no hunting. Dad was a gentle soul, and while he never remonstrated with any boy that I recall, his philosophy seemed to infuse itself into the groups that he guided over the rolling hills on these outings. There were a few squabbles, and he would turn an eye on the participants, apply a smile, and suddenly the steam would go out of the tussle. All the troops with Kenneth Sidey hustled along in good humor with a sharp eye out for the resident wildlife and an alert mind for discovering new dirt slides and pooled water that might harbor some minnows.

Even on these Sunday adventures the newspaper was not far from Dad's thoughts and actions. He frequently took his camera and he would not only experiment on the kids who accompanied but he would look for blossoms and clouds that might arouse his artistic interest. Before the age of eight and any personal commitment to the publishing business, my observations of my Dad were the things that formed my impression of newspapering. Much of the time a camera was at the center of the action, and the paper's darkroom was in the basement of our home; it was a niche of exquisite fascination when Dad began developing the pictures he took.

Photography in weekly newspapers was still something of a novelty in the early 1930s. If a local picture warranted printing, the photo had to be shipped off to be engraved and that took at least a week or two. Dad's interest in photography ripened into his conviction that the *Free Press* should have its own engraving system so that it could print pictures while they were in the news. So Dad made his own plant from reading and consulting the state's resident engraving authorities, of which there were mighty few then. He ordered the necessary trays, sheets of zinc, and the chemicals. He rigged up the rest of the machinery from scratch. Thus, in a tiny corner of our small basement Dad slowly accumulated the necessary skills to provide his own pictures every week. He would take the photographs, develop them, and make the prints. Then he would place the prints under arc lights and make half-tone negatives. He coated the zinc plates with a sensitive emulsion and transferred the images to the metal. Then, in the most sensitive routine of all, he would etch the pictures in fine dots, pausing repeatedly to make sure that the acid did not destroy the surface. The process was delicate. Humidity and temperature affected it; at first there seemed to be as many frustrations as successes. I believe it was during these engraving evenings that I learned my saintly father swore; not loudly but under his breath as he discovered that the chemistry of photoengraving was so capricious.

On those days when school or other activities did not demand my time, I sometimes got to ride along with Dad when he went on his picture-taking rounds. I can recall in the deep winters Dad parking his car beside twenty-foot-high drifts of snow that had been sliced through by a grader. He would then back off and take a shot of the snow-dwarfed auto. When grasshoppers were at their peak, he was diligent in scouting news of novel counterattacks against the insects. One original fellow had rigged up a net on the front of his Model A and he would rear around his pasture collecting the swarms of grasshoppers that were stirred up by the approaching car. He would then dump the mass of netted insects into a pile and spray them all. He claimed that he spared his pasture land, though as I look back the idea seems dubious. What he did do, however, was collect an impressive pile of squirming hoppers that made a good picture.

While I felt that my company on picture-taking missions surely was of great benefit to my Dad, I never considered that I really worked at the *Free Press* until what must have been the summer of my eighth year. My brother Ed, who was two years older, and I were recruited to help recover metal from what seemed like a mountainous pile of used plates stored in the dank recesses of the plant's basement. For years the illustrations for ads and the news pictures had been used and then taken to the basement and tossed in the corners. Why the sudden need to retrieve the metal just when my brother and I reached a coltish age and preferred the outdoors baffled me. It may have been the Depression and the feeling of desperation. In any event, we were led to those forbidding depths and given boxes to sit on. A couple of bare light bulbs hung from the ceiling, a criss-cross of massive timbers supporting the heavy machinery above. Cobwebs covered everything. There was only a dirt floor—and those piles of used plates. They were made of copper, lead, or zinc tacked onto hardwood blocks. The technique of separation was fundamental. I seized a plate, slammed it down repeatedly on the ground until the brads loosened along the edges, then took an old screw driver and pried the metal off. The metal was sorted and saved in gunnysacks, the wood blocks carefully stacked for reuse.

For hours, for days, for what seemed like weeks, the two of us trudged up to the office on summer mornings, headed down into the basement, and began thunking the plates one by one against the ground. It was my first introduction to real tedium, outside of church services. The piles of dirty old plates seemed not to shrink at all, but to grow bigger. There were plates hidden in corners and caverns of that basement that I had never imagined. Thunk, thunk, pry, pry. My recollection is that we were paid about fifty cents a day for this work, which was an exorbitant fee considering the times. That eased the thought of being separated from the outdoors and friends for those hours. But the dreariness of the labor and the surroundings impressed me mightily. To this day I still recall the job and how unpleasant it was. Now and then my grandfather, a tall and imposing Scotsman, would stalk down the stairs to see how his grandsons were coming along. He had a twinkle in his eyes and a good chuckle when I suggested that my life was not long enough to finish this job. Dad would make sure that the newly recruited labor force was reasonably happy. I could tell his foot on the steps as he began his descent. He hurried, both down and up. In fact, all of his life he took steps at an unusual pace, as if they were an obstacle that required an extra burst of energy. Even when he was past eighty and ailing, I remember coming home on a visit and lying in my old bed at night and hearing Dad come up the basement stairs. He still forced himself to take the same rapid pace, sole of shoe placed firmly on each board, the sound echoing through the stilled house, another of those small messages of family security.

In that summer of tedium my father would often bring down bottles of soda pop. We never had to ask. He just knew what it must mean for a couple of kids to be cooped up in a musty basement. We did not have to stay the entire day and usually at lunchtime the duty was ended. Coming up out of the basement into the full flood of summer light was a physical sensation. I felt lighter, ready to run.

The piles of old plates finally began to shrink. The veritable Everest which had dominated the scene was cleared away. The lesser peaks of the discard range began to recede. Then I received a major setback. My brother was taken from my side and assigned to more sophisticated duty topside. There I was still in the foothills of old plates, expected to finish the job alone. I whistled my way through the remaining duty. And I still remember that final plate. It was a big copper-covered ad for tires and I threw it triumphantly on the ground, beat it mercilessly until the nails popped out. I ripped the metal from the wood, took the sacks of separated plates and rushed up into daylight. Done, finished. I reported the triumph to my Uncle John and made a mental pledge to avoid all such work in the future.

I had learned a valuable lesson about the printing business. Much of it is monotonous. One by one. Sheet by sheet. Box by box. Hundreds. Thousands. There was no escape and if a fellow was to be a printer even part time, then he had better condition his body and mind to repetition. Numbers have never intimidated me since.

The next memorable duty was sweeping the floors. By this time I was advancing into my tenth year and my brother had been assigned the cleanup job in the front office, which entailed a nightly sweep through with lovely red sweeping compound and a reward at week's end of something like fifty cents. My assignment was the back shop, which I considered a bit more difficult because it was littered with paper scraps, had greasy boards for a surface, and far more equipment and tables to sweep around and under. But a salary was becoming a necessity with advancing maturity and so I entered the ranks of the employed with gusto. Besides, having a duty was a badge of honor in those days. It meant that I had to hurry home from school, change into my work clothes, then head back uptown for the job, which could be accomplished in a concentrated fifteen minutes but often took much longer because of the need to renew acquaintances with the staff and examine new developments in the back shop. I would scoop deep into the barrel of sweeping compound, sprinkle it liberally over the wooden floor, wait a few minutes for the oil to soak into the surface. Then I would push and pull, tap the broom firmly after each stroke to remove the clinging particles, speed down the aisles and around the table legs, up and down the ranks of type cases. I became an excellent broom man, complimented finally even by Uncle John. When I finally relinquished the job and went off to college one of the most prized compliments came from Millard Summers, Linotype operator and printer, who announced without any coercion, ''the place has not been clean since you quit sweeping out.''

I cannot recall just how I graduated into other duties besides sweeping the floors. But I became a printer, photographer, then pressman, and even an engraver. Nobody said to me, "Now, this morning I want you to learn to set type." It was, instead, by instinct. It was an established routine in any country newspaper family that the children all helped. Almost every such family in the southwest part of the state had boys and girls in the business. More than anything else, I suspect, it was simply the desire to help out my parents who had to work so hard. Though my mother did not have a job in the newspaper, she did almost everything at home but the heavy labor. Of course she had the household duties of cooking, sewing, cleaning, washing. But she also was the principal tutor, disciplinarian, encourager, musician, comforter, celebration organizer, fun maker. It was totally consuming. She stayed away from the newspaper. That was Dad's territory, almost exclusively.

While my early experiences around the office expanded with my age, it was pretty easygoing compared to what Dad had been through when he was a boy my age. I did not really hear many of those stories until I had grown up and left home. Then I got more interested. And as Dad grew older he talked more about his early life in Greenfield. While he could recount what had happened to him personally and what his father told him about the family roots, he did not bother with much research into the Sidey beginnings. I did more of that than he did.

My great-grandfather, a cobbler, had walked to Greenfield twenty miles from Stuart where the rails ended. He liked the town and there was work for him making shoes. He sent to Peterborough, Ontario, where the family had landed from Scotland, and Grandfather shepherded them along the way. The Sideys had found a place that suited their temperament. They stayed.

Not long after establishing himself in Greenfield, Great-grandfather decided that the town needed a Democratic newspaper. There were at least two Republican papers, a lopsided political equation that John Sidey intended to rectify. By then Grandfather had gone back to Boston and learned the printing trade, had come back to the state, and started a newspaper in Creston. He also printed the *Adair County Free Press* which Great-grandfather started. The family decided that the opportunity seemed best in Greenfield and so Grandfather moved up to develop his father's struggling business.

Soon my father was part of that weekly enterprise. The uncertainties of putting out a newspaper at the turn of the century were daunting except to such hardy adventurers. The type had to be set by hand. The printing equipment was unreliable. Acts of nature disrupted transportation with remarkable frequency. Deadlines were bent and broken in times of adversity and family life was geared to all these uncertainties. Putting out the paper then was more of a family act even than when I came along. Everybody had to work in order to keep the business going. My father, the accounts have it, used to be taken up to the office as an infant and put to sleep on the piles of newsprint when press night ran late. They claimed in later years that some place in the family records there was a photograph of Dad in short pants standing on a box so that he could reach the pile of papers and feed the folder in which the finished newspapers were creased and trimmed. It was established lore in the town that he learned the mechanics of presses and Linotypes better than anyone when he still was a high school student. The result was that Grandfather was always summoning Dad out of class to come to the shop to fix a Linotype or a press. He never could be a serious athlete because of his duties at the office.

Before the equipment was converted to electricity, the big press was driven by a steam engine. That piece of machinery proved to be the most cantankerous inhabitant of the back shop, according to legend. With an infuriating regularity, the steam engine would give out in the middle of the final press run. A strong man could lay his shoulder to the task and get the press drum moving with enough speed to complete the modest press runs of weekly papers. It became Dad's duty, when the steam engine balked, to seek out a town handyman noted for his great physical strength and endurance, but also for his taste for spirits. Thus, with the belching and wheezing of the old steam plant that signaled trouble ahead, Dad was sent through the darkened streets of the town to find the strong man. He developed sure instincts for locating the fellow, depending on the time of year, the relative prosperity of the town, and the time of night. Generally, Dad conceded later, he found the man in a tavern, well on his way to euphoria, but a person of such sweet disposition, drunk or sober, that he was ready to help anyone in distress. The giant would follow Dad back to the plant, take a firm grip on the flywheel crank, and heave his way through the night to sobriety and some extra money for the next evening's indulgence.

Dad never had a chance to be anything but a country editor and publisher, not that he would have wanted anything else had he had a choice. But choice was not easy for people to come by in a struggling farm town. They shared some of the exuberance of Theodore Roosevelt's age, and even some of the prosperity. But troubles with farm prices came early in the century; then the war took Dad and those his age away for a couple of years. Back home, the farm depression worsened despite the giddy excesses of the rest of the nation. Dad saved his money to go to the University of Missouri and study journalism. But Grandfather took his savings and plowed them into the paper. Dad got one year at Missouri and a summer at Northwestern and that ended his college days. He was ad salesman, reporter, mechanic, pressman, and then photographer. Of all the tasks that he undertook at the *Free Press,* the role of photographer seemed to gratify him the most. It was the combination of art and science, of eye and mechanics that so appealed to him. He loved the precision of the camera, the magic of the darkroom chemistry. He enjoyed recording history in such indisputable terms. And of course he liked the free-roaming life of a country photographer. His happiest moments came when he was off over a prairie road in quest of a picture, whether it was of a prize lamb or a church meeting or a flooded stream. His beloved camera would be in its case behind him, one of his sons beside him, and, a little later, Spot, the family dog, planted on the front seat pointing the way. Here was openness, sun and air, movement and adventure, and the sense of recording and creating.

I picked up that feeling for photography from Dad. Because he loved those delicate boxes, he figured his sons should, too. In the early 1930s Eastman Kodak was launching its series of inexpensive small cameras. My first, called the Bullet, came under the Christmas tree. Instead of the traditional bellows, its lens screwed out. Along with the camera I was given a developing kit. Because Dad had his darkroom in the basement, I immediately shot a roll or two of film, then locked myself in the darkroom and seesawed the film through developer, short-stop, and hypo to test my skill. The results were encouraging from the start. I began to take my camera on those excursions with Dad. My small prints of grasshopper damage or haystacks stood up well alongside his enlargements made for the paper. I began to sneak down to the darkroom on my own for photographic experiments. I enlarged my arsenal of cameras. I used to ask to be allowed into the dark room when Dad was enlarging and I silently studied the process. One day when Dad was not there, I went to the darkroom determined to try enlarging by myself. I never asked Dad's permission. Now that I think back on it, I understand that I always had it. His trust was total in all the skills that he wanted me to learn. He just assumed that when I felt ready to make enlargements I would do so. And I did. Again, my first experiments were gratifying. I made mistakes; exposed and wasted a considerable amount (for those days) of photographic paper and supplies. But there was never a complaint from Dad. He exclaimed over my handiwork, offered tips, bought more chemicals and paper to keep the flame alive.

Now and then one of my pictures would find its way into the newspaper. The group of Boy Scouts who went to summer camp posed for parental snapshots. My negative was borrowed and the picture printed in the paper. The quiet satisfaction of seeing one's work published was not something that a boy could explain but it was real from the start. For the next years much of my life centered around photography, learning to use bigger cameras, to be more skilled at making enlargements, establishing a lucrative trade in pictures of babies, weddings, and funerals. To this day I find few things more gratifying than driving and walking out over Adair County, photographing those shifting scenes of sky and land, then developing and printing the pictures.

By the time I reached high school, I was fully rated as a cameraman for the *Adair County Free Press*. Not only could Dad dispatch me with reasonable assurance of my competence to photograph groups, parades, games, and personalities, but he could turn over to me the weekend darkroom work. On Saturday afternoons I made the prints that we needed for the photoengravings. It was while sloshing developer and waiting for the images to loom out of the trays that I made the acquaintance of Ronald (Dutch) Reagan, a man I would encounter much later in life. He was then the sportscaster for Radio WHO. Dad had supplied the darkroom with a small radio because so many hours were spent there preparing the paper's pictures. Dad had listened to the news and the concerts as well as the humor shows. We could hear his chuckle drift up from below many a night as we huddled near the old cathedral radio listening to Fibber Magee and Molly and Jack Benny. But for me the radio meant a fifty-yard seat at Big Ten football, then the best in the nation. Dutch Reagan was my man. He was an articulate and passionate enthusiast for Iowa, one of the lesser teams in the awesome Big Ten. But Iowa was still capable of surprises and indeed during one of those years they went to the Rose Bowl and took Dutch along with them. He never came back. I never went to a Big Ten game while growing up in Iowa. But through the eyes of Dutch Reagan and later his brother, I learned of the strength of the Golden Gophers, the legacy that Red Grange left Illinois, the jinx that Iowa held on Notre Dame for years, and about the man I most admired in football and still do—Tom Harmon of Michigan. Dutch Reagan could make dull games bubble. His enthsiasm was infectious even down there in that cramped darkroom with the furnace pipe right over my head. I was far away from the world, but how close. When the crowds roared, when the runners broke through, Dutch Reagan went wild himself. The tiny radio would vibrate with sound and, who knows, maybe it was during one of those great games a crack appeared down the front of the plastic case and Dad had to put a piece of dark red paper over it to shield the sensitive photographic paper from the yellow light that showed through.

Without knowing it as I advanced through junior high school and high school I picked up a wide range of skills, all of it done casually, though out of a desire to help my hard-pressed Father through the years of World War II when skilled manpower was scarce. I did the stereotyping for the ads, testing the pot of molten lead with a piece of paper (if it turned brown at the point of insertion, the metal was about the right temperature) and then releasing the river of hot liquid that would form the image. Demand increased skill. Some Saturday mornings I would fill the basement stairs with heavy slabs of lead laid out to cool. Next, I conquered the art of trimming them with a metal saw. I tinkered with the Linotype and learned its mechanics, through I did not master the keyboard well enough to make me an efficient operator. I could set some of the lines that I needed when I began making up the pages of the paper and some of the ads. There was a certain visceral gratification in working with type. What began as nothing more than an idea scribbled down on paper (we did not have a layout department) came to life before my eyes as the small squares of lead were assembled. Typeface, size, space, all had to be calculated for pleasing visual impact. It proved to be a happy combination of physical and mental development.

I soon was learning about press work. My first job of feeding stacks of paper came on the old folder that my father had tended so many press nights. I found that I could master the quick twist of the wrist that floated the large sheets of paper down to the guides where they would be carried into the folding apparatus. Next I ventured up to the big Miehle and discovered that I could control that monster too. Finally, I was allowed into the job printing department where the paper was of a higher quality and the precision needed for finished work much greater. The automatic press was too complicated for a boy but the small hand-fed model, which we called the "snapper" for obvious reasons, was just right for young fellows. I soon could make up the forms for the printing jobs, get the press ready, select and trim the paper, and feed the stacks of stock with minimal misprints and breakdowns. I learned to judge the ink and add more when it began to run thin. I could lay out the fresh sheets like shingles on a roof to prevent the ink from smudging. Finally, I was taught how to assemble and, where needed, to pad and bind the finished products. Of course I was also the delivery boy, wrapping the completed jobs, marking them for the customers, and then hustling them around town.

I was vaguely aware of my good fortune at having a printing plant in the family with its variety of demands. My friends dug ditches or shoveled corn and they made a lot more money. But the few times that I entered their world I was appalled at the monotony of the duty. I could not define the satisfaction that I got from having started with a jumble of lead blocks with letters on their ends and finished with a crisp, clean stack of printed material, but it was down there inside me someplace. To be sure, there were moments when I wanted to rebel as in the days spent in the basement stripping plates. When Dad bought another used press and they delivered the abused machine in parts to the shop, the caked ink and accumulated grime which took two weeks to chip away and wash off nearly made me forget the joys of creation. And the time that Uncle John had me hand print 15,000 envelopes on the job press seemed to stretch to eternity. It was summer and the office windows were open. The outdoors was enticing. Friends passed up and down the town's streets, which I could not see from my spot in front of the press. For almost two days solid I stood rooted to the concrete and one by one thrust in those envelopes and retrieved them. Handful after handful passed through the press, box after box. When the end came I felt certain that my foot prints were surely in the cement. But the end had come, and perhaps that was some of the best training that I ever had in patience and endurance. Newspapering, printing, and photography could not yield instant gratification. Accumulated skills had to be orchestrated, bits and pieces assembled, time invested before there was a result. There were no shortcuts. Quality demanded strict attention to detail. Mistakes were costly in raw materials and time and certainly in pride. I was masterfully coaxed and chided along the way by Uncle John. He demanded improvement, but not too much. He could get angry just as he did when I placed a form in the press upside down and on the first imprint the type smashed into the guide pins, ruining the type and my exalted reputation as a fast learner. "You remind me of a cub bear," rasped my Uncle, jerking the form out of the press, resetting it, and handing it to me with withering contempt. "See if you can do it right this time." He soon mellowed but the lesson was learned. I made other mistakes, but I never got a form in a press upside down again.

Sometime in the midst of work and playing a little football and baseball with the Greenfield Tigers, the world took a more serious turn, and once again the guiding hand was the *Adair County Free*

Press. Every group of draftees who left for war service was photographed by my father. They gathered at the Trailways bus stop next to the office building and stood uncomfortably for the picture, then were sped to Des Moines, and on to the great crusade for freedom. I was soon helping Dad take those pictures that came with increasing regularity after Pearl Harbor. I had never witnessed such fundamental emotion on such a regular basis. Sometimes the buses left early in the morning, other times late at night. Husbands and wives clung together in their final embraces, mothers sobbed, and even some of those weathered faces of farmers whom I had known all my life were awash with tears. The power to separate families, to rend a small society like ours, was something I had never contemplated. It was in some ways even more intimidating than death. In Greenfield, as in all small towns, death is a part of life. From the age of seven I went regularly to funerals. As soon as I had established the fact that I could carry a tune and was singing in the Presbyterian Church choir, I was called upon to sing at funerals. Two of my best friends were drowned when I was nine and I was a pallbearer. One of my photographic duties was taking pictures of open, flower-banked caskets before the final rites. The inevitability of the end of life was thus set in my mind almost from the first years of awareness. But war and the demands from the federal government to fight it were new forces in my life.

I watched in my high school years the awakening of our small community from the icy grip of the Depression. The weather changed. Rains poured down over those fertile fields once again and as far as the eye could see there was green. Dust storms did not darken the sun. The proliferating farm ponds filled up with water. Grasshoppers retreated. The economy quickened as the nation began to gear up for war. Even with the shortages of materials, I could see the changes. We built an addition onto the *Free Press* building to house the new equipment. More new homes were constructed, streets repaired. People dressed better. The city fathers relented in their opposition to taking federal grants and allowed the WPA to build a town swimming pool. It was one of the last such projects in the county but it was one of the most important from my viewpoint. My love of water was natural and I soon developed a strong stroke. Toward the end of the first swimming season for the new pool I was asked to help lifeguard, a job I took with parental blessing, as long as I continued to help in spare hours at the newspaper. The early mornings at the pool were my special job. I arrived before any of the other hands, swept and disinfected the bath houses, backwashed the filters, and then before the swimming classes started, luxuriated a few minutes in the water by myself. I was like an otter, plunging and rising, turning and diving back, soaring between surface and bottom in the ten-foot section, like a bird, feeling the sweet ripple of water across my body. It was almost spiritual. Government had brought that possibility for pleasure, the same government that was claiming our boys for war.

I began to learn about conservation and breeding of fine livestock. The *Free Press* was filled with the new ideas that came out of the increasing number of trained agriculture experts. Production burgeoned during the war, the pace of life in Greenfield picked up even as we were denied the right to wander very far from town. Vacations were postponed, though that was not much of a sacrifice since the Depression had limited us to a few days at the north Iowa lakes. But distant hauls for football games and music contests were curtailed. We stayed in our small corner of prairie and we stayed close to each other.

Sixteen children who had entered kindergarten together graduated from high school together. The bonds established then endure today. We explored the back alleys together, we waded in ponds, and climbed the ice-rimmed snow banks. We played basketball and football together, and we were in the school plays and glee clubs. Life was close and sometimes cloying, but never beyond friendship. We stayed with each other, products of our land, a time, a nation. We went down in the books as the Class of 1945, brought to maturity just as World War II ended and Franklin Roosevelt died. I know all the names today. I can see the moments of exquisite joy and anguish along the way. That first day of kindergarten I found that Dick Bittner wore tennis shoes. I had never seen real tennis shoes. They were wonderful and I wanted some. I played marbles with Dick and went to his house. We hiked and camped together. Shortly after high school he was killed on a construction job. And I pondered again the equation of who should live and who should die. Dick Bittner, with his thick black hair, his exuberance for life. Why? I still recall the first day of school so long ago and that tiny boy with his tennis shoes and all the years between and how it ended. There were others and they moved away after 1945 as they planned it. Darlene and Becky, Bill and Jim and Wayne. Ordinary, yet special people. Deprived by Depression and war, ready for the new age.

I began to understand that for all of the open land and the newspaper that had been so much a part of me, the larger part of my background was a series of human encounters. The clouds and the sky were beautiful in the presence of my dad or my mother, or with the knowledge that the people of Adair County lived and worked among those low rolling hills. The machines of the back shop operated only under the skilled touch of the *Free Press* staff. Their labor and laughter bound the world together.

Mamie Lyman, the *Free Press* society reporter, painted the wooden wheel spokes of her old Studebaker pink, used a bear skin in the winter to keep the warm water she poured in the radiator from freezing, greeted me every day with a smile. Her life's work consisted of thousands of paragraphs about family dinners, deaths, and doings. She found endless satisfaction in the corners of plain people. And she herself became a stone sculpted by that society, many faceted, reflecting the eccentricities and the humanness of huddled village life. Each year when she went off on her bus trip around the country she left a full obituary with my father. It was written in cramped longhand, rolled-up pages of a girl's life on the farm and the adult existence in town. There was little that would excite the reader and yet I remember reading the full length of this tentative obituary (should the bus plunge off a Colorado cliff) one night during college, and finding the story deeply compelling. She had helped to anchor my life. She had resided at the desk beside the front window of the *Free Press,* her outrageous hats visible over the curtains, and her steady pecking at the typewriter and willingness to drop a compliment about a school play or concert into my hurried life were part of my own web of creation.

I remember those summer afternoons around the composing tables in the *Free Press* when it was Coke time. I would go across the alley to get the ice-cold bottles from Fry's Drug Store and the entire staff turned down the mechanical din and gathered for a few minutes. It always amazed me how we could find anything new about which to talk, having spent the day together. We always did. Jokes about the customers, tales from the old days when the tramp printers used to arrive seasonally for a few weeks' work before they went back on the bottle and disappeared on the train, speculation about the fall's football team, and stories told and retold about the town's great lovers and the loved. Was anything so rich, so intensely human? Even on the Great Wall of China or in the White House lobby nothing has been quite so meaningful as those memories.

The branches of my family resided in every quadrant of the town and while their scrutiny was sometimes uncomfortable, their presence was strength, depth, obligation, duty, and a charter from the past, no matter how murky, to march proudly into the future. For all its strains, there was a bond, no matter how modest, that allowed for flaws and praised accomplishment. Forced by circumstances and the act of creation to be together, the people of Greenfield rarely denied the dark shadows that clouded their existence, but their smallness and their closeness demanded a compensating sense of care. These moments whether around the town square or in the Presbyterian church or the high school or leaning on the composing stone in the *Free Press* or walking through the evening silently with my father after press night—these were distilled droplets of life at its best.

JOSEPH LANGLAND

To the midwestern generations that grew up before
1940, horses were as much a part of the rural scene as cattle and hogs.
Every farm had its permanent bluegrass pasture and its horse barn. Until
the 1930s, the farm machines—plows, drags, discs, seeders, reapers—were
drawn back and forth over the fields by patient teams. Horse-drawn
wagons, rather than trucks and pickups, hauled the farmer's crops to
town and the goods he bought back to his farmstead. In towns and cities
horse-drawn vehicles picked up freight at railroad depots and hauled it to
the stores and shops; grocers and dairies delivered food and milk to individual homes using wagons that made daily deliveries. As late as 1927
the business men of one midwestern city, while agreeing that the
automobile was here to stay, still thought that the motortruck was a
novelty, unlikely to replace the horse-drawn dray.

The horse was even a part of the educational scene. Schoolchildren
of Langland's generation knew the Horse Fair and other paintings of
horses by the French artist, Rosa Bonheur; copies of her painting hung on
classroom walls. The popularity of her work in America can be measured
by the space the Chicago Art Institute accords her work; one wall is
literally covered with Rosa Bonheur originals.

No wonder then that the memory and imagination of Joseph Langland, who was born in 1917 and grew up in the rural Midwest, came to
be fascinated by horses, as his essay and poem emphasize.

The poems in the "Sacrifices" section of his Wheel of Summer also
reflect his boyhood on a farm near the Minnesota border in Winneshiek
County, Iowa. Langland is the author of For Harold (n.d./n.p.), The
Green Town (1956), A Little Homily (1962), An Interview and Fourteen
Poems (1973), and Iowans in the Arts (1977). With Paul Engle he edited
Poet's Choice (1962); with James B. Hall he edited The Short Story
(1956); with Aczel and Tikos he edited Poetry from the Russian
Underground (1973). He is an adjunct professor of English at the Univer-
sity of Massachusetts, Amherst.

A Dream of Love

A PREPARATORY NOTE. When I was in the second grade in Bekkan School, a one-room schoolhouse in Winneshiek County, Iowa, I discovered a fine fairy tale in our very small school library, "The Princess on the Glass Hill." That is where I let this poem begin. And in another idealized sense, more oriented to religion and medieval romance, that is where the poem ends, also. The locale, in my mind, is always Iowa.

I am one of nine children. One of our games in the Depression years was called "horse-stick." We would select various cane-length sticks, often with a little irregularity near the bottom which we likened to hooves and hocks, and we would set up whole stables of these horse-sticks, with names, colors, speeds, and imagined qualities. Then we would race them and trade them. My own favorite was named "Blue Streak," and for a little while I managed to make him the envy of all others.

Both from the actual horses on the farm, and from our own trotting and galloping with those magical sticks, I have taken the whole basic rhythm of this poem, the galloping three-beat line with which I have gathered together most of the narrative.

I begin with naming all the actual horses I can remember from that childhood and on up through our working adolescence on Valley View Farm in Highland Township, Winneshiek County, Iowa. That farm has been in the family since 1877, and on December 6, 1978, it was named the winner of the state of Iowa's Soil Conservation Achievement Award. The farm is now run by my brothers, Maurice and Walter, and their wives and children. It is, of course, the "home" farm, and it has been the imaginative landscape of many of my poems. . . .

The poem has so many references to horses which I came to know through picture, song, and story while growing up in Iowa that I can mention only a few. Our one-room rural school, for some unknown reason, had a huge brown sepia reproduction of Rosa Bonheur's "The Horse Fair" on one schoolhouse wall. It was magnificent; I used to study it for hours. Books such as *Black Beauty* came out of its small and rather beat-up library in a little oak case at the front of the room. *Smoky, the Cowhorse* was read to us, day by day, by the teacher, Albert Thornton of Postville, Iowa. I tried to imagine how that book might end, and he told me that the last two words were "full size," which was baffling to a ten-year-old boy. Now I know how that was, and I have put even that in this poem.

Then I remember a fine pictorial film short of horses running. I have put that there. And of stories from *The Youth's Companion,* read by my mother at the supper table, and newspaper accounts read by my father later in the dining room. The essence of some of that is there. And in this way, the poem radiates out from that local farm scene and education on into the sophisticated adult world of art and literature and experience and knowledge and historical and even geological time, keeping the prancing rhythm, with free verse interludes, of our childhood horse-sticks and the horses, themselves, in our fields and barns and meadows and timber and bottomlands.

Finally, the poem returns, in a kind of secular high gothic style, to northeastern Iowa. And there it ends, with the echoes of years of religious services in our local rural church "galloping away in the shadows," through those wooded hills and down those streams and valleys to the Upper Iowa and the Mississippi and the sea.

Once upon a time
three brothers kept three horses
in a farmyard near a forest not far from a magnificent castle.
According to the old story,
one was black, one brown, and one white.
Each night one of the brothers caught his own horse in the early
      evening,
and in the glimmering darkness
he tried to ride it up a great glass hill
into that fairy kingdom.

And somewhere three beautiful horses,
with stars just under their forelocks
and hooves aglow in the moonlight,
nicker out of my childhood
and neigh in the distant meadows.
They stand at night in the pastures
with Bell and King and Beauty,
with Czar and Kate by the river
munching the grass by the timber
in the hills of northeastern Iowa,
wild in the harness of springtime,
tame in the woodland of summer;
with May and June, gray-dappled,
mild in their stalls in the winter,
trotting with sleighs and wagons,
straining at tugs in the snowdrifts,
farting out loud in the village,
working and sweating and sleeping;
with Roxy and Trixy and Mable,
biting and pawing and snorting
when led to the western stallion,
ears flat on their foreheads, breeding,
their nostrils flaring, kicking,
till their hind legs set like pillars;
with Daisy and Bill and Lady
chucking for oats in the morning,
chortling for hay in the evening,
and at county fairs with sulkeys
racing the silver jockeys
and galloping over the hillsides.

Left to right: NOBLE, QUEEN, BLOSSOM, DAISY. VALLEY VIEW
(LANGLAND FARM), WINNESHIEK COUNTY, IOWA, 1946.

My hands still fiddle with those bridles still,
the steel bits sliding over the white shining teeth,
past the dark elastic lips and pink tongues
swallowing into their soft throats.
I pull the reins taut; my arms tighten on their sleek muscles,
and again the polished hooves go clattering
out of the moonlit barnyard and on to the glass hill
where the breathless lady waits with her gossamer gowns and pale
    lips, chill as the night,
for the breath of her one true lover.

Daisy and Lady and Beauty,
we curry your hair in the morning,
your manes in the morning combing,
braiding your tails in the morning,
your velvet nostrils rubbing,
your rumps all silken, slapping;
on your barrel backs still climbing
I bury my face in your manes.
I snuggle my crotch on your withers,
my legs on your rib-flanks wrapping
to touch my feet to your belly.
And we walk and trot and gallop
out of the barns to the roadway
and up the road to the mailbox
and over the hills to the neighbors,
then back again to the barnyard
where I clean your stalls of manure
and bed you down for the evening
in bundles of golden straw.

Black Beauty, I think, is still whinnying in the orchards and
        weeping by waterfalls.
Postillions, coaches and schooners are running wild in their old
        tracks.
Flicka has tossed her tail up again west of Cheyenne and is headed
        into the mountains.
Smoky the Cowhorse is languishing in his harness,
trying to make that shriveled heart grow back again to full size.

The Red Pony and spotted horses are asleep in the bookshelves,
and Rosa Bonheur has scribbled magnificent horses all over the
        one-room schoolhouse wall.

Horses are standing by roadways,
charging over the sage-brush
in their oiled and studded saddles;
they are swimming the swollen rivers
through Wyoming, leaping and bucking
and plunging the dust-storms of cattle;
Old Paint is off to Montana,

walking the tourists in mountains
and standing by livery stables
and threshing grain on the prairies.

And somewhere in the local theaters of Spring Grove, Minnesota,
    and Decorah, Iowa,
legions of horses are rising and leaping out of the wild Atlantic
onto the Brittany beaches.
Their sea-weed manes are rising and falling, their hooves
rising and falling, the wind-driven grass rising
and falling over the dunes,
and the dark French rustlers with their stiff black hats
are throwing silver lariats everywhere out of the hills.

And the Good Men are riding their horses,
and the Bad Men riding their horses,
the stage coach is whipping its horses,
and the Indians are riding their horses,
and the Tartars are riding their horses,
and Ghenghis Khan and the Chinese
emperors riding their horses.
And horses are guarding the palace,
and Lawrence is riding his horses
with all his Arabians running
to the muffled drums of the sand.

And the great blue horses of Franz Marc
stand in Bavaria near Benedicktbeuren with their strict geometric
    rumps,
and Dutch horses wait near courtyards fat as burghers.
By the hay wains set by streams, horses are no more than a mound
    or a lamp-post.
And where is that young blue Spanish boy with his elegant mare?
Are they dreaming of blankets of flowers
falling over the pastel horses charging through steeple-chases out
    of the suburbs of Paris?
Or the cavalry milling by Moscow, the horses like dreary plains?
Or horses like trumpets and bugles falling, blood-stained, out of
    the sky?

There are princes arriving on chargers
and departing, forever and ever,
where the farm boys sleep with their horses,
and horses hidden in thickets
while the cavalry passes on horses,
and horses pressed against boulders
while the posse passes on horses,
and horses stilled in the hemlocks
while the murderers spur at their horses,
and the hunters go by on their horses
past rivers and castles and mountains.

And still the corporal is rearing upon his stallion in the Louvre,
and the generals sit stiffly astride their bronze studs
in all the public squares of Europe,
and Xanthus sulks with Achilles,
and Pegasus rides from the sea foam,
Al Borak carries Mohammed,
Bucephalus, Alexander,
and Sleipnir trots with Odin
out of the fjords to the ocean;
then out of the long processional friezes
where the marble horses twist and prance for the proud cities
Apollo rides straight up like thunder into the skies.

And the horses rear in the passes
with the horn of Roland winding
and Charlemagne riding his horses
And Joan of Arc at the crossroads
and the highwaymen riding their horses.
Brazilian horses are running,
and the listener sits in the moonlight,
alone on his horse in the moonlight.
Eohippus sleeps in the lavas,
and the Hittites' horses are running;
Mesohippus sleeps in the lavas;
the Persian horses are running.
In the steppes the horses are plunging,
with stars just under their forelocks;
they are galloping over the tundra;

they are leaping from mountain to mountain
with hooves aglow in the moonlight.
They have harnessed the waves of the ocean.
They are riding up over our beaches.
They are running wild in our cities.
I love you! I love you!

And then the brown horse and the black horse and the white
     horse
leaped so high in the moonlight that when they came back down
     there was only a dappled one,
and he floated up out of the back pastures over the hills of
     northeastern Iowa.
And when he came to your garden
where you sat in a blue dress on a pallet on the lawn,
his hooves rang like polished bells,
and he knelt on his silken hocks and knees by your side,
laid his slender head gently upon your lap,
looked up at your face with his marble eye,
then folded the silver membrane of his eyelid down,
and slept,
scarcely hearing the apocalypse
galloping away in the shadows.

DOLORES A. QUINN

By comparison with most of the authors in this collection, Dolores A. Quinn has not strayed far from Chicago's South Side where she was born just as the Century of Progress was ending its second season. Her maternal grandparents, like many Chicagoans at the turn of the century, were immigrants from Ireland. Her paternal grandfather was one of the city's first motion picture projectionists. His wife worked in the ballroom of White City, the amusement park left over from the 1893 Columbian Exposition.

Although she grew up in the Windy City and attended St. Theodore's Parochial School as her mother had, Dolores Quinn is as much a Chicago tourist in many respects as are all perennial visitors to this "heart" of the Midwest. In an autobiographical letter she wrote to me that she rode "the rocking red street cars to the sandy shores of Lake Michigan's 76th Street Beach." She rode, unchaperoned she emphasizes, "the trembling elevated trains across the city and into the damp, tunneled subway stations for a tour of Chicago's Loop." She "enjoyed endless days of prowling the posh hotels and huge department stores of downtown Chicago, explored the Museum of Science and Industry, the Field Museum, the Shedd Aquarium, the Adler Planetarium." But she "shied away from the Art Institute after being shocked and made giggly by the naked statues that flanked the exhibition halls." Like all tourists, she "took in all the sights of this marvelous city; the Lincoln Park Zoo and Buckingham Fountain were just an elevated train ride away."

Chicago's attractions were inexpensive in those days; they could be enjoyed for a day's expenditure of fifty cents, mostly gleaned from returning empty pop and milk bottles. Riverview Amusement Park, which became the big attraction for kids of all ages after White City closed, was a special bargain on Tuesdays, two-cents day.

The tamest rides were all 2¢ on Tuesdays, but even the daring roller coaster rides, the Bobs, the Blue Streak and the Silver Streak were only a nickel. One could be scared silly for at least two weeks to come with one stop at the Park's famous spook house, Aladdin's Castle. She squealed on the Flying Turns, the Parachute Drop, and airplanes that turned her upside down, back and forth, and spun around faster than the speed of light. For fifty cents, if she took a brown bag lunch, she could spend the whole day at Riverview Park and ride the Western Avenue streetcar back to the South Side just as the street lights would warn her she was late for dinner."

Dolores Quinn had the time of her life in the toddlin' town—not only on State Street, that Great Street, but all over town.
"How Green Was My Alley" is her first published story of Chicago. The editor of the Chicago Tribune Magazine *(which first printed this story) and I are hoping she'll write more.*

How Green Was My Alley

IF WE WERE a little apprehensive about taking the giant step to suburbia, it was only because we had both been born and raised in an aging Chicago neighborhood, and every house, every crack in the sidewalk, every church, school and store, were faithfully familiar. But our old, two-story frame home was forever in need of repair, and the new suburban home with its gleaming aluminum siding and double-pane windows would be a snap to maintain. We were comfortable enough in this new sculptured setting; decorating and unpacking brought additional excitement and a rush of activity.

It was while I was unpacking and trying to get rid of empty crates and boxes that I felt the first pains of homesickness and frustration. Something was missing here: the odorous main artery, the posterior of all city dwelling, was absent from the suburban scene. Our unassuming, versatile, beloved alley was gone, and I was reminiscently depressed.

The alley was our Disneyland to all us kids growing up in Chicago in the 1940's; certainly it was infinitely more important than a place for discarded rubbish. It was our perpetual playground. Although we didn't have plastic swimming pools or backyard swing sets, we did have the supreme pathway to excitement—"our alley."

To a passer-by it was just another alley, lined with garbage cans, garages, and, in season, gardens of hollyhocks and phlox. To us, however, it was an enchanted castle, a frontier fort, a yellow brick road.

Towering over the far end of our alley stood a forbidding red-brick wall, an imposing structure, at least nine feet tall, flanked by two grotesque lion heads. A mammoth wooden gate, bolted tight on the inside, secured the courtyard of a huge apartment building against the taunting eyes of unwelcome intruders. The wall and the gate challenged the imagination of all of our neighborhood's mighty-mites. Ghost stories came alive as we hoisted one another higher and higher to the top of the grim wall. A quick glance beyond the maze of graying wooden porches and then the startled gasp of the viewer. "It's him, Crazy John." I could hear his thunderous roar as the gate bolt slid open and I tumbled to the ground. Crazy John, the caretaker, came running in murderous pursuit, threatening us with his broom and shouting obscenities after us as we fled down the alley. I was running so fast I though my heart would burst from my body. Safely inside my own back yard, I threw myself on the grass to catch my breath. I knew that tomorrow we'd go back to the great brick wall and start the game again.

In the early predawn hours, unburdened by mischievous offenders, the chalk-white milk truck rolled daily into our alley. It moved quietly to its prearranged stops, making its predictable deliveries. But the milkman would whistle and hum in perfect rhythm with the containers clinking behind him in his truck. His snow-white uniform and cap matched the contents of the bottles. He maneuvered his truck gracefully, one hand braced against the always-open door, his derriere just barely touching his stool-like seat, his body tilting forward at a slight angle—he drove in a standing position. In a few quick strides he could reach each back porch; then, taking two steps at a time, he'd be at the back door. If there was no one there to take the creamy milk, he would slip the bottle into an insulated metal box provided for that purpose. How I loved to get to the milk before my Mother and sip the cream that rose to the top of the bottle.

Later in the morning we'd hear "Rags, old iron, rags, old iron." It was the junkman, clip-clopping and chattering in his rickety wagon, drawn by two even more rickety mares. The junkman himself matched the stuff he picked up, and I was a little afraid of him—but not so afraid that I didn't run to the alley when I heard his call. Horses in the alley were always exciting, and all of us neighborhood

DOLORES QUINN, RIVERVIEW PARK, MAY 1948, AND THE RIVERVIEW PARK ROLLER COASTER, 1930s.

kids turned out to see those work-worn creatures, swishing their tails and stomping their hooves to discourage the army of flies which had taken up residence on their hides. Looking at us, the horses would roll their heads from side to side and grin widely to show huge, yellowed teeth. Behind them, the wagon was piled high with old, rusty bed springs and bundles of old Chicago newspapers. As the junkman moved on down the alley, we'd mock his call in the alley's own language: "Rags, o-lion, rags, o-lion."

In those days, many of the neighborhood families, like our own, still used wooden ice-boxes. It was the super treat of the day to catch Joe's ice truck making deliveries. Joe was a grumbly character, and we'd hide behind the garage when we saw him coming along the alley. His truck had thick wooden walls and was open at the top and back. His cold, crystal cargo was covered with an aging, smelly tarpaulin. Joe was a somber hulk of a man who wore a thick, gray quilted pad over one shoulder and down his back. We'd watch in silence as he stepped up to the high flatbed of his truck and begin chopping away at a block of ice, using a menacing-looking ice pick. Shoving the ice block to the edge of the truck, he would grasp it firmly with his great iron tongs and sling it deftly to his padded shoulder. As soon as Joe headed into the yard we'd make our move: a quick dash to the truck to relish those slivers of ice left from the chipping. But Joe was fast, superfast, and before we could get our hands and mouths full of those tingly ice chips, he was back. He would be raving mad, shouting after us as we ran down the alley and darted between garages and fences. We didn't look back until we heard the roar of his engine moving on to the next stop.

Darkness promised new adventures as all the kids gathered to play "kick the can" or "hide and seek." At night, the alley was forbiddingly dark and spooky; we loved it. There were dim street lights on the far corners; their eerie, mellow glow dared the timid to enter. In the summer we could stay up later, unnoticed by our parents who were escaping the heat visiting with friends out on the front porches. "Kick the can" was the noisy favorite in our alley; and sometimes a garbage can or two got knocked over in the excitement and tomatoes growing too near a back fence had a way of disappearing. Often kids from surrounding blocks joined in the fun. "Olee, olee, all in free; new player." I waited to hear this call so I could come out of my hiding place and the game could start anew. I always thought the call was "olee, olee, ocean free," but my husband says it was "all in free"; his version, at least, makes sense.

We played basketball, jump-rope and hopscotch, but the most rewarding and spirited fun of all came from "alley picking." For this, we often strayed from our own alley because "the grass was always greener." We searched through discarded boxes and bags to find our treasures: a rollerskate, a chipped bowl, half a can of paint, bicycle handlebars, a doll's head, an old motor. For longer excursions we pulled a trusty red wagon; on one of these my best friend and I came upon the most unforgettable find of all. It was a tall, marble-like vase with a heavy metal base; the opening at the top had been sealed. Centered on one side was an ornate, golden oval frame, surrounding the photo of a lovely lady. Gently and with great care we rushed our prize home, sure that its value was priceless. But when we confronted my mother with our magnificent vase, her face was a sight to behold. She gasped and screamed and made the sign of the cross (mothers did not practice psychology when we were growing up). "Get it out of here. It's a funeral urn. Take it back where you found it." Her voice was threatening, but I had never heard of a funeral urn so I pursued the issue. In a wavering choke, she reluctantly explained that the vase contained the ashes of a dead person, the lady in the photograph. Now it was our turn to have the daylights frightened out of us. The entire story sounded weird in our ears. Sadly my girlfriend and I went out the back door, carrying our now-depressing treasure back to its resting place in the alley. Mother's tirade, however, led us into a discussion of the ashes of the deceased. In school we had learned about ashes to ashes and dust to dust, but never had we been told about ashes being put into a beautiful vase. In the end we decided that my mother had lost a marble or two and that the best solution was to smash the vase and resolve the dilemma. And that's just what we did. With a quick thrust, we shattered the vase, spewing a small pile of ashes across the alley. How innocent and irreverent we were. The alley that had been our playground was now the lovely lady's cemetery.

The alley was our short-cut to the corner grocer's and to my girl-friend's house, and it was our passage to adventure. It was the place where Dads fixed cars on Saturdays, and where the neighbors held alley rallies with beer, soda and games. The alley was mysterious, festive, and fun, and was a place where I could have put all those empty crates and boxes.

Garrison Keillor was born in 1942 in Anoka, a Minneapolis suburb, and grew up in another northwestern suburb, Brooklyn Park, in a big white house his father built. "It was a lovely green place," Keillor recalls in an article entitled "What Do You Do? (How much do you earn?)" published for Minnesota Public Radio in 1977, "with a cornfield across the road, a deep twisting ravine behind the house and dry creek bed with big rocks where we made camps and forts, and just over the hill the Mississippi to swim in and skate and skip stones."

His father, a free-lance carpenter, was also a clerk in the Railway Mail Service. He rode the Great Northern's Empire Builder from St. Paul to Jamestown, North Dakota, threw off the heavy sacks of mail at small towns, and wore a .38 revolver strapped to his hip. "I was proud of him," Keillor wrote.

Despite his father's two occupations, there were worries about money. Yet the family's lack of money didn't become terribly important to Keillor until he was in high school. Somehow making a connection between money and intelligence, between money and culture, Keillor began buying The New Yorker *and carrying it openly "as a sign of Class." But he also read the magazine and began cultivating an ambition to write for it.*

In sharing such ambitions with other children of the working class, Keillor suggests that he and his peers betrayed their own class; they viewed its members as "not too bright. The secret desire [is] to be like the Kennedys, graceful and easy and liberal and rich."

Keillor went to the University of Minnesota and earned a B.A. in English in 1966. He continued graduate studies until 1968 and at the same time worked as an announcer for the university radio station. In his own words, he "lucked" into an announcing and producing job with Minnesota Public Radio.

Keillor presently lives on the St. Croix River thirty-odd miles north of the studios of KSJN, Minnesota Public Radio, in downtown St. Paul. Four mornings a week he leaves home at 4:00 A.M. because from 6:00 to 9:00 A.M.—prime time in radio—he conducts the "Prairie Home Morning Show." Saturday evenings he works late—his "Prairie Home Companion" radio show, originally heard all over Minnesota and in parts of the Dakotas, Wisconsin, and Iowa, is now heard nationally. It's the entertainment descendant of such old-time radio greats as the "Grand Ole

Opry" and the "Louisiana Hayride." It can now be seen and heard in a touring version personally conducted by Keillor.

Keillor, tall (over six feet), black bearded, and gentlefaced, comments that as an announcer on public radio he is a poorly paid radio personality entertaining the wealthy; if he were on commercial radio, he'd be a wealthy man entertaining the working class!

Keillor recognizes the irony of having to take time off from his radio work to further his career as a writer. Writing time is not easily come by; "If you do radio work well," he admits, "you have little time for anything else."

Since 1969 Keillor has published over fifteen stories and a few poems in his old high school handbook, The New Yorker, and stories and poems in other periodicals. William Shawn, editor of The New Yorker, which Keillor calls "A hard-working magazine devoted to writers," likes Keillor's work, although he often returns the original manuscript with "dozens of simple and direct queries" blue pencilled in the margins.

For artists and writers, Keillor acknowledges "the pleasure is in the doing, not in talking about it or being done with it." When he does talk about writing, he's concerned about writers who "mingle with wealth." He thinks that writers and artists may have a lot more in common with the working class than with bankers and businessmen. The latter have too much "concern with goals, with status, with accomplishment." Writers, artists and workers "just do the work and get out."

Drowning 1954

WHEN I WAS TWELVE, my cousin Roger drowned in Lake Independence, and my mother enrolled me in a swimming class at the Y.M.C.A. on La Salle Avenue, in downtown Minneapolis. Twice a week for most of June and July, I got on the West River Road bus near our home in Brooklyn Park township, a truck-farming community north of Minneapolis, and rode into the stink and heat of the city, and when I rounded the corner of Ninth Street and La Salle and smelled the chlorine air that the Y.M.C.A. breathed out I started to feel afraid. After a week, I couldn't bear swimming class anymore.

Never before had I stood naked among strangers (the rule in the class was no swimming trunks), and it was loathsome to undress and then walk quickly through the showers to the pool and sit shivering on the cold tiles along the edge with my feet dangling in the water (Absolute Silence, No Splashing) and wait for the dread moment. The instructor—a man in his early twenties, who was tanned and had the smooth muscles of a swimmer (he wore trunks)—had us plunge into the pool one at a time, so that he could give us his personal attention. He strode up and down the side of the pool yelling at those of us who couldn't swim, while we thrashed hopelessly beneath him and tried to look like swimmers. "You're walking on the bottom!" he would shout. "Get your legs up! What's the matter, you afraid to get your face wet? What's wrong with you?" The truth was that my cousin's death had instilled in me a terrible fear, and when I tried to swim and started to sink it felt not so much like I was sinking but as if something was pulling me down. I panicked, every time. It was just like the dreams of drowning that came to me right after Roger died, in which I was dragged deeper and deeper, with my body bursting and my arms and legs flailing against nothing, down and down, until I shot back to the surface and lay in my dark bedroom exhausted, trying to make myself stay awake.

I tried to quit the swimming class, but my mother wouldn't hear of it, so I continued to board the bus every swimming morning, and then, ashamed of myself and knowing God would punish me for my cowardice and deceit, I hurried across La Salle and past the Y and walked along Hennepin Avenue, past the pinball parlors and bars and shoeshine stands, to the old Public Library, where I viewed the Egyptian mummy and the fossils and a facsimile of the Declaration of Independence. I stayed there until eleven-thirty, when I headed straight for the WCCO radio studio to watch "Good Neighbor Time."

We listened regularly to this show at home—Bob DeHaven, with Wally Olson and His Band, and Ernie Garvin and Burt Hanson and Jeanne Arland—and then to the noontime news, with Cedric Adams, the most famous man in the upper Midwest. It amazed me to sit in the studio audience and watch the little band crowded against the back wall, the engineers in the darkened booth, and the show people gliding up to a microphone for a song, a few words, or an Oxydol commercial. I loved everything except the part of the show in which Bob DeHaven interviewed people in the audience. I was afraid he might pick me, and then my mother, and probably half of Minnesota, would find out that I was scared of water, and a liar to boot. The radio stars dazzled me. One day, I squeezed into the WCCO elevator with Cedric Adams and five or six other people. I

RAILROAD MAIL CLERKS ABOUT 1900.

stood next to him, and a sweet smell of greatness and wealth drifted off from him. I later imagined Cedric Adams swimming in Lake Minnetonka—a powerful whale of happiness and purpose—and I wished that I were like him and the others, but as the weeks wore on I began to see clearly that I was more closely related to the bums and winos and old men who sat around in the library and wandered up and down Hennepin Avenue. I tried to look away and not see them, but they were all around me there, and almost every day some poor ragged creature, filthy drunk at noon, would stagger at me wildly out of a doorway, with his arms stretched out toward me, and I saw a look of fellowship in his eyes: *You are one of us.*

I ran from them, but clearly I was well on my way. Drinking and all the rest of the bum's life would come with time, inevitably. My life was set on its tragic course by a sinful error in youth. This was the dark theme of the fundamentalist Christian tracts in our home: one misstep! A lie, perhaps, or disobedience to your mother. There were countless young men in those tracts who stumbled and fell from the path—one misstep!—and were dragged down, like drowning men, into debauchery, unbelief, and utter damnation. I felt sure that my lie, which was repeated twice a week and whenever my mother asked about my swimming, was sufficient for my downfall. Even as I worked at the deception, I marvelled that my fear of water should be greater than my fear of Hell.

I still remember the sadness of wandering in downtown Minneapolis in 1954, wasting my life and losing my soul, and my great relief when the class term ended and I became a kid again around the big white house and garden, the green lawns and cool shady ravine of our lovely suburb. A weekend came when we went to a lake for a family picnic, and my mother, sitting on the beach, asked me to swim for her, but I was able to fool her, even at that little distance, by walking on the bottom and making arm strokes.

When I went to a lake with my friends that summer, I did get it—the crawl and the backstroke and the sidestroke, all in just a couple of weeks. I dived from a dock and opened my eyes underwater and everything. The sad part was that my mother and father couldn't appreciate this wonderful success; to them, I had been a swimmer all along. I felt restored—grateful that I would not be a bum all my life, grateful to God for letting me learn to swim. It was so quick and so simple that I can't remember it today. Probably I just stood in the water and took a little plunge; my feet left the bottom, and that was it.

Now my little boy, who is seven, shows some timidity around water. Everytime I see him standing in the shallows, working up nerve to put his head under, I love him more. His eyes are closed tight, and his pale slender body is tense as a drawn bow, ready to spring up instantly should he start to drown. Then I feel it all over again, the way I used to feel. I also feel it when I see people like the imperial swimming instructor at the Y.M.C.A.—powerful people who delight in towering over some little twerp who is struggling and scared, and casting the terrible shadow of their just and perfect selves. The Big Snapper knows who you are, you bastards, and in a little while he is going to come after you with a fury you will not believe and grab you in his giant mouth and pull you under until your brain turns to jelly and your heart almost bursts. You will never recover from this terror. You will relive it every day, as you lose your fine job and your home and the respect of your friends and family. You will remember it every night, in your little room at the Mission, and you will need a quart of Petri muscatel to put you to sleep, and when you awake between your yellow-stained sheets your hands will start to shake all over again.

You have fifteen minutes. Get changed.

JOHN R. POWERS

![decorative flower ornament] *Although John R. Powers (whose real name is John J[ames] Powers) graduated in the bottom twentieth of his Chicago parochial high school class, and was the only student in the school's history to flunk music appreciation, he managed in the next dozen years to earn a Ph.D.* from Northwestern University, to become a professor of speech at Northeastern Illinois University, to become a columnist for the Chicago Daily News, *and to publish three books. The first two were fictionalized memoirs of his twelve years of Catholic grade and high school education:* The Last Catholic in America *(1973) and* Do Black Patent Leather Shoes Really Reflect Up? *(1975). The third, a novel,* The Unoriginal Sinner and the Ice-Cream God *(1977), focuses on the college training of a Chicago South Side Catholic, Tim Conroy, in a near North Side city college. The popularity of Powers's books is shown by their continuing publication in paperback form. A musical comedy version of* Do Black Patent Leather Shoes Really Reflect Up? *began an extended run in Chicago's Forum Theater in 1979; the play was scheduled for a Broadway premiere in late 1980.*

*Powers's trilogy is the second literary trilogy to focus on the adolescence of a South Side Chicago Catholic youth. Forty years earlier, James T. Farrell, in his Studs Lonigan trilogy (*Young Lonigan: A Boyhood in Chicago *[1932];* The Young Manhood of Studs Lonigan *[1934];* Judgement Day *[1935]) had traced with comprehensive realistic detail the fantasies and self-destructive tendencies that led to Studs's untimely death. Powers's memoirs focus on the misadventures of Eddie Ryan, a bumbling boy in the antihero tradition of current literature. Both Studs and Eddie have problems with the institution of parochial education: Studs's antagonists at St. Patrick's grammar school are Battleaxe Bertha and Father Gilhooley. Eddie's tormentors at St. Bastion's grade school are Dynamite Diane, Cyril the Savage, Boom Boom Bernadine, and ninety-year-old Sister Lee. When Studs thinks of his schoolday experiences he thinks of them with rancor; Eddie reacts to his teachers with sharp wit and a smart tongue.*

Tim Conroy, the college student–narrator of Powers's third book, is a grown-up Eddie Ryan who sandwiches four love affairs between slices of education and finds more guidance in Caepan, a gas station owner, than he does from his teachers. Caepan is the God of the novel, and he and Conroy constantly exchange notes:

Dear God:
>I didn't go to mass last Sunday morning.
>Signed: Conroy

Conroy:
>Don't worry about it. It was a nice day. I don't know who built the church but I made the sunshine.
>Signed: God

So far, Powers's needling of three major American institutions—the Roman Catholic Church, the Cub Scouts, and college education—has not led to excommunicaton, expulsion, or any other form of retribution. Quite the opposite has taken place; higher education has made him a part of the institution. The Catholic Sentinel *has praised him, saying that "John Powers does for Catholics what Erma Bombeck does for house-wives." (My own analogy would have utilized Art Buchwald.) And* Scouting, *the official organ of the Boy Scouts of America, spread "Some Great Moments in Sloppy Scouting" over its centerfold.*

Some Great Moments in Sloppy Scouting

CONTRARY TO POPULAR FOLKLORE, Cub Scouts do not spend all their time helping old ladies cross the street. In my neighborhood, they couldn't have. There weren't enough old ladies to go around. Larry Gogel, who lived a few doors down from me, owned one. She was his grandmother, I think. All she ever did was sit in the kitchen. She had no desire to cross the living room much less the street.

In the neighborhood of Seven Holy Tombs, Cub Scouting was a lot more than simply collecting bundles of old newspapers on Saturday mornings. It was the training wheels of life and was as much a part of growing up as breaking bones and getting pimples. There was something wrong with a boy's glands if he didn't become a Cub Scout. Boys who didn't join Scouting seemed to grow up strangely. But then, how can you expect a kid to mature properly when he's never dressed like an Indian?

It was Sunday afternoon and my eighth birthday, the age when one normally joins the Cub Scouts. I was due to be initiated into the Scouts the following day. As I walked through the kitchen, my mother told me that my father, who was outside in the backyard painting the fence, wanted to see me.

The first eight years of my life had been somewhat less than impressive. In school, I had started out in the highest reading group, the Robins, but was quickly demoted to the Sparrows. My nun once remarked that she was thinking of creating a new group just for me called the Droppings. My mother made me quit the Pee Wee Baseball League because I kept getting lost on the way home from the park. I even got the feeling that some of my imaginary friends considered me a loser.

When I got to the backyard, my father was squatting next to the fence, painting the pickets.

"You wanted to see me, Dad?" He didn't look up. He just kept painting.

"Yes, son," he said. "Tomorrow is a real big day in your life, as you know. Tomorrow night, you'll wear the blue and gold uniform of a Cub Scout. Your mother and I feel this is a very important step in your life. It's a sign that you're maturing, that you're growing up. You know what I mean, son?"

"Yeah, Dad, I know what you mean." I leaned on the fence.

"I realize that things in the past have not always worked out for you," my father said as he continued to paint the fence, "but I'm sure that as a Cub Scout, you're going to make everyone very proud of you." He looked up from the picket he was painting and saw me leaning on the fence.

"Hey, get your hand off the fence. I just painted there."

I jerked my arm away and looked at my hand. It was loaded with paint. "Sorry, Dad."

He mumbled something about illegitimacy and went back to painting the pickets.

My father was right. I had blown the first eight years of my life. It was time to grow up. I went next door to find out from Demented David, who had already been a Cub Scout for two years, how one went about making it big in the Scouts.

"Nothin' to it," Demented David told me. "All you have to do to impress your parents is to get Mr. Barnum, the pack leader, to think you're a hotshot. Do a nice job in something, like singing or hiking. If Mr. Barnum notices you, at the next pack meeting he'll lead the whole pack in giving you three cheers." Demented David demonstrated, flinging his fist into the air each time he yelled, "Hip hip hurrah, hip hip hurrah, hip hip hurrah. Most of the parents go to the pack meeting," Demented David continued, "and when they hear their kid getting hip hip hurrahed, they go wild."

"What's a pack?" I asked.

"All the Cub Scouts in each neighborhood made up a 'pack,' which has as its name a four-digit number," Demented David said. "Then each pack is divided into a number of dens made up of nine or ten guys and a den mother."

"And all I have to do to get hip hip hurrahed at a pack meeting is to have Mr. Barnum notice me doing a nice job in something?"

"That's all," said Demented David.

The pack meeting that Monday night was held in the parkhouse. The meeting began with the Pledge of Allegiance and then Mr. Barnum handed out badges to about twenty different Cub Scouts. After each Cub Scout received his badge, Mr. Barnum would yell, "How about three cheers for . . ." (whoever it was) and while punching our fists into the air, we'd all yell, "Hip hip hurrah, hip hip hurrah, hip hip hurrah." After about forty thousand "hip hip hurrahs," Mr. Barnum welcomed us new Cub Scouts.

"As Cub Scouts, boys," said Mr. Barnum, "you will acquire many new skills that you, as an adult, will need later on in life. You'll be taught to make model airplanes, shoeshine kits, and Mother's Day cards. You will learn how to survive in the wilderness with nothing but two sticks and a Clark Bar."

Mr. Barnum went on to teach us the Cub Scout pledge, sign, handshake, and the secret writing. Mr. Barnum also told us about the three Cub Scout books: the *Wolf Book,* the *Bear Book,* and the *Lion Book.* We would receive badges for completing the exercises and challenges in each book, Mr. Barnum said. Actually, the books sounded like parents between covers.

Mr. Barnum also informed the new members of Pack 3838 that the key word in Cub Scouting was "akela," which was the "secret" word used to refer to a good leader. A good leader included Mr. Barnum, den mothers, parents, and basically anyone taller than a Cub Scout.

"Of course," said Mr. Barnum, "as Cub Scouts you will be trained to be good followers. Good leaders," said Mr. Barnum, "are good followers."

Later in life, I discovered that statement to be untrue. Good leaders are rotten followers because they're always gunning to be leaders.

SCOUTING.

"Now," said Mr. Barnum, "we're going to do something that all Cub Scouts love to do, sing." He held up his hands as if he were allowing them to drip dry. "And remember, men, use those hands to express the words of the song."

This was what I had been waiting for: an area of skill in which I could immediately establish my supremacy. I limbered up my fingers, ready to perform to perfection the dictations of the song.

Mr. Barnum started us off. "One, two, three . . ."

> Do your ears hang low,
> Do they wobble to and fro,
> Can you tie them in a knot,
> Can you tie them in a bow.
> Can you throw them over your shoulders
> like a Continental soldier, do your ears hang low.

That is not an easy song in which to excel. At first I was panic-stricken. I couldn't do any of the things the song said. My ears didn't hang low, they didn't wobble to and fro. I couldn't tie them in a knot or tie them in a bow. I looked around at the other Cub Scouts.

They weren't doing any of those things either. They were just waving their hands around their ears as Mr. Barnum was doing up in front of us.

The next song consumed by our lungs was the national anthem of all Cub Scouts, the "Itsy Bitsy Spider" song.

> The itsy bitsy spider ran up the water spout,
> Down came the rain and washed the spider out.
> Up came the sun and dried up all the rain,
> And the itsy bitsy spider crawled up the spout again.

We sang the "Itsy Bitsy Spider" song about fourteen times, each round faster than the previous one. This entire song is accompanied by intricate finger movements, none of them obscene. Such intricate finger movements are not learned in one night of "Itsy Bitsy Spider" singing. Considering I was a novice, I did fairly well except when "the itsy bitsy spider ran up the water spout." I almost broke my thumb. You do not get cheered for that, not even in the Cub Scouts.

I was assigned to Mrs. Dunnewater's den and a week later attended my first den meeting.

Mrs. Dunnewater was perhaps the only woman in the world to ever earn a double-figure income as a crossing guard. She had a habit of throwing herself in front of cars and collecting the insurance money. People became suspicious when she managed to get herself run over on a Saturday afternoon. After suddenly finding herself retired from the crossing-guard force, Mrs. Dunnewater, her fortune made, turned philanthropist and became a den mother for Pack 3838.

Demented David was in my den. He was convinced that the Cub Scouts were destined to become a military power and, marching to the "Itsy Bitsy Spider" song, go off and totally annihilate the Girl Scouts from the face of the earth, among them Demented David's older sister, who, I admit, deserved to be annihilated. Two other members of the den were Bobby Felgen, a massive piece of flesh whose personality was very much like those who leave money under your pillow when you lose a tooth, and Anthony Trielli, who wanted nothing more out of life than to be vice-president of the United States.

At the den meeting, Mrs. Dunnewater announced that Pack 3838's candy drive was beginning. We could pick up our boxes of candy at the next meeting.

This was my chance. I would become a super salesman and lead the pack in selling Cub Scout candy. No doubt I would be rewarded by a standing ovation of three cheers at the next pack meeting. I realized that this would be no minor achievement as Cub Scout candy tasted like chocolate-covered grease. But I knew I could do it. Besides, I had a lot of relatives living in the neighborhood.

On the way home from the meeting, I told Demented David of my plans.

"Forget it," he said, "you'll never beat Alex Schietzer."

"Why? Does he have that many relatives in the neighborhood?"

"No," Demented David said, "he can actually sell the stuff to total strangers. Really, I've seen him. He gets this sappy look on his face and just about cries on the front porch if someone says no to him."

It wasn't even close. Alex beat me by forty-seven boxes and three hip hip hurrahs.

Every year, Pack 3838 marched in the Fourth of July parade. Mr. Barnum always gave an award, and three cheers, to the Cub Scout who was the best marcher or, as Mr. Barnum said, "demonstrated the best cadence." That year, I was determined to win it. I needed the three cheers.

For an entire week before the parade, I practiced marching in the backyard. In order to simulate the actual marching conditions of a parade, I got up early one morning before school and marched in the deserted street in front of my house. I was unable, however, to simulate the marching conditions created by walking directly behind an elephant, which was where I marched that Fourth of July. Marching elephants have a way of destroying one's cadence. Fortunately, at the next pack meeting, the elephant did not received three cheers for his efforts. Unfortunately, neither did I.

In late August, Pack 3838 held its annual Pow Wow Weekend. Pow Wow Weekend was a time when all good Cub Scouts and their parents left the comfort of their homes to dress up like Indians and spend two days in a flat-chested, pock-marked forest preserve. It was forty-eight hours of dodging falling tent poles and two-hundred-pound mosquitoes while consuming metallic well water, warm pop, cold hot dogs, and charcoal-coated hamburgers.

During Pow Wow Weekend, there were two excellent opportunities to earn three cheers. The first was in the softball game against another Cub Scout pack, Pack 3841. The second opportunity came at the very end of the Pow Wow Weekend, when the Indian-dancing contest was held.

There was little chance to grab glory in the softball game. Our pack leader, Mr. Barnum, didn't believe in having anyone ride the bench, so he played everyone in the pack for the entire game. Instead of nine men on the field, we had seventy-five.

In the first inning, thirty others and I were standing in left field. A fly ball was hit right at me. As is customary in the softball world, I yelled, "I've got it," so that no one would run into me. Simultaneously, I heard seventy-four other guys rushing at me yelling, "I've got it." No one got it.

I didn't get to bat. With seventy-five kids in the lineup, the average player got to swing a bat for Pack 3838 once every two years.

We lost, 33 to 12, a relatively tight game by Cub Scout standards. Naturally, we gave the other team three cheers for beating us to death. Hip hip hurrah, hip hip hurrah, hip hip hurrah.

The softball game was played on Friday night. Saturday and Sunday of Pow Wow Weekend progressed smoothly. Only three kids had to be carried off by ambulance. Two of them ran into trees and the third kid managed to swallow the apple during the apple-bobbing contest.

All kinds of things went on during those two days: gunny-sack races, pie-baking contests, tugs-of-war. But I was after bigger things. I spent the two days inside my tent practicing my Indian dancing in preparation for the Indian-dancing championship that was to be held Sunday night at the close of the Pow Wow Weekend.

A rigid training schedule was followed. First, I would spend twenty minutes Indian dancing: my body crouched appropriately, the head bobbing, the tails of the Indian headdress weaving behind my back, the mouth producing perfect Indian grunts as my hand rhythmically shuttered over it, and the gym shoes shuffling smoothly under my body. The next twenty minutes would be spent doing push-ups and running around the tent. Conditioning is very important in Indian dancing.

Jerome Bizybinski had won the Indian-dancing championship for the past two years. It wasn't a case of Jerome being so good as it was of Jerome's competition being so bad. Kids who had seen both of us dance said that I definitely had Jerome outclassed. Already I could hear Mr. Barnum announcing me as the new Indian-dancing champion, followed by three lusty cheers from my fellow Cub Scouts. Hip hip hurrah, hip hip hurrah, hip hip hurrah.

I wasted no time during the Pow Wow Weekend going to the outhouse. Unlike the bathroom at home, the outhouse didn't smell of Lysol. Besides the odor, there were hundreds of flies around the outhouse. Most of the guys who used the outhouse held their breaths the whole time they were in there. I couldn't hold my breath that long so I figured I'd just skip the whole process until I got back home.

Demented David warned me that it wasn't a good idea to do that. He had done the same thing the previous year and had gotten a case of constipation that crippled him for two weeks.

The Indian-dancing contest was the climax of the Pow Wow Weekend. After dark, a big bonfire would be built and all the members of the pack would sit in a large circle around it. Each contestant would then stand up and do his stuff. After the winner was announced, the entire pack would Indian-dance around the bonfire. It was a very impressive sight.

The first five contestants were strictly passé. Then Jerome Bizybinski came on. Jerome's dancing was good. Not great, but good. He had a few cute twirls and he kept his head bobbing nicely. But his dance fell far below the routine I was about to unravel around that campfire.

As I was watching Bizybinski dance, I suddenly realized that my legs were turning to concrete. Gastric pains were spreading from the base of my neck to my ankles. My mouth was dehydrating.

Jerome Bizybinski finished dancing and received healthy applause from the circle around the campfire. I tried to stand up but the pain in my stomach forced me into a crouch. Fortunately, a good Indian dancer performs in a crouch so this was no problem. As I shuffled toward the campfire, I noticed the hungry look of anticipation on my fellow Scouts' faces. Word of my skill had spread. They were waiting to witness an upset.

I slowly began dancing. My feet were hardly leaving the ground. I was afraid that if I bobbed my head, it would fall off. There was stunned silence. This was the man who was going to replace Jerome Bizybinski as the Indian-dancing champion of Pack 3838?

Mr. Barnum coughed nervously, stood up, and said mechanically, "Very, very good. Now, Scouts, let's sing a few songs around the campfire while the judges decide who is going to be the new Indian-dancing champion of Pack 3838."

A few speckles of applause bid me farewell as I crawled through the circle of singing Cub Scouts and into my tent. I lay coiled on the ground, my Indian headdress hovering over my forehead. Through the blur of agony I could hear them chant.

"The itsy bitsy spider ran up the water spout, down came the rain and washed the spider out, up came the sun and . . . Let's have three cheers for Jerome Bizybinski! Hip hip hurrah, hip hip hurrah, hip hip hurrah."

GWENDOLYN   BROOKS

Karl Shapiro, formerly editor of Poetry *magazine, suggests that "Poetry, as we know it, remains the most lily-white of the arts." He might have supported his assertion by naming the few well-known black women poets—Margaret Walker, Toni Morrison, Lerone Bennett, Sonia Sanchez, and Gwendolyn Brooks. Of these, the name that most people would recognize would be that of Gwendolyn Brooks.*

Gwendolyn Brooks was born in 1917 in Topeka, Kansas, but soon moved with her family to Chicago. In her home the black American author Paul Lawrence Dunbar was a household idol and all of his two-dozen books were available. She wrote her first sheet of rhymes at seven, had a few poems published in black newspapers when she was eleven, and had her poem "Eventide" published in American Childhood Magazine *when she was thirteen.*

She graduated from Chicago's Wilson Junior College in 1936 and in 1939 married Henry L. Blakely. The Blakelys have two children, Nora and Henry L. Although some women authors have said they had to make a choice between motherhood and authorship, Gwendolyn Brooks concludes that being a wife and mother enriched and nourished her work.

Her first book of verse, A Street in Bronzeville, *was published in 1945, the year* Madamoiselle *magazine named her one of its Ten Women of the Year. Bronzeville is the term applied to the predominantly black South Side neighborhood of Chicago that centers on Forty-seventh Street and the former South Parkway, now Martin Luther King Drive. The lines that follow are from "Of DeWitt Williams on His Way to Lincoln Cemetery" in* A Street in Bronzeville:

> Drive him past the Pool Hall.
> Drive him past the Show.
> Blind within his casket,
> But maybe he will know.
>
> Down through Forty-Seventh Street:
> Underneath the L,
> And—Northwest Corner, Prairie,
> That he loved so well.

Don't forget the Dance Halls—
Warwick and Savoy,
Where he picked his women, where
He drank his liquid joy.

Several awards followed the generally favorable reviews of her first book; in 1946, a creative writing award from the American Academy of Arts and Letters and a Guggenheim fellowship for creative writing in 1946 and 1947. Her next volume of verse, Annie Allen *(1949) won her the 1950 Pulitzer Poetry Prize:*

Maxie Allen always taught her
Stipendiary little daughter
To thank her Lord and lucky star
For eyes that let her see so far,
For throat enabling her to eat
Her Quaker Oats and Cream of Wheat,
For tongue to tantrum for the penny,
For ear to hear the haven't-any.
For arm to toss, for leg to chance,
For heart to hanker for romance.

Recognition has continued for Gwendolyn Brooks—the Anisfield-Wolf Award in 1969, and in that same year, selection as Poet Laureate of Illinois to succeed the late Carl Sandburg.

She recalls her life and experience in the Midwest as a "peoply" one, and concludes that people in the Midwest pay more attention to people *than to* nature.

Her later books are Maud Martha *(novel, 1953);* Bronzeville Boys and Girls *(children's verse, 1956);* Bean Eaters *(1960);* Selected Poems *(1963);* In the Mecca *(1968);* Riot *(1969);* Family Pictures *(1970);* Aloneness *(1971);* Report from Part One *(autobiography, 1972). She has also edited the magazine* The Black Position *and has taught poetry writing at several Chicago area colleges and at seven or eight prisons and penitentiaries.*

"The Life of Lincoln West," like Langston Hughes's "One Christmas Eve," shows blacks trying to cope in a world where white values and antiblack attitudes predominate. But Lincoln West has a problem that many of us, black or white, will be able to empathize with.

The Life of Lincoln West

Ugliest little boy
that everyone ever saw.
That is what everyone said.

Even to his mother it was apparent—
when the blue-aproned nurse came into the
northeast end of the maternity ward
bearing his squeals and plump bottom
looped up in a scant receiving blanket,
bending, to pass the bundle carefully
into the waiting mother-hands—that this
was no cute little ugliness, no sly baby waywardness
that was going to inch away
as would baby fat, baby curl, and
baby spot-rash. The pendulous lip, the
branching ears, the eyes so wide and wild,
the vague unvibrant brown of the skin,
and, most disturbing, the great head.
These components of That Look bespoke
the sure fibre. The deep grain.

His father could not bear the sight of him.
His mother high-piled her pretty dyed hair and
put him among her hairpins and sweethearts,
dance slippers, torn paper roses.
He was not less than these,
he was not more.

As the little Lincoln grew,
uglily upward and out, he began
to understand that something was

wrong. His little ways of trying
to please his father, the bringing
of matches, the jumping aside at
warning sound of oh-so-large and
rushing stride, the smile that gave
and gave and gave—Unsuccessful!

Even Christmases and Easters were spoiled.
He would be sitting at the
family feasting table, really
delighting in the displays of mashed potatoes
and the rich golden
fat-crust of the ham or the festive
fowl, when he would look up and find
somebody feeling indignant about him.

What a pity what a pity. No love
for one so loving. The little Lincoln
loved Everybody. Ants. The changing
caterpillar. His much-missing mother.
His kindergarten teacher.

His kindergarten teacher—whose
concern for him was composed of one
part sympathy and two parts repulsion.
The others ran up with their little drawings.
He ran up with his.
She
tried to be as pleasant with him as
with others, but it was difficult.
For she was all pretty! All daintiness,
all tiny vanilla, with blue eyes and fluffy
sun-hair. One afternoon she
saw him in the hall looking bleak against
the wall. It was strange because the
bell had long since rung and no other
child was in sight. Pity flooded her.
She buttoned her gloves and suggested
cheerfully that she walk him home. She

started out bravely, holding him by the
hand. But she had not walked far before
she regretted it. The little monkey.
Must everyone look? And clutching her
hand like that . . . Literally pinching
it . . .

At seven, the little Lincoln loved
the brother and sister who
moved next door. Handsome. Well-
dressed. Charitable, often, to him. They
enjoyed him because he was
resourceful, made up stories. But when
their More Acceptable friends came they turned
their handsome backs on him. He
hated himself for his feeling
of well-being with them despite—
Everything.

He spent much time looking at himself
in mirrors. What could be done?
But there was no
shrinking his head. There was no
binding his ears.

"Don't touch me!" cried the little
fairy-like being in the playground.

Her name was Nerissa. The many
children were playing tag, but when
he caught her, she recoiled, jerked free
and ran. It was like all the
rainbow that ever was, going off
forever, all, all the sparklings in
the sunset west.

One day, while he was yet seven,

MAXWELL STREET, CHICAGO'S WEST SIDE, 1947.

a thing happened. In the down town movies
with his mother a white
man in the seat beside him whispered
loudly to a companion, and pointed at
the little Linc.
"THERE! That's the kind I've been wanting
to show you! One of the best
examples of the specie. Not like
those diluted Negroes you see so much of on
the streets these days, but the
real thing.

Black, ugly, and odd. You
can see the savagery. The blunt
blankness. That is the real
thing."

His mother—her hair had never looked so
red around the dark brown
velvet of her face—jumped up,
shrieked "Go to —" She did not finish.
She yanked to his feet the little
Lincoln, who was sitting there
staring in fascination at his assessor. At the author of his
new idea.

All the way home he was happy. Of course,
he had not liked the word
"ugly."
But, after, should he not
be used to that by now? What had
struck him, among words and meanings
he could little understand, was the phrase
"the real thing."
He didn't know quite why,
but he liked that.
He liked that very much.

When he was hurt, too much
stared at—
too much
left alone—he
thought about that. He told himself
"After all, I'm
the real thing."

It comforted him.

JOLIE PAYLIN

When we speak of frontiers and migrations in the Midwest, some of us think of Frederick Jackson Turner's "rolling frontier"—the westward movement of people across woodlands, prairies, and plains from the colonial era onward. But there were also migrations within the Midwest from south to north.

A significant northward migration came in the early years of this century, two decades or so after the prairies and plains had been finally converted to cornbelt and wheatbelt. Land agents, with their eyes open for the "main chance," looked to the "northwoods" of Wisconsin, Minnesota, and Michigan's Upper and Lower peninsulas. There they saw vast areas of "cutover country" that had once been forested by magnificent pines. It stood abandoned by the timber barons who had logged everything that stood up straight from the ground, leaving the land barren of all but stumps and second growth.

Their nimble-minded public relations specialists named this land Cloverland, hoping to catch the attention of romantics with the implied promise that because forests had flourished there, cash crops, dairy herds, and chicken flocks would also. They began promoting the imaginary potential of this new Garden of Eden among Iowa, Illinois, and Indiana farmers, weary of mud, humid summers, and endless horse-farmed fields. Their Cloverland *magazine presented the merits of diversified farming with stories and pictures of pleasant homes, happy families, and an easier, more fruitful way of life.*

Hundreds, perhaps thousands of disenchanted prairie farmers gave up their struggles in the cornbelt and moved their families, willing or not, north. Many of these settlers carved fine potato and dairy farms from the former forestlands; others, discouraged and homesick, gave up the struggle and went back where they came from.

In "The Facts of Life in Cloverland," we see a young girl's version of a portion of her family's first year in what the girl's mother often saw as an alien land. For Jolie Paylin, who continues to live on the Wisconsin-Michigan border, that first year was an introduction to the complexities of living that she would face as an adult.

Jolie Paylin is the pseudonym of Mrs. Archie Behrend of Menominee, Michigan. She has published two novels about her Cloverland experiences: Cutover Country: Jolie's Story *(Iowa State University Press, 1976); and* Nels Oskar *(Iowa State University Press, 1979).* Cloverland Magazine *was published at Menominee from January 1913 to June 1924.*

The Facts of Life in Cloverland

I RAN BAREFOOT through the dew drenched grass to the little house by the backyard fence. The breaking day was heavenly fresh and peaceful, chorused about with birds' songs and touched by a breeze so perfect in temperature that I felt only the slightest caress on my skin. Later it would be a hot day in the sugar beet field.

Something was sucking deep breaths and thumping in the garden beyond the fence. At first I thought the heifers were in Mama's vegetables; then I heard the jingle of a chain. Something had been caught in the trap Papa had set for a bean-bent woodchuck!

The scythed grass along the sod path to the garden gate was tall again and soaked the skirt of my nightgown as I ran to investigate. The wetness reminded me that the precious phenomenon of dew sustained plants and wildlife during a dry spell like this one. I was sorry if any creature had been suffering in our cruel trap, but Papa had to defend our vegetables by any means he had. Mama was determined to have fresh produce when Grandpa came from Illinois to visit.

The weighted, wood-slat garden gate was fastened with a chain and harness snap. When I went through the creaking entrance, there was a renewed commotion at the far end of the plot. I'd gone this far, I'd run down the side path of the garden along the dewy plumes of asparagus and the rhubarb where I'd stashed the poor pine snake and I'd see if something was actually in the trap before I told Papa. He'd be most annoyed at being taken from his milking.

A tawny white-tailed doe was hurling herself against the woven wire fence at the rear of the garden. The chuck trap was fastened on one of her front feet below the dewclaws. I knew better than to go near the deer's sharp hooves. It would take some doing for grown men to extricate the frenzied, big-eyed doe without hurting her.

I hated to have to go to the barn and tell Papa. Of late, before breakfast he was inclined to be cranky and prematurely burdened by the problems of the day. He wanted me to help him milk in the mornings, as I did at night; but Mama had put her foot down on that, saying it was too early for a child to do barn.work. I felt most alive in the dawn hours and it was good to have time to enjoy them.

Well, no matter how busy Papa was, the doe would have to have help or she'd thrash herself to pieces. Why didn't Papa hear the animal himself when he and Spark went to the barn? Homer Martin had said a deer would make no sound if a dog was near; maybe that was it. Deer would even come right up to humans to escape dogs, preferring to be shot rather than ripped alive by dogs who lacked the instinct to kill their prey at once.

When I appeared in the alleyway behind the cows, Papa was finishing the hard milker he tackled first while he had optimum strength in his hands and arms. It distressed me that he somehow blamed the Holstein for her disability.

"Now what? Why ain't you dressed?" he demanded.

"There's a deer in that chuck trap in the garden. We have to do something before she breaks her leg."

"Well, I'll just go get my gun and shoot it. I can't stand around here all day with a cussed deer. I got to milk these cows and start blocking beets if the Craniak kids're going to help us with the thinning."

"I'd expected irritability from Papa under these circumstances, but his callous attitude shook me. "It's a doe. She's got babies. I saw she was giving milk when she fell on her side," I explained in one breath. I should've taken time to get Mama to go to the barn and break the news.

"Well, I can't just stand here," Papa said and started to the house with his one full pail of milk. "Lock that dog up," he added.

When he joined me in the garden, we could see the doe had done most of her struggling in the cabbages after consuming the much relished table beets. Both could still be replanted.

I knew Papa itched to shoot the disheveled but appealing doe and have the problem dispatched forthwith.

"There's nothing else to do. I'll have to put her out of her misery," he declared. If we try to take that trap off, she'll pound the whole works in the ground."

Mama had come to the garden and now she remonstrated. Her voice was appalled and urgent. "Dan Paylin! I give up right now if you shoot that mother deer!"

Mama was right—if Papa was so overworked and upset that he'd shoot a doe with babies, we might as well go back home. But I couldn't go; I'd had my eleventh birthday and had thrust a tenacious taproot into the soil of the pine-scented Cloverland.

Max had heard the disturbance and was standing inside the gate with the freed dog by the collar. Suddenly Spark broke loose and sailed at the doe's head, probably believing his family was menaced.

Without thinking, Mama dashed, nightgown billowing, into the melee to drag the dog away from the deer.

Papa exploded, jerked both Mama and the dog away and fired orders to his family. "Jolie, you get dressed and go on that pony for Homer. Tell him to bring a long rope. Max, lock that dog up and keep him locked up. Van, you go in the house where you belong, put some clothes on and make breakfast. We'll let the critter calm down—I'll milk till Homer comes."

The doe sat on her haunches, panting and gathering her stength until the last moment when the men moving across the garden would attack her. I'd booted Bill into the barn and was standing a prudent distance away so I'd not be noticed and sent to the house.

Homer Martin was tall and thin. He looked like he'd break in two in the middle, but I'd heard Papa say he was as tough as a whang string. "This is a humdinger of a situation, all right," he was saying. "That doe's not going to sit up and say, 'Pretty please, take this thing off of my leg.' "

Papa admitted, "I wanted to shoot her, but Van and the kids wouldn't let me. I reckon the doe's got young ones that can't fend for themselves."

"That she has. They'd die or fall to the coyotes without her. We'll have to try and rope her, tie her feet, and lug her out of the garden. She's too scared and weak to jump back over the fence."

As he was speaking, Homer was tying a noose in his rope. He drew a shorter length of rope from his hip pocket and tossed it to Papa. "We'll do it this way," he said. "If I catch her by the neck, I'll keep the slack out of the rope. You throw her and tie her hind feet. I'll help you with the front ones. Look out! She's going to spook! Ready? Now!"

The rope looped through the air in a five-foot oval and settled over the doe's head. She sprang into the air and would have shot through the rope, but the trap chain held to the stake and she fell hard on her side.

Instantly, Papa, Homer, and fourteen-year-old Franz Martin pinned her to the ground. With both sets of her feet tied, Papa hand-compressed the trap and freed the heaving doe's foot. Now the worst was over. The trap had cut the deer's skin and was working into a joint, but she would certainly heal to raise her fawns.

"Franz, you open the team gate," Homer told his son. "We

have to put her out where she can find her young ones.''

I watched the men carry the doe like a slain carcass, her long, white-throated neck lolling and her tongue scraping the dirt from the ground. Was it too late? Would she ever be able to get up and zigzag across another field?

Through the wide field gate, I saw the doe lying on the cropped grass of the meadow with her eyes closed.

''Now, we'll take off the ropes, shut the gate, and see what happens,'' Homer said.

Mama, dressed in her work clothes, breathlessly joined us with the small children. One second the doe lay stretched out in a posture of death, the next, she arched into full flight, her powerful haunches propelling her ivory and russet body over the green field like an arrow shot from a bow.

It seemed that it took only the time of a long-drawn breath for the deer to reach the sugar beet field fence. Would she be pitifully trapped again without a reserve of energy to clear the barbed wire? Would she be cut to ribbons by the wicked barrier? The white flag flew high and she was airborne. The doe had one more hurdle, the pasture fence, then freedom.

Where had the time gone? I knew the cream separator, the tyrant of the kitchen, should have been assembled and ready for the milk. But I'd been fixing breakfast while Mama worked on an oven baked lunch she could bring to the field for the beet blocking and thinning crew.

Papa would be in from the barn in a minute and it would be hard to predict his mood except, paradoxically, he was often in better spirits *after* an annoying emergency.

Della was fussing. ''Jolie,'' Mama said, ''if you can put the separator together, I'll change and dress the baby.'' Anything was better than tending a night sopped baby.

Mama had suddenly quit nursing Della and now we had to boil cow's milk and bottles besides. I'd heard Mama tell Mrs. Martin, ''This is the second time it didn't work for me. I'd hoped so much to be safe for another year.'' Now, I knew Mama meant safe from having another baby, but what nursing had to do with it was a mystery.

I worked carefully with the numbered pieces of the De Laval. If the machine was not assembled in precise numerical order, the worst mess in the world could result. I certainly was not going to rile Papa again with a sloppy job on the separator.

Papa hated milking as most men did, probably subconsciously considering the task woman's work. It disgruntled him to be so delayed when he could be in the fields with a team doing what a man should do. I asked Mama why we couldn't have one of the new milking machines, but she said Papa thought they were apt to ruin cows.

Well, I could think of cows that had been mistreated in other ways. Their udders were often subjected to painful manipulation as was the case of Papa's hard milker. I myself was careful that my fingernails were trimmed short before I milked my three strippers at night.

After breakfast Papa went for the Craniak children in the car and I walked with Max to the beet field. Too much of the cool of the day had already been wasted with the doe in the garden. Mama was still baking McGinty pies and apple butter tarts in the wood range oven.

As I worked, I looked up occasionally at Antonia, Stanis, and Papa who were clipping through the light green rows of four-inch-high sugar beet plants with sharp hoes. They were leaving clusters of the best plants at blade-width intervals. The thinnners, coming behind, were to pull out all but one robust plant.

I'd maneuvered myself into a row behind Stanis. I hadn't seen him to talk to since the last day of school. Maybe he'd forgotten that I was an odious kid.

George Craniak followed Papa while Max and Edward alternated on Antonia's row. The thinners were being paid fifty cents a day, but Stanis and Antonia would each earn a dollar. It wasn't fair for the stand-uppers to get twice as much as the crawlers.

In half an hour I'd made myself thirsty thinking about ice. The night before Homer Martin had brought us a big chunk in a washtub covered with wet gunny sacks. At eleven-thirty, Mama would come to the beet field with our lunch and some field ginger, a drink made from ginger, sugar, cider vinegar, and, today, ice.

By nine o'clock the pain had set in. It was hard to say which was going to hurt worse, my legs, back, or shoulders. Max and Edward were falling behind. I'd be expected to come back on their row when mine was done. Did Papa realize how much Max and I were physically hurting to help him succeed at this new kind of farming?

It had been idle to hope to talk to Stanis by taking his row. Working erect, he'd forged far ahead of me as I stooped, squatted, crawled, and knelt, changing positions to relieve my misery.

There were enough fine stones in the sandy loam to cut and bruise my bare knee caps when I was reduced to walking on them. It

was better when I discovered I could have more comfort by knee-walking in Stanis's packed foot tracks. It was a frivolous thing to worry about compared to the shoes Antonia needed, but how many times would I have to walk across that quarter-mile-long field on my middle leg joints to earn a dollar and nineteen cents for a box of oil paints?

Coming back across the field, Stanis stepped aside to check his brothers' work. The surviving beet plants had to be pressed firmly into the ground or they would dehydrate in the friable soil. "Tough job, eh?" he said as he passed me.

That was what he respected, someone who could work and suffer without flinching. Well, I could; I'd show him. "I think it's easy," I scoffed, straining out the sarcasm before I said it.

"Tomorrow, you won't hurt so much," he said, walking away, flicking at missed weeds with his hoe. "Anyway, you don't have to

CLOVERLAND.

go clear to the end of the rows," he added. "The deer have eaten all the beets by the back fence."

Kneeling again and lurching on, I saw the dark area of trampled earth and the telltale, pointed hoof tracks of varied dimensions. What would Papa do? He couldn't let them eat every plant in the narrow field.

You could have a lifetime of picnics and not have one as satisfying as the lunch we had under a scrub oak tree in the fence row. Mama had packed everything around Della in the wicker perambulator and pushed it across the meadow.

A restful, mattressed couch was formed by flattened timothy grass and clover in the field margin. The little boys were capering around to unkink their muscles, but I lay flat on the sod watching Mama unpack the warm chicken and asparagus pies. Their fragrance revived me; I sat up and pressed my throbbing spine against the trunk of the tree and ate. I looked around and saw that hard work had made one family out of the Bohemian Craniaks and the Appalachian-English Paylins.

Antonia was visiting easily with Mama about the new baby brother at their house, but babies were boring compared to the things Stanis and Papa were talking about. They had quit discussing the deer and Stanis was telling Papa he already had a job for the winter.

"I'll be swamping brush at Mayer's logging camp. It's just over the state line," he said, attempting a matter-of-fact tone. "If I save every cent I earn, I can buy a retired team of logging horses in the spring."

"That's the way to think," Papa encouraged him.

"Then I can really start to farm," Stanis went on, "but it worries me that I don't know much about driving."

"We'll begin haying as soon as we're done with the beets," Papa told him. "You'll soon learn to drive in the field."

Stanis thanked Papa, settled his back against a fence post and reached for another chicken pie. "Our mother makes these out of wild rabbit and sauerkraut," he said.

Papa had no reason to worry about working the Craniaks too hard; they were ready to return to the field before he was. The low pain in my back failed to subside and, abruptly, it struck me that it was no use—with their peasant capacity for fun and hard work, the Craniaks would outlast and outdo us Paylins. Their dream could come true long before ours did.

Our dream had become a nightmare of dawn to dark labor. What was the use in living in a new and exciting land if there was less and less time to enjoy it? Mama *was* right. It'd be better to go back home in the fall than to try to meet Papa's "We'll stick out this diversified farming for one year then we'll be used to it," goal for his family.

That evening, coming home from taking the wash to Mrs Deckler's with Papa and Max in the Ford, I was glad when the car turned in to the Stenbockers'. A few hours' rest and the ride had refreshed me and I felt like living again. It would be fun if Allan and Norma would show us the sharp-nosed, nervous silver foxes they raised.

What were our fathers talking so earnestly about as we took our leave? Why was Webb going to follow us with the long flashlight and short rifle he had put in his Dodge sedan?

At home, Max went upstairs to read a book, but I pestered Mama about Papa's and Webb's activities: "Why're they both going to take blankets and sleep in the pasture when it gets dark?"

Mama gave lame answers when she was perturbed. "They're just camping out for the night."

"Then why can't Max and I go?"

"Because this outing is only for men."

"Are they taking guns because they're afraid of something? I wouldn't be."

"No, they're not afraid. They've some business to attend to."

What kind of work could be done in the black of night? Suddenly, with a wrenching of loyalties, I knew what the men were going to do. Why did the beautiful deer have to eat sugar beets when there was a field of alfalfa alongside? Wasn't there a law against shooting deer out of season, especially with a light?

Papa had always been meticulous about the law. He'd bend over backward to see justice done, but now I knew he planned to be a violator like the moonshiners. What was the difference? It was plain that Mama was upset, but I couldn't help asking her, "Will somebody come and arrest Papa if he kills one of those deer in the beet field?"

Mama gave me a look that told me she wished I'd go to bed, but she explained, "We hope not. This is a serious situation. Homer says the price of potatoes is so low, the beet crop may bring us our only cash money this year."

"If they kill one of the beet field deer, are we going to eat it?"

"I guess your father thinks we will, though I'm sure the meat will be divided around the neighborhood."

"Are we going to give the Craniaks some?"

"No."

"Why? They need the meat."

There was pure bitterness in Mama's voice for the first time I could remember. "Because, in this wild land, they break the law in their way, making wine; and we do it in ours, killing deer out of season."

When darkness fell, I heard Papa speak to Mama in the kitchen. The message was relayed with a rising inflection as Mama came to the door of the dining room where I was aimlessly reading, hoping to stay as close to the action as possible. "Jolie, you're to go upstairs with Max. You're to go to bed and stay in bed, no matter what. And I mean in bed."

"No matter what," could mean anything. How could I lie down and go to sleep after that kind of an announcement?

The dining room clock struck nine o'clock, ten o'clock. Max was asleep, but I'd never been so awake. Before, I'd never noticed the variety and busyness of nocturnal birds. Eleven o'clock. There it was! A series of staccato reports and the conversing birds were still. Did they stick a deer like butchering a hog? I'd eat cornmeal mush three times a day before I'd eat meat from a lovely animal like a deer.

Half an hour later, there was quiet but purposeful activity in the kitchen and the smokehouse; then Webb's car left the yard. Limbering my tensed muscles. I crept to my out-of-bounds listening post at the head of the stairs.

Papa was saying, "I'll fetch Greta the first thing in the morning. She'll show you how to can some of the meat in the wash boiler. You'll have to fix us a cold lunch to take to the sugar beet field. It's the only way we can keep Jolie from catching on to what we're doing.

"What kind of deer was it?" Mama asked.

"A yearling buck."

"With two livers?"

Papa groaned. "That's why I feel so bad. One was a big doe. She stepped right in front of the second buck we were going to shoot. Her front legs were both broken. Webb shot her."

"*Not* the doe in the garden?"

"No."

I went back to my bed in a daze. After trying so hard to save the doe in the garden, fawns were orphaned anyway. I began to strain my ears for the furious feeding of coyotes and it was morning before I went to sleep.

Stanis had told the truth, the second day of thinning beets, your muscles didn't trouble you quite so much. Besides, a machine didn't hurt; and that was what my body was, a pair of mechanical hands operating independently of a fawn filled brain.

I had to try and find the baby deer before another night turned the coyotes loose. I'd fill up on egg sandwiches, baked beans, and molasses cookies at noon so I could take right off on Bill when we quit working in the field at three o'clock. The cows would have to be hunted and brought home before I could ride out again in search of the fawns. I'd have to sneak away the second time; Mama and Papa didn't know I knew about the orphans.

Back in the hinterland, unseen by my parents, I deliberately fired up the Indian pony. I began to rein him in a grid, starting two rods from the fence, and endeavored not to let my course be deflected by logs, stumps, or trees.

The most likely places for the young deer were under drooping hemlocks, in a hazel thicket, or in a stand of big-leaved poplar saplings. Surely the doe would not have hidden the fawns on wet ground, but she'd keep working toward the creek. The weather had been summer-dry for a couple of weeks. Maybe she'd been staying near water.

Bill was sweating profusely and becoming irritated with this second, seemingly senseless foray into the brush. After a few minutes of stiff-legged crow hopping and balky changes of leads, he pitched me over his head without warning. One of my hands clung to a rein, and he was brought up short with pain on his lower jaw bar.

Lying on my back in the crushed sweet fern, worn out from the day's labor, I looked up at the horse towering above me. I began to sob like any other little girl, shaken up, bruised, disappointed, and mad. I'd find a better switch, but the truth was, I already had more horse than I could handle.

Doggedly, I mounted the snorty horse from a stump. I'd make one more try for the fawns for my own peace of mind. Calming Bill with long strokes on his neck, I rode slowly in the opposite direction from my first series of loops. Finally I faced up to something I'd been pushing out of my consciousness all day long—what would I do with the fawns if I found them? Grandpa Martin had said hand raised fawns became as destructive as billy goats around the yard.

Was that all worth the worry my unexplained absence was giving Mama who was innocent of doe killing in the first place?

I rode back to the gate and rubbed Bill with handfuls of dry grass, obliterating most of the evidences of hard riding except for a darkening of his golden hide and the distension of his flanks. I'd go home and, if I was lucky, manage to get in my bed unpunished. I was too weary to eat. I barely had enough bounce in my rubber legs to mount the pony from the top of a dead furrow.

JAMES HEARST

James Hearst was born, he will tell you, on the family farm near Cedar Falls, Iowa, on the eighth day of the eighth month under the sign of the threshing machine. The Hearsts have always been farmers and Hearst was the third generation on the present Maplehearst Farm, founded by his grandfather after the Civil War. Hearst's father, Charles E. Hearst, was a vice-president of the American Farm Bureau from 1932 to 1936.

A crippling accident when he was a young man did not keep him from actively farming, though it did keep him from medical school. His mother and his college teachers encouraged him to write, and in college he learned a valuable lesson: a writer should write from his own experience. In time, Hearst became a teacher of creative writing at his college, now the University of Northern Iowa. There he and Ruth Suckow became close friends.

His verse, published over the years in a half-dozen slender volumes, has consistently demonstrated that the midwestern soil can be as fertile for the poetic imagination as it is for pigs and corn. The best of his work can be inspected in Snake in the Strawberries (1979) where Hearst's metaphorical views of man's relations with nature are laid out, as in "To an Old Sow":

> At times I see in you, old sow, ways like mine too clearly,
> You won't jump to attention when someone blows his horn
> As if he ran the township—don't chomp your jaws at me!
> The Lord had trouble with nature the day when you were born.

Here for the coda to this collection we see Jim Hearst as both poet and teacher. Retired from teaching, but not from the world of the poet's mind, Hearst must have seen the experience recounted here on more than one occasion—including, perhaps, his own case.

"OLD MAIN."

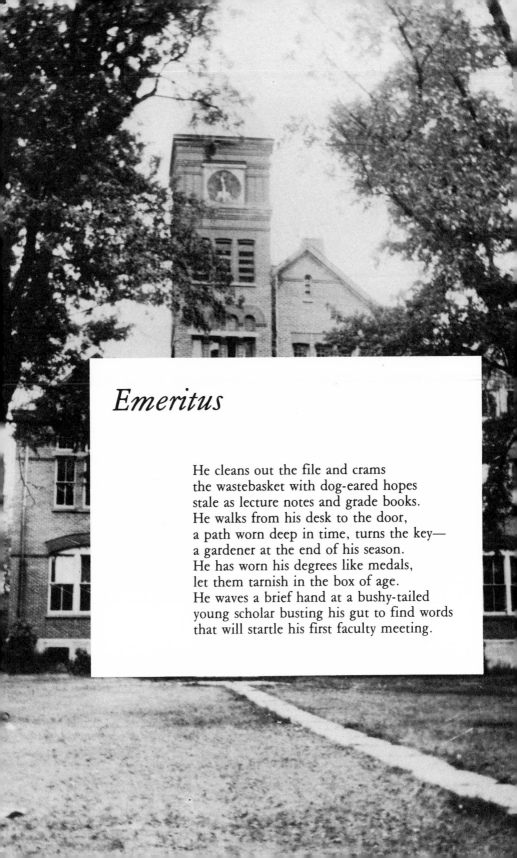

Emeritus

He cleans out the file and crams
the wastebasket with dog-eared hopes
stale as lecture notes and grade books.
He walks from his desk to the door,
a path worn deep in time, turns the key—
a gardener at the end of his season.
He has worn his degrees like medals,
let them tarnish in the box of age.
He waves a brief hand at a bushy-tailed
young scholar busting his gut to find words
that will startle his first faculty meeting.